CW00735469

Dordogne/Lot Lifeline

by
Val Gascoyne

SURVIVAL BOOKS • LONDON • ENGLAND

First published 2004

Copyright © Val Gascoyne 2004
Cover photograph: Roger Moss (🖥 www.picturefrance.com)

Survival Books Limited, 1st Floor,
60 St James's Street, London SW1A 1ZN, United Kingdom
☎ +44 (0)20-7493 4244, 🖷 +44 (0)20-7491 0605
✉ info@survivalbooks.net
🖥 www.survivalbooks.net
To order books, please refer to page 300.

British Library Cataloguing in Publication Data.
A CIP record for this book is available
from the British Library.
ISBN 1 901130 28 2

Printed and bound in Finland by WS Bookwell Ltd

ACKNOWLEDGEMENTS

A huge thank-you to Chris, who was always there with support, and Barnaby, who was convinced that his mum was just a mirage when he woke in the night – thank you both for your understanding. Thanks also to Dad, who dropped everything at a moment's notice to come over and drive me around the area. Sightseeing was forbidden, as were leisurely lunches and lie-ins, but it was really appreciated – thank you. Another thank-you to my editor, Joe Laredo, for knocking my text into shape and bullying me for details and to his wife and colleague, Kerry, for designing and laying out the pages, producing the index and checking the proofs. A final thank-you to Jim Watson for his superb illustrations, maps and cover design.

OTHER TITLES BY SURVIVAL BOOKS

The Alien's Guide To Britain;
The Alien's Guide To France;
The Best Places To Live
In France; The Best Places To
Live In Spain; Buying, Selling &
Letting Property; Foreigners In
France: Triumphs & Disasters;
Foreigners In Spain: Triumphs
& Disasters; How To Avoid
Holiday & Travel Disasters;
Costa Del Sol Lifeline; Lifeline;
Poitou-Charentes Lifeline;
Renovating & Maintaining
Your French Home;
Retiring Abroad;
Rioja And Its Wines;
The Wines Of Spain

Living And Working Series

Abroad; America; Australia;
Britain; Canada; The Far East;
France; Germany; The Gulf
States & Saudi Arabia; Holland,
Belgium & Luxembourg;
Ireland; Italy; London; New
Zealand; Spain; Switzerland

Buying A Home Series

Abroad; Britain; Florida;
France; Greece & Cyprus;
Ireland; Italy;
Portugal; Spain

Order forms are on page 300.

What Readers & Reviewers Have Said

If you need to find out how France works, this book is indispensable. Native French people probably have a less thorough understanding of how their country functions.

LIVING FRANCE

This book is a Godsend – a practical guide to all things French and the famous French administration – a book I am sure I will used time and time again during my stay in France.

READER

I would recommend this book to anyone considering the purchase of a French property – get it early so you do it right!

READER

Let's say it at once: David Hampshire's *Living and Working in France* is the best handbook ever produced for visitors and foreign residents in this country. It is Hampshire's meticulous detail which lifts his work way beyond the range of other books with similar titles. *Living and Working in France* is absolutely indispensable.

RIVIERA REPORTER

I found this a wonderful book crammed with facts and figures, with a straightforward approach to the problems and pitfalls you are likely to encounter. It is laced with humour and a thorough understanding of what's involved. Gets my vote!

READER

I was born in France and spent countless years there. I bought this book when I had to go back after a few years away, and this is far and away the best book on the subject. The amount of information covered is nothing short of incredible. I thought I knew enough about my native country. This book has proved me wrong. Don't go to France without it. Big mistake if you do. Absolutely priceless!

READER

If you're thinking about buying a property in France, Hampshire is totally on target. I read this book before going through the buying process and couldn't believe how perfectly his advice dovetailed with my actual experience.

READER

About Other Survival Books on France

In answer to the desert island question about the one how-to book on France, this book would be it.

The Recorder

It's just what I needed! Everything I wanted to know and even things I didn't know I wanted to know but was glad I discovered!

Reader

There are now several books on this subject, but I've found that this book is definitely the best one. It's crammed with up-to-date information and seems to cover absolutely everything.

Reader

Covers every conceivable question concerning everyday life – I know of no other book that could take the place of this one.

France in Print

An excellent reference book for anyone thinking of taking the first steps towards buying a new or old property in France.

Reader

Thankfully, with several very helpful pieces of information from this book, I am now the proud owner of a beautiful house in France. Thank God for David Hampshire!

Reader

I saw this book advertised and thought I had better read it. It was definitely money well spent.

Reader

We bought an apartment in Paris using this book as a daily reference. It helped us immensely, giving us confidence in many procedures from looking for a place initially to the closing, including great information on insurance and utilities. Definitely a great source!

Reader

A comprehensive guide to all things French, written in a highly readable and amusing style, for anyone planning to live, work or retire in France.

The Times

THE AUTHOR

Originally from Hertfordshire, Val Gascoyne worked as a retail manager before returning to college to qualify as an administrator and going on to run her own secretarial business for five years. Having spent most of her earnings on travelling, she eventually moved to France for fresh challenges, a calmer life and French neighbours. There she set up Purple Pages (see below). This book and its companion, *Poitou-Charentes Lifeline*, are a development of that activity and are the first Val has written for Survival Books.

Purple Pages
Grosbout, 16240 La Forêt de Tessé, France
☎ 05 45 29 59 74, UK ☎ 0871-900 8305
🖳 www.purplepages.info

This company produces tailored directories, unique to each family, which are the result of exhaustive research and contain everything you could possibly need to know about an area – from when the dustmen call and where the nearest English-speaking doctor is to be found to facilities and services for specific medical needs or sporting passions.

CONTENTS

1 Introducing Dordogne/Lot & Lot-et-Garonne 17

2 Dordogne 89

3 Lot   173

IMPORTANT NOTE

Every effort has been made to ensure that the information contained in this book is accurate and up to date. Note, however, that businesses and organisations can be quite transient, particularly those operated by expatriates (French businesses tend to go on 'for ever'), and therefore information can quickly change or become outdated.

It's advisable to check with an official and reliable source before making major decisions or undertaking an irreversible course of action. If you're planning to travel long-distance to visit somewhere, always phone beforehand to check the opening times, availability of goods, prices and other relevant information.

Unless specifically stated, a reference to any company, organisation or product doesn't constitute an endorsement or recommendation.

Author's Notes

- As the three departments covered by this book are in two regions, they're referred to collectively as 'the area'.

- Times are shown using the 12-hour clock, e.g. ten o'clock in the morning is written 10am and ten in the evening 10pm.

- Costs and prices are shown in euros (€) where appropriate. They should be taken as guides only, although they were accurate at the time of publication.

- Unless otherwise stated, all telephone numbers have been given as if dialling from France. To dial from abroad, use your local international access code (e.g. 00 from the UK) followed by 33 for France and omit the initial 0 of the French number.

- His/he/him/man/men (etc.) also mean her/she/her/woman/women (no offence ladies!). This is done simply to make life easier for both the reader and, in particular, the author, and isn't intended to be sexist.

- Warnings and important points are shown in **bold** type.

- The following symbols are used in this book: ☎ (telephone), 🖹 (fax), 🖥 (internet) and ✉ (email).

- British English is used throughout. French words and phrases are given in italics in brackets where appropriate and are used in preference to English where no exact equivalents exist.

- If there isn't a listing for a particular town under a given heading, this facility or service wasn't available in or near that town at the time of publication. For facilities and services that are available in most towns or are provided on a regional basis and are therefore not listed individually in the department chapters, see **Chapter 1**.

Montignac

INTRODUCTION

If you're thinking of living, working, buying a home or spending an extended holiday in Dordogne, Lot or Lot-et-Garonne, this is **the book** for you. *Dordogne/Lot Lifeline* has been written to answer all those important questions about life in this region that aren't answered in other books. Whether you're planning to spend a few months or a lifetime there, to work, retire or buy a holiday home, this book is essential reading.

An abundance of tourist guides and information about these departments is available, but until now it has been difficult to find comprehensive details of local costs, facilities and services, particularly in one book. *Dordogne/Lot Lifeline* fills this gap and contains accurate, up-to-date, practical information about the most important aspects of daily life in the Dordogne/Lot area. If you've ever sought a restaurant that's open after 10pm, a 24-hour petrol station or something to do with your children on a wet day, then this book will become your 'bible'.

Information is derived from a variety of sources, both official and unofficial, not least the hard-won experiences of the author, her friends, family and colleagues. *Dordogne/Lot Lifeline* is a comprehensive handbook and is designed to make your stay in the region – however long or short – easier and less stressful. **It will also help you save valuable time, trouble and money, and will repay your investment many times over!** (For comprehensive information about living and working in France in general and buying a home in France, this book's sister publications, *Living and Working in France* and *Buying a Home in France*, written by David Hampshire, are highly recommended reading.)

The Dordogne/Lot area is a popular holiday destination (particularly for adventure holidays) and has long been a magnet for discerning holiday homeowners: it enjoys long hot summers and its rugged countryside and medieval villages are among the most beautiful in France; the delicious local cuisine (the best of country fare) and wine are a magnet for foodies; and the relaxed lifestyle and quality of life attract an increasing number of foreign residents. I trust this book will help make your life easier and more enjoyable, and smooth the way to a happy and rewarding time in Dordogne/Lot.

Bienvenue en Dordogne/Lot!   **Val Gascoyne**
                                                      April 2004

St Cirq-Lapopie

1

Introducing Dordogne, Lot & Lot-et-Garonne

This chapter provides a general introduction to the area covered by this book and a brief description of each of its three departments and their main towns (see Overview below). This is followed by information about getting to (and from) the area and getting around by public transport once you're there (see page 24). The section headed General Information (see page 45) contains information relating to the whole area, in alphabetical order; detailed information relating to each department is contained, under similar headings, in Chapters 2 to 4.

OVERVIEW

As the departments of Dordogne, Lot and Lot-et-Garonne are in different regions of France (Dordogne and Lot-et-Garonne in Aquitaine, Lot in Midi-Pyrénées), the term 'area' is used to refer to all three in order to avoid confusion. The location of the area in relation to France is shown below. Relevant airports outside the area are shown here; those within the area are shown on the map opposite.

The map below shows the area as a whole; detailed maps of each department are included in **Chapters 2, 3** and **4**.

In each department, a selection of main towns has been made and facilities and services in these towns highlighted, although others are included where appropriate. The selected towns are geographically spread, so at least one of them should be reasonably close wherever you choose to stay or live. The selected towns are as follows:

Dordogne (24)

- **Bergerac**
- **Montpon-Ménestrérol**
- **Périgueux**
- **Sarlat-la-Canéda**
- **Le Bugue**
- **Nontron**
- **Ribérac**

Lot (46)	**Lot-et-Garonne (47)**
● **Cahors**	● **Agen**
● **Figeac**	● **Marmande**
● **Gourdon**	● **Nérac**
● **Saint Céré**	● **Villeneuve-sur-Lot**

Dordogne

This department is often referred to as Périgord, which was the name of the ancient province covering more or less the same area, and has recently become divided into four areas:

● **Black Périgord** (representing the forests) in the east and south-east;

● **Green Périgord** (representing the fields) in the north;

● **Purple Périgord** (representing the vineyards) in the south and south-west;

● **White Périgord** (representing limestone) in the centre and west.

With hill-top chateaux and medieval towns, this is a beautiful region of France. Although renowned for walnut oil and tobacco, it's most famous for truffles and *foie gras*, with specialist markets across the department. Those who are partial to the latter should note that the practice of force-feeding geese in order to produce the delicacy may soon be outlawed by European law.

Bergerac

This town developed around the first bridge over the Dordogne river. It was a prosperous city in the Middle Ages but lost a lot of its population to emigration in the 17th century, later reviving its fortunes as a wine-shipping and tobacco-growing centre. The medieval town is now surrounded by a thriving modern town, which in the summer is vibrant with festivals of art, music, theatre and gastronomy.

Le Bugue

This is a small market town on the river Vézère in a region inhabited for more than 10,000 years. The town is surrounded by evidence of its past, with numerous caves, museums and prehistoric art. Le Bugue also offers facilities for water sports, camping and other leisure activities whilst striving to protect and promote its traditions and history.

Montpon-Ménestérol

Montpon stretches between the river Isle and the railway line along the route between Bordeaux and Périgueux. This is an area with a wide variety of local produce from honey and cheese to apples, jams and wine. Ménestérol is a large village north of Montpon, on the other side of the river, with a leisure lake and beach. Montpon-Ménestérol is hereafter referred to simply as Montpon.

Nontron

Ideally placed for those who wish to explore several departments, Nontron is in northern Dordogne near its borders with Charente to the north-west, Haute-Vienne to the north-east and Corrèze to the east and lies in the heart of the Périgord Limousin natural park, which offers a host of outdoor activities. In the town itself you can visit the workshops that have been producing hand-crafted knives since1653.

Périgueux

This is the capital of Dordogne and has a medieval centre overlooking the river Isle. The twice-weekly market spills out across the central boulevards and across various areas in the pedestrian quarter. Périgueux is a large and lively agricultural centre where the region's specialities – truffles, *foie gras*, honey and liqueurs – are readily available.

Ribérac

The main road through Ribérac is the busy commercial route from Angoulême to Bergerac. However, the real centre of the town is to one side – an area of open spaces, restaurants and cafes with outside seating, where open-air concerts and performances take place during the summer months.

Sarlat-la-Canéda

Officially the most attractive medieval town in France, Sarlat-la-Canéda has managed to preserve its ancient buildings and cobbled side streets. The town grew up around a Benedictine monastery founded in the ninth century. Unlike most other towns in the area, it isn't to be found on a hilltop but in a bowl-like dip in the landscape, which made it reliant on ramparts for protection during the various wars in its history.

As Sarlat-la-Canéda isn't on a waterway, it didn't become a major industrial area and this may have helped the town to preserve its character, buildings and calm way of life. A walk along Rue de la République will lead you to many quiet alleyways and to an unusual statue of three geese symbolising the old goose market.

Lot

Lot (the final T is pronounced) is one of eight departments that make up France's largest region, Midi-Pyrénées, whose capital is the city of Toulouse. Lot is famous for caves and châteaux, both of which are plentiful. The river from which the department takes its name and its many tributaries mean that you're never far from water, and the varied landscape offers plenty of sport and leisure opportunities, from the traditional boules and fishing to pot-holing and canyoning. More leisurely pursuits include riding on a horse-drawn caravan through the countryside at four miles per hour and tasting locally made *foie gras* and wine.

Cahors

The capital of Lot, Cahors is a thriving town that has developed since Gallo-Roman times within a deep loop of the river. There are only three bridges that cross it, the westernmost, now closed to traffic, being the world's only fortified bridge with three towers in the world. With the ultra-modern architecture of the new library on Avenue Jean Jaurès, it's a town of great diversity, with bustling markets filling the streets and squares, and many gastronomic restaurants in quiet side streets or overlooking the river.

Figeac

Like many towns in this department, Figeac has a central square surrounded by half-timbered buildings. Similar buildings line the tiny streets and alleys leading off the square and Boulevard Juskiewensky ends in a flight of distinctive zigzag steps. To mark Figeac as the birthplace of the Egyptologist Jean-François Champollion is an enlarged replica of the Rosetta Stone, whose hieroglyphics he deciphered in the 1820s: a huge slate laid flat on the Place des Ecritures.

Gourdon

Gourdon is a well preserved hilltop town with a spider's web street plan. It's a steep climb to the central church of Saint Pierre, where you're rewarded with magnificent views. The houses in the central area are beautifully kept and Gourdon's various commercial enterprises and tourist office are tucked away in the tiny roads leading to it.

Saint Céré

This medieval town was once called 'Sainte Sperie', which is still the name of the main church. The church was severely damaged by fire during the religious wars but has since been rebuilt. However, the town contains numerous examples of ancient architecture: on Rue Paramelle, for example, is a collection of 15th and 16th century houses, one of which used to be a convent (founded in 1683), and a 12th century column window. Guided tours of Saint Céré can be booked at the tourist office.

Lot-et-Garonne

Like Lot, Lot-et-Garonne is a department with water at its heart; there are extensive navigable waterways and many lakes, ponds and streams on which to relax, paddle, swim or row. The surrounding countryside is made up of rolling hills, which in spring and summer are full of corn and sunflowers. The variety of local produce includes *foie gras*, plums and Armagnac. There are also many châteaux to visit, ranging from imposing ruins to magnificent houses complete with elaborate furnishings.

Agen

Agen is the capital of Lot-et-Garonne and a city of great variety. In the 19th century, its importance was largely due to the 200km (125mi) Garonne Lateral Canal, but now Agen is well situated for all modes of transport: rail (Agen is four hours from Paris by train), road (the A62 from Bordeaux to Toulouse is only a few kilometres to the south) and air (Agen has its own small airport). Agen is the heart of French rugby country, the local team having won the French championship eight times. With the recent arrival of a new university and modern architecture, the town continues to grow and develop.

Marmande

Marmande originated in the ninth century as a group of houses. The subsequent building of a fortress, a spell of English rule and periods of strong economic growth have made it the historic and lively town it is today. The river Garonne has always played an important part in the life of the town, originally providing transport and power for its mills and now lending itself to flourishing leisure and tourist activities. The best way to explore Marmande is on a Discovery Tour, whose route takes you along alleys of half-timbered houses, down to the river and into cloisters and formal French gardens.

Nérac

A small town but one full of character, as the main road bypasses its centre, leaving it undisturbed. The château of Henri IV nestles in the very centre of Nérac with views over the Baïse river towards the Eglise Notre Dame, which dominates the skyline to the east.

Villeneuve-sur-Lot

Villeneuve-sur-Lot has a pedestrian area, with side streets full of small shops and a wide variety of restaurants. The town is steeped in history and this is evident in the architecture, which consists of half-timbered buildings overhanging the tiny streets. Place Lafayette, for example, resembles a huge courtyard enclosed by medieval houses and shops in the galleries below.

GETTING THERE & GETTING AROUND

Getting There By Air

There are several airlines that fly direct to this region, as well as numerous flights from Paris, which is accessible from a variety of UK airports. From Paris you can hire a car (or a helicopter, if money is no object) or complete your journey by rail. Details of all three options are given in this section.

Airports

There are three major airports in the area and several others nearby, as listed below (department numbers are given in brackets).

Agen (47)	Aéroport d'Agen There are currently no commercial flights to or from this airport but they may resume to Paris in summer 2004.	☎ 05 53 77 00 88
Bergerac (24)	Aéroport de Bergerac Roumanière	☎ 05 53 22 25 25
Bordeaux (33)	Aéroport Bordeaux Mérignac	☎ 05 56 34 50 50
Brive-la- Gaillarde (19)	Aérodrome Brive-Laroche	☎ 05 55 86 88 36
Limoges (87)	Aéroport International de Limoges	☎ 05 55 43 30 30
Périgueux (24)	Aéroport de Périgueux Bassillac	☎ 05 53 02 79 71
Rodez (12)	Aéroport Rodez-Marcillac, route Decazeville, Salles-la-Source	☎ 05 65 76 02 00
Toulouse (31)	Aéroport Toulouse-Blaynac	☎ 05 61 42 44 00

Although budget airlines can offer cheap fares, the scheduled airlines also offer some good prices and are sometimes cheaper than the budget airlines if you're booking either late or well in advance. In early 2004, the majority of the flights listed below were under £200 return.

The following tables list direct routes from England, Scotland and Ireland (North and South) that were in service in early 2004. These are intended only as a guide, as airline services are constantly changing, and you should check with the relevant airports or airlines (see below) for the latest information.

England

From	To	Airline
Birmingham	Paris	British Airways & Air France
	Toulouse	Flybe.com
Bristol	Bergerac	Flybe.com
	Bordeaux	Flybe.com
	Paris	Air France
	Toulouse	Flybe.com
Leeds	Paris	British Midland
Liverpool	Paris	Easyjet
Luton	Paris	Easyjet
London City, Gatwick & Heathrow	Paris	British Airways & Air France
London Gatwick	Bordeaux	British Airways, Air France & Flybe.com
	Toulouse	British Airways
London Heathrow	Toulouse	Air France & KLM
London Stansted	Bergerac, Limoges & Rodez	Ryan Air
Manchester	Paris	Air France
	Toulouse	British Airways & KLM
Newcastle	Paris	Easyjet & Air France
Southampton	Bergerac	Flybe.com
	Paris	Air France
	Toulouse	Flybe.com

Ireland

From	To	Airline
Dublin	Paris	Air France & Ryan Air

Scotland

From	To	Airline
Aberdeen	Paris	Air France
Edinburgh	Paris	British Airways, British Midland & Air France
Glasgow	Paris	British Airways, British Midland & Air France

Regular flights from Paris include the following:

From	To	Airline
Paris	Bergerac (daily)	Airlinair
	Brive-la-Gaillarde (six days a week)	Airlinair
	Périgueux (daily)	Airlinair

Airline	Website	UK ☎	French ☎
Air France	🖳 www.airfrance.com	0845-359 1000	08 20 82 08 20
Airlinair	🖳 www.airlinair.com		08 20 82 08 20
British Airways	🖳 www.britishairways.com	0870-850 9850	
Easyjet	🖳 www.easyjet.com	0870-600 0000	
Flybe.com	🖳 www.flybe.com	0871-700 0535*	
Ryan Air	🖳 www.ryanair.com	0871-246 0000	08 99 70 00 07

* Note that calls to Flybe.com cannot be made from outside the British Isles (☎ 1890-925 532 from Ireland), although it's possible to send a fax on 🖩 +44 1392 266650.

The following websites may help you to find low-cost flights with scheduled airlines:

🖳 *www.cheapflights.co.uk*

🖳 *www.ebookers.com*

🖳 *www.expedia.co.uk*

🖳 *www.flightline.co.uk*

🖳 *www.travelocity.co.uk*

Plane & Helicopter Hire

Air Angoulême	Aérodrome, Champniers Private planes and helicopters.	☎ 05 45 69 81 92
Airways	Aéroport la Garenne Aeroplane taxis.	☎ 05 53 68 18 18
Aéro Charter Darta	Aéroport du Bourget, Le Bourget Plane and helicopter taxis.	☎ 01 48 62 54 54
Avialim Charter	Aéroport Limoges Bellegarde, Limoges Aeroplane taxis to destinations all over Europe.	☎ 05 55 48 05 61
On Top Aviation	L'Aérodrome, Missé	☎ 05 49 96 20 94
Périgord Hélicopt'Air	42 rue 4 Septembre, Montignac Hire of helicopters and light aircraft.	☎ 06 08 32 64 02
Héli-Périgord		☎ 05 53 57 70 46

Car Hire

The larger towns have several car hire companies; listed below are the main companies in each town. The websites of the 'big five' companies are as follows:

Avis	🖳 *www.avis.fr*
Budget	🖳 *www. budget.fr*
Car'Go	🖳 *www.cargo.fr*
Europcar	🖳 *www.europcar-atlantique.com*
Hertz	🖳 *www.hertz-grand-ouest.com*

Airport-Based

Agen	Alamo, Aéroport Agen la Garenne	☎ 05 53 48 11 04
Bergerac	Europcar, Aéroport de Roumanière	☎ 05 53 61 61 61
Bordeaux	Hertz, Aéroport Bordeaux Mérignac	☎ 08 25 00 24 00
Brive-la-Gaillarde	ADA, 139 avenue Georges Pompidou	☎ 05 55 88 33 28
Limoges	Avis, 1ter avenue Général de Gaulle	☎ 05 55 33 36 37
Périgueux	Rent-a-Car, 163 avenue Maréchal Juin	☎ 05 53 05 00 50

Dordogne

Bergerac	Europcar, 3 avenue du 108ème RI	☎ 05 53 58 97 97
Le Bugue	Garage Marty, route de Campagne	☎ 05 53 07 21 58
Montpon	Garage Gaillard, avenue Georges Pompidou	☎ 05 53 80 40 20
Nontron	Carrosserie Cadas, route Piégut	☎ 05 53 56 02 24
Périgueux	Europcar, 7 rue Denis Papin	☎ 05 53 08 15 72
Ribérac	Garage Raymond, rue André Cheminade, ZA des Chaumes Nord	☎ 05 53 90 06 85
Sarlat-la-Canéda	Budget, Centre Commercial du Pontet	☎ 05 53 28 10 21

Lot

Cahors	ADA Location, 52 avenue Anatole de Monzie	☎ 05 65 35 06 66
Figeac	Avis, 1 avenue Georges Pompidou	☎ 05 65 34 10 28
Gourdon	Budget, route de Cahors	☎ 05 65 41 03 95
Saint Céré	Avis, Garage Payrot, route de Gramat	☎ 05 65 38 01 07

Lot-et-Garonne

Agen	ADA Location, 381 avenue du Maréchal Leclerc	☎ 05 53 96 96 40

Marmande	Hertz, Garage Ford, ZAC de Girouflat	☎ 05 53 83 34 72
Nérac	Budget Pujol Location, route de Condom	☎ 05 53 65 62 55
Villeneuve-sur-Lot	Avis Location, route Bordeaux	☎ 05 53 49 21 44

Taxis

Dordogne

Bergerac		☎ 05 53 23 32 32
	This is a central number for all taxis in Bergerac	
Le Bugue	Taxi Dupuy, La Faure	☎ 05 53 07 22 97
Montpon	Allô Taxi, Le Petit Bigotas	☎ 05 53 80 39 17
	Roger Naboulet, le Petite Jarrauty	☎ 05 53 80 32 19
Nontron	Taxi Michel, 2 place de l'Eglise	☎ 05 53 56 06 90
Périgueux	Allô Taxi, place Bugeaud	☎ 05 53 09 09 09
	Station de Taxis, place Bugeaud & rue Denis Papin	☎ 05 53 53 27 00
Ribérac	Allô Ribérac Taxis, 1 bis rue Pierre Serbat	☎ 05 53 90 07 72
	B. Moulinier, 3 rue des Mobiles	☎ 05 53 90 11 99
	Taxi Byl, les Fougères	☎ 05 53 90 41 53
Sarlat-la-Canéda	Allô Allô Taxi Sarlat, Moussidière	☎ 05 53 59 02 43
	Allô Philippe Taxi, le Bras de l'Homme English spoken	☎ 05 53 59 39 65
	Bernard Brajot, la Trappe	☎ 05 53 59 41 13
	Eric Faugère, impasse de l'Hôpital	☎ 05 53 31 62 43
	Sarlat Taxi, Grojeac English spoken	☎ 05 53 59 06 27

Lot

Cahors	Allô Taxi, 742 chemin des Junies	☎ 05 65 22 19 42
	Taxi Baptiste, 70 allées Fénelon	☎ 06 74 88 62 08
	Taxi Gérard, Peyrolis	☎ 05 65 22 04 10
Figeac	Claude Busson, 2 avenue Jean Jaurès	☎ 06 08 42 38 24
	J.M. Luc, avenue de Nayrac	☎ 05 65 50 00 20
	Taxi Radio Figeac, 18 boulevard Juskiewenski	☎ 05 65 50 01 73
Gourdon	Castelnau Taxi, Croix de Pierre	☎ 05 65 41 64 68
	Gambetta Taxi, Lot. Hermissens	☎ 05 65 41 02 68
	Pasteur Taxi, 5 avenue Anciens Combattants	☎ 05 65 41 08 63
	Taxi Bourian, 14 avenue Léon Gambetta	☎ 05 65 41 17 57
	Taxi Mistecki Michel, le Bourg, St Clair	☎ 05 65 41 90 55
	Transport Gelis, les Hermissens	☎ 05 65 41 36 31
Saint Céré	Albine Belounis, 6 rue Gare, Biars-sur-Cère	☎ 05 65 38 43 95
	M. Pascal, avenue de la Libération, Bretenoux	☎ 05 65 10 90 90
	Taxi Saint Céréen, 54 rue de la République	☎ 05 65 38 36 36

Lot-et-Garonne

Agen	Agen Banlieue Taxi, 20 rue Arthur Rimbault	☎ 05 53 96 04 04
	Agen Taxi Gare, 1 place Rabelais	☎ 05 53 66 39 14
	Allô Taxi Agenais, 25 rue de La Couronne, Boé	☎ 05 53 96 76 19

	Bruno Taxi, 94 rue Emile Zola	☎ 06 08 57 32 15
	Taxi Boudignon, 34 rue Jeanne d'Arc	☎ 05 53 98 14 95
Marmande	J.C. André, Beyssac Turon	☎ 05 53 20 76 76
	P. Bouchard, 2 impasse Honoré Daumier	☎ 05 53 64 73 29
	M. Ducan, Rieutord	☎ 05 53 20 05 44
	P. Jamme, 14 impasse Frédéric Chopin	☎ 05 53 89 17 80
	J.M. Pages, 13 rue Tombeloly	☎ 06 17 18 79 61
Nérac	Taxi Lafage, 31 allées d'Albret	☎ 05 53 65 02 31
	Taxi Néracais, 14 boulevard 8 Mai 1945	☎ 05 53 65 35 04
Villeneuve-sur-Lot	AATV Taxi Roucaud, boulevard Palissy	☎ 05 53 40 26 95
	ARTL Taxi Lyneel, 19 allée des Cèdres	☎ 05 53 40 18 18
	S. Boutié, boulevard Palissy	☎ 06 86 49 10 57
	Guillaume Taxi, boulevard Palissy	☎ 05 53 40 11 51
	J.C. Hasse, rue des Etoiles	☎ 05 53 40 14 62
	Taxi André, 33 rue Colonel Robinet, Bias	☎ 05 53 40 20 99

Trains

There are trains direct from Charles de Gaulle airport in Paris to Bordeaux, from where you can connect to Agen and other towns in the region. Alternatively, you can take the underground or bus or a taxi to the relevant station in Paris for trains southbound. For details, contact the SNCF:

SNCF   ☎ 08 92 35 35 35
🖳 *www.voyages-sncf.com*
The website has an English option and enables you to look up and book train travel both to and within France.

Getting There By Car

Channel Crossings

Travelling to the area from the UK by car you have the option of crossing the channel by Eurotunnel, which is a quick crossing but a long drive on the French side, or by ferry, which takes longer but involves less driving through France, unless you cross to Calais, which is slightly further from the region than the Channel Tunnel terminal. The most popular routes for those travelling to the region are to Calais, Caen, Cherbourg, Dieppe and St Malo, and the main carriers are detailed below. The routes into St Malo provide the shortest drive once in France.

There are also crossings from Weymouth to St Malo via Guernsey or Jersey between mid-March and the beginning of November, but these routes require a change of vessel on the relevant island.

Another option is to take a longer sea crossing down the west coast of France to Bilbao or Santander in Spain and have a shorter drive to the area.

Route	Journey Time
Dover/Calais by Channel Tunnel	35 minutes
Dover/Calais by Seacat	1 hour
Dover/Calais by standard ferry	1 hour 15 minutes
Newhaven/Dieppe by Seacat	Around 2 hours
Portsmouth/Caen by fast ferry	3 hours 30 minutes
Portsmouth/Caen by standard ferry	6 hours daytime 7 hours 30 minutes overnight
Poole/Cherbourg by ferry	2 hours 15 minutes daytime 6 hours 15 minutes overnight
Dublin & Rosslare/Cherbourg by ferry	18 hours
Portsmouth/St Malo by ferry	9 hours daytime 11 hours 30 minutes overnight
Poole/St Malo by Seacat	4 hours 35 minutes
Portsmouth/Bilbao by cruise liner	36 hours
Plymouth/Santander by cruise liner	24 hours

Dover/Calais

Tunnel	Eurotunnel	*UK* ☎ 0870-535 3535

💻 *www.eurotunnel.co.uk*
Lines open Mondays to Fridays 8am to 7pm, Saturdays 8am to 5.30pm, Sundays 9am to 5.30pm. There are two or three crossings per hour during the day and less frequent crossings during the night.

Eurotunnel Property Owners'
Club   *UK* ☎ 0870 538 8388
Five return crossings must be purchased initially, at £129 each for long-stay or £99 for short-stay – an excellent saving if you want to travel at peak times, as the tickets are vastly cheaper than an ordinary peak-time fare, but on the other hand you don't get a discount for travelling at 6am in the middle of winter! The tickets are 'fully flexible'. There's an initial administration fee of £30 plus an annual membership fee of £35. Membership of the Property Owners' Club allows you to use the Club Class check-in and entitles you to a 20 per cent discount off bookings for friends and relatives.

Seacat	Hoverspeed	*UK* ☎ 0870-240 8070
	💻 *www.hoverspeed.com*	*France* ☎ 03 21 46 14 54

The Seacat operates from mid-March to mid-December, hourly from 5am to 8pm in high season.

Ferry	P&O Ferries	*UK* ☎ 0870-520 2020
	💻 *www.poferries.com*	*France* ☎ 01 55 69 82 28

	Sea France	*UK* ☎ 0870-571 1711
	💻 *www.seafrance.co.uk*	*France* ☎ 03 21 46 80 00
		or 08 25 82 60 00

Crossings all year, at least one every hour in high season.

Newhaven/Dieppe

Seacat	Hoverspeed	*UK* ☎ 0870-240 8070
	💻 *www.hoverspeed.co.uk*	*France* ☎ 03 21 46 14 54

This service operates from the beginning of April to the first week in October, offering up to two crossings a day, depending on the time of year and day of the week.
Frequent User membership is free but you need to provide three booking references from the previous six months as proof of regular travel. Membership entitles you to a 20 per cent discount.

Portsmouth/Caen

Fast Ferry	P&O Ferries	*UK* ☎ 0870-520 2020
	💻 *www.poportsmouth.com*	*France* ☎ 01 55 69 82 28

This fast ferry operates from April to September with an average of two crossings a day.

Standard Ferry   Brittany Ferries   *UK* ☎ 0870-366 5333
                 💻 *www.brittany-ferries.co.uk*   *France* ☎ 08 25 82 88 28
                 These ferries operate all year with at least two sailings a day.

                 Brittany Ferries Property Owners'
                 Travel Club   *UK* ☎ 0870-514 3555
                 Brittany Ferries' Property Owners' Travel Club offers savings of
                 up to 33 per cent on passenger and vehicle fares and three
                 guest vouchers for friends, providing up to 15 per cent savings
                 on standard fares. There's a one-off registration fee of £35 and
                 a £40 annual membership fee.

Poole/Cherbourg

Ferry   Brittany Ferries   *UK* ☎ 0870-366 5333
                 💻 *www.brittany-ferries.co.uk*   *France* ☎ 08 25 82 88 28
                 This service runs from mid-February to mid-November, with at
                 least one daytime crossing every day.
                 For details of the Property Owners' Travel Club, see above.

Dublin & Rosslare/Cherbourg

Ferry: P&O Irish Sea   *UK* ☎ 0870-242 4777
                 💻 *www.poirishsea.com*   *ROI* ☎ 1800-409049
                 This is an 18-hour service from Dublin, some ships travelling
                 via Rosslare. Phone lines are open Mondays to Fridays from
                 7.30am to10.30pm, and Saturdays and Sundays from 7.30am
                 to 8.30pm.

Portsmouth/St Malo

Ferry   Brittany Ferries   *UK* ☎ 0870-366 5333
                 💻 *www.brittany-ferries.co.uk*   *France* ☎ 08 25 82 88 28
                 There's at least one daytime crossing every day from January
                 to mid-November. Overnight sailings depart at 8.30pm to arrive
                 at 8am the next day.
                 For details of the Property Owners' Travel Club, see above.

Poole/St Malo

Seacat   Condor Ferries   *UK* ☎ 0845-345 2000
                 💻 *www.condorferries.co.uk*
                 Office open Mondays to Fridays from 8.30am to 7.30pm,
                 Saturdays from 8.30am to 5.30pm, and Sundays from 9am to
                 5pm in summer; Mondays to Fridays from 8.30am to 5.30pm,
                 and Saturdays and Sundays from 9am to 5pm in winter.
                 This service operates from the end of May to the
                 end of September.
                 Frequent Traveller Membership entitles you to a 20 per cent
                 discount on all Channel crossings and a 10 per cent discount
                 between the Channel Islands and France. Annual membership
                 costs £66 for an individual plus a £20 for a spouse.

Portsmouth/Bilbao

Ferry   P&O Portsmouth   *UK* ☎ 08705-202020
💻 *www.poportsmouth.com*
This route decreases the long drive through France and delivers you directly to Bilbao, one of northern Spain's major cities. The crossing takes around 36 hours on the luxurious Pride of Bilbao, which is a cruise liner rather than a ferry. There are two crossings per week.

P&O Portsmouth Traveller
Loyalty Scheme   *UK* ☎ 08706-008008
'Traveller' is a new loyalty scheme available exclusively to property owners abroad. There's no registration fee but a £35 annual membership fee. A photocopy of a utility bill is required with your application form. Membership currently entitles you to the following:

- Up to 45 per cent off your fares and up to 30 per cent discount on guests' fares;

- 10 per cent off meals and commission-free exchange;

- Points collected with each booking (on average you can earn one free crossing for every four booked).

The Traveller call centre is open Mondays to Fridays 8am to 8pm, weekends 8am to 6.30pm.

Plymouth/Santander

Ferry   Brittany Ferries   *UK* ☎ 0870-366 5333
💻 *www.brittany-ferries.co.uk*   *France* ☎ 08 25 82 88 28
This 24-hour cruise is a shorter crossing than Bilbao but with a slightly longer drive from Santander into France. Two sailings a week from Plymouth.
For details of the Property Owners' Travel Club, see above.

Booking

As an alternative to booking direct with the ferry company, you can use one of several companies that will help you to obtain the cheapest fare. These include:

💻 *www.ferrycrossings-uk.co.uk*   *UK* ☎ 0871-222 8642
💻 *www.cheap4ferries.co.uk*   *UK* ☎ 0870-700 0138
💻 *www.ferry-crossings-online.co.uk*

Suggested Routes

Suggested routes to the most central main town in each department from each port are described below. These are based on an average driving speed of 120kph (75mph) on motorways and 80kph (50mph) on other roads, and costs are based on fuel at €1.10 per litre and fuel consumption of 30mpg in towns and 40mpg on the motorway. The toll charges given are approximate, as charges on motorways south of Paris can vary by around €5 according to the day and time of travel.

From Calais

Depending on the time you 'hit' Paris, your journey time can vary by anything up to one and half hours. Times to avoid are 7 to 10am and 3 to 7pm (not least because your chance of being involved in a crash are even higher at those times than at others!). If you aren't familiar with driving on the Paris ring road (*périphérique*) or other motorways near Paris, pay attention to the signposts, as the junctions are close together and you have little warning of the next one. In fact, if you aren't familiar with driving on the Paris ring road, you might be better advised to choose another route!

● **Calais ➜ Périgueux**

Suggested Route
A 26 to Béthune
A1 to Paris
A3 southbound towards Paris
A86 to Bordeaux (around Paris)
A186 to Bordeaux (around Paris)
A10 to Orléans
A71 to Vierzon
A20 to junction 33, Limoges
N21 to Périgueux

Summary
Distance: 775km (485mi)
Time: 7 hours, 40 minutes
Cost: €62 plus tolls (€33)

● **Calais ➜ Cahors**

Suggested Route
A 26 to Béthune
A1 to Paris
A3 southbound towards Paris
A86 to Bordeaux (around Paris)
A186 to Bordeaux (around Paris)
A10 to Orléans
A71 to Vierzon
A20 to junction 57, north of Cahors
N20 into Cahors

Summary
Distance: 865km (540mi)
Time: 8 hours, 20 minutes
Cost: €69 plus tolls (€40)

● **Calais ➜ Agen**

Suggested Route
A 26 to Béthune
A1 to Paris

Summary
Distance: 950km (590mi)
Time: 8 hours, 55 minutes

A3 southbound towards Paris
A86 to Bordeaux (around Paris)
A186 to Bordeaux (around Paris)
A10 to Orléans
A71 to Vierzon
A20 to junction 57
N20 down into Cahors
D653/D656 past Tournon and into Agen

Cost: €76 plus tolls (€48)

From Dieppe

● **Dieppe ➜ Périgueux**

Suggested Route
N27 ➜ A151 ➜ A150 towards Rouen
A13 to Paris
Périphérique east (around Paris)
A6 towards Nantes
A10 to Orléans
A71 to Vierzon
A20 to junction 33, Limoges
N21 to Périgueux

Summary
Distance: 670km (420mi)
Time: 7 hours, 10 minutes
Cost: €55 plus tolls (€17)

● **Dieppe ➜ Cahors**

Suggested Route
N27 ➜ A151 ➜ A150 towards Rouen
A13 to Paris
Périphérique east (around Paris)
A6 towards Nantes
A10 to Orléans
A71 to Vierzon
A20 to junction 57, north of Cahors
N20 into Cahors

Summary
Distance: 760km (475mi)
Time: 7 hours, 40 minutes
Cost: €60 plus tolls (€22)

● **Dieppe ➜ Agen**

Suggested Route
N27 ➜ A151 ➜ A150 towards Rouen
A13 to Paris
Périphérique east (around Paris)
A6 towards Nantes
A10 to Orléans
A71 to Vierzon
A20 to junction 57
N20 down into Cahors
D653/D656 past Tournon and into Agen

Summary
Distance: 840km (525mi)
Time: 8 hours, 15 minutes
Cost: €67 plus tolls (€32)

From Caen

● **Caen ➔ Périgueux**

Suggested Route
N158 from Caen towards Falaise
Continue on N158 to Sées
N138 to Alençon
A28 past Le Mans, exit at Ecommoy
N138 to Tours
E502 to A10
A10 to Poitiers
N10 south to Angoulême
D939 to Périgueux

Summary
Distance: 545km (340mi)
Time: 6 hours, 30 minutes
Cost: €47 plus tolls (€17)

● **Caen ➔ Cahors**

Suggested Route
N158 from Caen towards Falaise
Continue on N158 to Sées
N138 to Alençon
A28 past Le Mans, exit at Ecommoy
N138 to Tours
A10 to Poitiers
N147 to Limoges
A20 to junction 57, north of Cahors
N20 into Cahors

Summary
Distance: 640km (400mi)
Time: 7 hours, 30 minute
Cost: €58 plus tolls (€20)

● **Caen ➔ Agen**

Suggested Route
N158 from Caen towards Falaise
Continue on N158 to Sées
N138 to Alençon
A28 past Le Mans
A11 to Angers
D761/D938 down to Niort
A10 to Bordeaux
A62 to Agen

Summary
Distance: 710km (445mi)
Time: 7 hours, 10 minutes
Cost: €52 plus tolls (€40)

From Cherbourg

● **Cherbourg ➔ Périgueux**

Suggested Route
N13 to Valognes, D900 to Coutances
D971/D973 to Avranches

Summary
Distance: 655km (409mi)
Time: 8 hours, 25 minutes

A84 towards Rennes
N137 to Nantes
Ringroad west around Nantes in the direction of the airport
A83 past Niort to the A10
A10 to junction 34, St Jean d'Angély
D939 past Angoulême and on to Périgueux

Cost: €53 plus tolls (€17)

● **Cherbourg ➔ Cahors**

Suggested Route
N13 Cherbourg to Caen
N158 from Caen towards Falaise
Continue on N158 to Sées
N138 to Alençon
A28 past Le Mans, exit at Ecommoy
N138 to Tours
A10 to Poitiers
N147 to Limoges
A20 to junction 57, north of Cahors
N20 into Cahors

Summary
Distance: 760km (476mi)
Time: 9 hours, 20 minutes
Cost: €67 plus tolls (€20)

● **Cherbourg ➔ Agen**

Suggested Route
N13 to Valognes
D900 to Coutances
D971/D973 to Avranches
A84 towards Rennes
N137 to Nantes
Ringroad west around Nantes in the direction of the airport
A83 past Niort to the A10
A10 to Bordeaux
N230 around Bordeaux
A62 to Agen

Summary
Distance: 775km (485mi)
Time: 8 hours, 45 minutes
Cost: €63 plus tolls (€30)

From St Malo

● **St Malo ➔ Périgueux**

Suggested Route
N137 to Nantes
Ringroad west around Nantes in the direction of the airport
A83 past Niort to the A10
A10 to junction 34, St Jean d'Angély
D939 past Angoulême and on to Périgueux.

Summary
Distance: 520km (325mi)
Time: 6 hours 20 minutes
Cost: €42 plus tolls (€13)

- **St Malo ➔ Cahors**

Suggested Route
N137 to Nantes
Ringroad west around Nantes in the
    direction of the airport
A83 past Niort to the A10
A10 to Bordeaux
N230 around Bordeaux
A62 to Agen
D656/D653 to Cahors

Summary
Distance: 730km (455mi)
Time: 7 hours, 10 minutes
Cost: €57 plus tolls (€18)

- **St Malo ➔ Agen**

Suggested Route
N137 to Nantes
Ringroad west around Nantes in the
    direction of the airport
A83 past Niort to the A10
A10 to Bordeaux
N230 around Bordeaux
A62 to Agen

Summary
Distance: 640km (400mi)
Time: 6 hours, 40 minutes
Cost: €51 plus tolls (€20)

From Bilbao

- **Bilbao ➔ Périgueux**

Suggested Route
A8 from Bilbao (Spain) into France
A63 to Bayonne
N10 to Bordeaux
N230 around Bordeaux
A89/N89 to Périgueux

Summary
Distance: 455km (285mi)
Time: 5 hours
Cost: €36 plus tolls (€25)

- **Bilbao ➔ Cahors**

Suggested Route
A8 from Bilbao (Spain) into France
A63 to Bayonne
A64 to Toulouse
A20 north to Cahors

Summary
Distance: 545km (340mi)
Time: 5 hours
Cost: €43 plus tolls (€20)

- **Bilbao ➔ Agen**

Suggested Route
A8 from Bilbao (Spain) into France
A63 to Bayonne

Summary
Distance: 370km (230mi)
Time: 4 hours

N10/N124 to Mont-de-Marsan   Cost: €29 plus tolls (€30)
D933/D665 to Nérac
D656 to Agen

From Santander

● **Santander ➜ Bilbao**

Suggested Route   **Summary**
Leave Santander on the A8 eastwards   Distance: 90km (55mi)
   towards Bilbao   Time: 1 hour
From Bilbao follow the route given   Cost: €7 plus tolls (€1.50)
   above to the relevant destination

Télépéage

If you're travelling regularly on French motorways, it's worth considering Télépéage. This involves a one off fee of €30 for the disc that fits to your windscreen, then €20 a year. An invoice is sent out monthly and you can arrange to pay by direct debit from a French bank account, in which case there's no charge for the disc.

With the standard contract there's no discount on tolls, but you no longer have to queue to pay, as you can use a dedicated lane. In fact, you don't even need to wind down your window as you go through a toll point. The same disc can be used on all French motorways. There are contracts that give discounts of up to 20 per cent on tolls, but these are primarily for commuters.

Apply online (🖳 *www.cofiroute.fr* – click on 'liber-t' in the French-language version) or go to the office at any toll point – usually near the kiosks.

Getting There By Rail

Eurostar

   🖳 *www.eurostar.co.uk*   *UK* ☎ 08705-186186
                                France ☎ 08 92 35 35 39

The Eurostar travels from Waterloo (London) and Ashford to both Lille and Paris. However, there are no direct routes from Lille to this area, so it's better to travel to Paris, from where you can travel down to Dordogne, Lot and Lot-et-Garonne. There are one or two trains per hour and journey time to Paris Gare du Nord is around three hours. You must then take the underground or a bus or taxi to the relevant station for a southbound train, as shown below.

Destination	Paris Station	Route
Dordogne		
Bergerac	Montparnasse	Change at Libourne or Bordeaux
Le Bugue	Austerlitz	Change at Périgueux or Limoges
Montpon	Montparnasse	Change at Limoges, Périgueux or Bordeaux
Périgueux	Austerlitz	Direct trains (journey time around 4 hours 15 minutes)
Sarlat-la-Canéda	Austerlitz or Montparnasse	Change at Libourne or Souillac

(There are no stations at Nontron or Ribérac.)

Lot		
Cahors	Austerlitz	Direct trains (journey time around 5 hours 15 minutes)
Figeac	Austerlitz	Direct trains (journey time around 6 hours)
Gourdon	Austerlitz	Direct trains (journey time around 5 hours)
St Céré (Bretenoux-Biars)	Austerlitz	Change at Brive-la-Gaillarde
Lot-et-Garonne		
Agen	Montparnasse	Direct trains (journey time around 4 hours)
Marmande	Montparnasse	Change at Bordeaux
Villeneuve-sur-Lot	Montparnasse	Change at Agen

(There's no station at Nérac.)

For details of mainline train services, contact the SNCF:

🖳 *www.voyages-sncf.com*   ☎ 3635 or 08 92 35 35 35
The website has an English option and enables you to look up and book train travel both to and within France.

The following telephone numbers are for stations in the area; some station offices are open limited hours.

Dordogne

Bergerac	☎ 05 53 63 53 81
Le Bugue	☎ 05 53 07 20 05
Montpon	☎ 05 53 80 32 54
Périgueux	☎ 05 53 06 21 57
Sarlat-la-Canéda	☎ 05 53 59 00 21

Lot

Cahors	☎ 05 65 23 33 50
Figeac	☎ 05 65 64 94 55
Gourdon	☎ 05 65 41 02 19
St Céré	☎ 05 65 10 31 04

Lot-et-Garonne

Agen	☎ 05 53 77 81 65
Marmande	☎ 05 53 20 45 63
Villeneuve-sur-Lot	☎ 05 53 70 00 35

Getting Around

Buses in the region are primarily to serve the schools and colleges and so the routes pass not only the schools but in many cases railway stations as well. Unfortunately, this also means that there's drastic reduction (if not a total cessation) in services on some routes during school holidays. Timetables are usually displayed at bus stops and can be obtained from tourist offices or the relevant transport company's offices. For details of taxi services, see page 29.

Local Trains

Ter Auvergne operates a local rail network in conjunction with the SNCF.
     🖳 *www.ter-sncf.com/auvergne*   ☎ 08 92 35 35 35

Other Public Transport

Dordogne

Transport in and around Bergerac is organised by Transports Urbains de Bergerac/TUB (☎ 05 53 74 66 40). Various operators provide services between Bergerac and other towns in the department, including the following:

Bergerac	Les Cars Boullet	☎ 05 53 61 00 46
	Services include Bergerac to Cadouin.	

Les Cars Bleu d'Eymet   ☎ 05 53 23 81 92
Services include Bergerac to Marmande.

CFTA   ☎ 05 53 08 43 13
Services include Bergerac to Périgueux.

Périgueux   Péribus, cours Montaigne   ☎ 05 53 53 30 37

Sarlat-la-Canéda CFTA Périgord, avenue Aristide Briand ☎ 05 53 08 43 13

Lot

General   Le Bus du Lot   ☎ 05 65 53 27 50

Figeac   Le Bus Figeac, Mairie, rue de Colomb   ☎ 05 65 34 81 93
This bus service has many routes in and around the town and
is free to everyone. Timetables are available from the *mairie*.

Cahors   Bus Evidence   ☎ 05 65 53 07 07
A town bus service – timetables available from the
tourist office.

Lot-et-Garonne

There are various bus companies that operate across this department, the
majority going through or starting from Agen, including the following:

General   Autocars Pascal   ☎ 05 53 98 50 60
Services include Agen to Villeneuve-sur-Lot.

Citram Aquitaine   ☎ 05 56 43 68 68
Services include Agen to Nérac.

Transports Sivadon   ☎ 05 53 65 53 60
ervices include Agen to Barbaste.

Citram Pyrénées   ☎ 05 59 27 22 22
Services include Agen to Pau.

Transports Bajolle   ☎ 05 62 28 04 82
Services include Agen to Condom.

Transports Casteran   ☎ 05 53 85 20 78
Services include Agen to Clairac.

Transports Rivière   ☎ 05 62 05 46 24
Services include Agen to Auch.

Transports Serag   ☎ 05 58 75 22 89
Services include Marmande to Mont Marsan.

Agen   Trans Bus, 121bis boulevard Carnot   ☎ 05 53 48 90 10
                      Operates in and around Agen.

Camper Van Hire

General   Camping Club de France, 5bis
                      rue Maurice Rouvier, 75014 Paris   ☎ 01 58 14 01 23
                      🖳 *www.campingclub.asso.fr*

Dordogne

Brantôme   Font Vendôme, route de Nontron   ☎ 05 53 05 78 13
                      🖳 *www.font-vendome.fr*

Lot

Cahors   Sport 2000, 759 chemin Belle Croix   ☎ 05 65 22 12 40
                      (behind the Carrefour hypermarket)
                      Open Mondays to Saturdays 10am to 12.15pm
                      and 2 to 7.15pm.

Lot-et-Garonne

Villeneuve-sur- Allez et Cazeneuve, route de Bordeaux ☎ 05 53 01 02 00
Lot   (west of the town)

GENERAL INFORMATION

Accommodation

Camping

                      Camping Qualité, 105 rue La Fayette,
                      Paris   ☎ 02 40 82 57 63
                      🖳 *www.campingqualite.com*
                      This organisation holds information on campsites
                      all over   France.

Châteaux

                      Bienvenue au Château
                      🖳 *www.bienvenue-au-chateau.com*
                      This website is available in English and gives details of
                      château accommodation in western France.

Gîtes And Bed & Breakfast

Tourist offices have lists of bed and breakfast facilities (B&B) in the area
and may display one in their window. Some communes have *gîtes* available
for rent via the *mairie*.

Many *gîtes* owners are members of Gîtes de France, 25 rue Wilson, Périgueux (☎ 05 53 35 50 24, 🖳 www.gites-de-france.fr), through which you can book accommodation throughout France.

Internet Booking

The websites below have *gîte* and B&B accommodation listed and bookings are made direct with the owners via the site, where contact details are given.

French Connections
🖳 *www.frenchconnections.co.uk*

Holiday Homes France
🖳 *www.holidayhomes-france.co.uk*
For both *gîtes* and B&B.

Pour Les Vacances
🖳 *www.pour-les-vacances.com*
A British site for B&B accommodation.

Hotels

National Chains

The following hotels can be found throughout France:

Formule 1   ☎ 08 92 68 56 85
🖳 *www.hotelformule1.com*

Hôtel de France   ☎ 01 41 39 22 23
🖳 *www.hotel-france.co*m

Hôtel Première Classe   ☎ 08 25 00 30 03
🖳 *www.hotelpremierclasse.f*r

Ibis Hotels   ☎ 08 92 68 66 86
🖳 *www.ibishotel.com*

Mercure   ☎ 08 25 88 44 44
🖳 *www.mercure.com*

Novotel   ☎ 08 25 88 44 44
🖳 *www.novotel.com*

Administration

Regional Capitals

Bordeaux is the capital of the Aquitaine region, which includes the departments of Dordogne and Lot-et-Garonne.

Conseil Régional d'Aquitaine,
Hôtel de Région, 14 rue François de
Sourdis, Bordeaux   ☎ 05 57 57 80 00
💻 *www.cr-aquitaine.fr*

Toulouse is the capital of the Midi-Pyrénées region, which includes Lot.

Conseil Régional Midi-Pyrénées,
22 boulevard Maréchal Juin, Toulouse   ☎ 05 61 33 50 50
💻 *www.cr-mip.fr*

Préfectures

The *préfecture* is the administrative centre for each department and is
located in the department's main city. You may need to contact or visit the
préfecture or *sous-préfecture* (see below) if you apply for a residence permit,
register ownership of a new car or apply for planning permission.

Dordogne   2 rue Paul Louis-Courier, Périgueux   ☎ 05 53 02 20 20
💻 *www.dordogne.pref.gouv.fr*

Lot   place Jean Jacques Chapou, Cahors   ☎ 05 65 23 10 00
💻 *www.lot.pref.gouv.fr*

Lot-et-Garonne place Verdun, Agen   ☎ 05 53 77 60 47
💻 *www.lot-et-garonne.pref.gouv.fr*

Sous-Préfectures

Dordogne

Bergerac   place Gambetta   ☎ 05 53 61 53 00

Nontron   12bis boulevard Gambetta   ☎ 05 53 60 83 60

Sarlat-la-Canéda place Salvador Allende   ☎ 05 53 31 41 00

Lot

Figeac   22 rue Caviale   ☎ 05 65 34 04 15

Gourdon   62 boulevard Aristide Briand   ☎ 05 65 41 00 08

Lot-et-Garonne

Marmande   rue de la Libération   ☎ 05 53 76 01 76

Nérac   avenue Maréchal Foch   ☎ 05 53 65 03 18

Villeneuve-sur-   rue Cieutat   ☎ 05 53 49 03 16
Lot

Town Halls (Mairies)

All French towns have an *hôtel de ville*, which is the equivalent of a town hall, and most villages have a *mairie*, which has no equivalent in the UK (and certainly isn't a 'village hall'!). To avoid confusion, we have used the French word *mairie* to apply to both town hall and *mairie* unless otherwise specified.

Although town halls are usually open Mondays to Fridays, the opening hours of *mairies* vary greatly and in small communes they may be open only two or three hours each week at set times (usually on two days). There's usually a function room (*une salle des fêtes* or *salle polyvalente*), attached to the town hall/*mairie* or close by. Notice boards at the town halls/*mairies* are used for formal notices, while local shops usually display a variety of posters for local events.

The 'mayor' of a town or village is *Monsieur* or *Madame le Maire* (yes, even a female mayor is '*le Maire*'!).The *Maire* is the equivalent of a British mayor but is usually more accessible and has more immediate authority in the community. If you buy or rent a property in a small community, you should visit the *mairie* at the earliest opportunity to introduce yourselves to the *Maire*.

If you're considering making any alterations to your house or boundaries, it's **essential** to contact the *Maire* **before** undertaking any work or even drawing up plans. Full details of the required procedures are described in ***Renovating & Maintaining Your French Home*** (see page 300).

The *mairie* should also be your first port of call if you need any advice, as they're a mine of useful information and, if they haven't got what you need, will either get it for you or point you in the right direction.

Embassies & Consulates

British Embassy, 35 rue du Faubourg
St Honoré, Paris   ☎ 01 44 51 31 00
🖳 *www.britishembassy.gov.uk*

British Consulate-General,
353 boulevard du Président Wilson,
BP91, 33073 Bordeaux   ☎ 05 57 22 21 10

Banks

The majority of French banks close for lunch and are open Saturday mornings. Banks are rarely open on Mondays and in small towns may be open only in the mornings or even just a few sessions a week. Below are the names of the most commonly found banks, with a web address and a contact number (if available) to allow you to find the branch closest to you.

Banque Populaire   🖳 *www.banquepopulaire.fr*   ☎ 05 55 45 33 00

BNP Paribas   🖳 *www.bnpparibas.ne*t   ☎ 08 20 82 00 01
To find your nearest branch click on 'toutes les agences et leurs régions'.

Banque Tarneaud   🖳 *www.tarneaud.fr*   ☎ 08 10 63 28 28
Open Mondays to Fridays 7.30am to 10pm, Saturdays 9am to 5pm.

Caisse d'Epargne   🖳 *www.caissedepargne.co*m   ☎ 05 49 44 50 00

Crédit Agricole   🖳 *www.creditagricole.fr*
To find your nearest branch, on the front page of the site use the box in the top right corner with the map of France. There are some English pages available on this website.

Dordogne   ☎ 05 45 20 49 60
This is an English-language helpline open Monday to Friday 10am to 5pm.

Lot   ☎ 08 90 71 20 71

Lot-et-Garonne   ☎ 08 10 81 06 15

Crédit Lyonnais   🖳 *www.creditlyonnais.fr*   ☎ 08 21 80 90 90
English option on the website.

Crédit Mutuel   🖳 *www.cmso.com*   ☎ 08 21 01 10 12
To find your nearest branch click on '*où nous trouver*'.

Société Générale   🖳 *www.societegenerale.fr*   ☎ 05 49 55 57 00
To find your nearest branch on the website go to '*trouver une agence*'.

English-Language Bank

Britline, 15 esplanade Brillaud de Laujardière, 14050 Caen Cedex   ☎ 02 31 55 67 89
🖳 *www.britline.com*
Britline is a branch of Crédit Agricole and is located in Caen.

It's an English-language bank with some of its forms in English, although most forms and its newsletter are in French. However, an English-speaking teller always answers the telephone.

Note that branches of Crédit Agricole in Dordogne, Lot and Lot-et-Garonne (and elsewhere) aren't familiar with dealing with Britline and, as it's in a different department, you cannot pay in cheques at your local branch. To pay a cheque into your Britline account you need to post it to Britline at the above address. Withdrawals, however, are possible through any Crédit Agricole cash machine. As more and more Crédit Agricole branches have English-speaking staff, you may find opening an account locally more advantageous.

General Information

French banking is quite different from banking in the UK. The most noticeable differences are the following:

- French cheques are laid out differently (the amount **precedes** the payee), and you must state the town where the cheque was written. Note also that, when writing figures, a comma is used in place of a decimal point and a point or space instead of a comma in thousands, e.g. €1.234,56 or €1 234,56.

- You must usually press a button or even enter a code to gain access to a bank.

- Most banks have open-plan desks with receptionists, who handle minimal amounts of cash, most cash transactions being carried out by machine.

- Some banks don't have any cash at the counter. When withdrawing money, you're given a card, which you take to a cash machine to obtain the money. This system doesn't always enable you to withdraw the exact amount you want, e.g. €20 or €40, but not €30.

- Receipts aren't always issued when paying in money without a paying-in slip, so ask for a paying-in book (or simply ask for a receipt – *un reçu*).

- When you open an account, you will be given copies of your *relevé d'identité bancaire* (normally called *un RIB* – pronounced 'reeb'), which contains all your account details. As you will need to provide a *RIB* when setting up a direct debit or an account (e.g. with a shop) and when asking anyone (e.g. an employer) to pay money into your account, it's wise to take extra copies.

- There are no cheque guarantee cards, although many shops now insist on identification with cheques.

- Cheques are guaranteed for payment in France, but if you write a cheque without sufficient funds in your account (unless you have an authorised overdraft facility) it may result in a registered letter being sent by the bank demanding that funds are paid into the account within 30 days. If this happens again within 12 months, the account will be closed and you will be unable to hold any account in France for a year and will be blacklisted for three years. **You have been warned!**

- It's wise to keep at least €30 in your account at all times to cover any unexpected charges. For example, some banks charge to transfer money between accounts of the same bank while others charge you each time you access your account online.

- If your cheque book is lost or stolen, irrespective of which bank you use, call ☎ 01 42 41 22 22 between 8am and 11pm.

Opening a French bank account will provide many benefits – not least the provision of a debit card (*une carte bleue*), which has a microchip and requires you to enter a four-digit PIN rather than sign a receipt. Such a card enables you to use automated petrol pumps (see page 64) and will save you embarrassment and hassle in shops where the staff are unfamiliar with UK credit cards and either won't accept them or don't know how to 'swipe' them. Most *cartes bleues* can be used all over Europe.

Moneo

Moneo is a system designed to eliminate the need to carry small change. A Moneo card has an initial cost of €8 and is then 'charged' with up to €100 and can be used to buy a newspaper, a loaf of bread or even a bar of chocolate in shops, cafés, newsagents and bakeries displaying the Moneo sign, of which there's an increasing number. The card can be used for purchases up to €30 and, once the credit is used, it can be re-charged at banks and post offices. Cards are ordered from your bank and you must have a French bank account to obtain one.

Business Services

Employment Agencies

Agence Nationale pour l'Emploi (ANPE)
🖳 *www.anpe.fr*

ANPE is the national employment agency. The main offices of ANPE are listed in the relevant chapter. Independent companies, **which are allowed to offer only temporary employment**, include the following:

Adecco	🖥 *www.adecco.fr*
Manpower	🖥 *www.manpower.fr*
Vedior Bis	🖥 *www.vediorbis.com*

Communications

Telephone

Fixed Line Telephone Services

Telephone installations must be carried out by France Télécom, but telephone services are also available from a number of other operators, some of which are listed below.

France Télécom ☎ 1014
🖥 *www.francetelecom.fr*   *From abroad* ☎ 00 800 44 33 22 11
The website has an English option and France Télécom has an English-language helpline (☎ 08 00 36 47 75)

One.Tel ☎ 08 25 92 55 55
🖥 *www.onetel.fr*

Tele2 ☎ 08 11 24 00 10
🖥 *www.tele2.fr*

Primus Telecom ☎ 05 53 05 47 82
🖥 *www.as24telecom.com*
An excellent English-language service provided by
Andrew Martin.

These companies can prove to be cheaper than France Télécom, especially for international calls, which are often the same tariff day and night, but you should always compare before deciding. France Télécom's standing charge is payable for the line, even if you use another service provider. It's worth noting that some UK non-geographical numbers (e.g. beginning 0870 or 0345) are accessible only via a France Telecom connection.

Useful Numbers

Directory Enquiries ☎ 3212
For international dialling information.

BT Direct ☎ 08 00 99 00 44
For making reverse-charge calls to the UK, etc.

Mobile Telephones

Mobile phone (*portable* or, increasingly, *mobile*) shops are found in most town centres, and hypermarkets sell a good selection of handsets and connection packages. Reception in rural areas can be poor, with some quite large areas having no reception at all. There are just three service providers in France: Bouygues, Orange and SFR. If your mobile phone is lost or stolen, contact the appropriate number below:

Bouygues	☎ 08 00 29 10 00
Orange	☎ 08 25 00 57 00 (*from abroad* ☎ +33 6 07 62 64 64)
SFR	☎ 06 10 00 19 00 (*from abroad* ☎ +33 6 10 00 19 00)

Public Telephones

These are located all over towns and villages and in railway stations, bars and cafés. The new kiosks are Perspex and usually accept only cards; however, if there's a group of three or more kiosks, one may accept coins. All public phones allow international calls and there's a button with a double flag symbol, which you can press for the telephone display to appear in different languages.

Telephone cards are available from post offices, railway stations, cafés, banks and anywhere you see the sign *Télécarte en vente ici*. Cards don't have a standard design, as they're used for advertising. You often need a telephone card for internet access at a public facility such as the post office.

Telephone Directories

Directories are no longer available from France Télécom stores. If you don't have a directory or would like a copy for a neighbouring department, they can be obtained by phoning ☎ 08 10 81 07 67 and cost between €7.50 and €12 depending on size. The line is often busy, so keep trying: choose option 2, then hold until the message finishes and (eventually) you will be put through to an operator.

Directories usually incorporate both yellow pages (*les pages jaunes*) and white pages (*l'annuaire* or *les pages blanches*) in a single book, back to back, although they can be ordered separately. All listings in the residential section are alphabetical order within each commune, so you need to know the name of the commune where the person you want to call lives.

Special Rate Phone Numbers

Special rate numbers normally start with 08 or 09 (mobile numbers start 06). Numbers beginning 09 are charged at high rates and are to be avoided if possible. The cost of calls to numbers beginning 08 varies greatly (see below), and you're advised to be wary of numbers for which the charge isn't specified. You should also avoid numbers starting with 00, as calls may be routed via another country. Common 08 prefixes include the following:

- 0800, 0805, 0809 – free call (known as *numéros verts*);

- 0810, 0811 – local call rates (known as *numéros azur*);

- 0836 – calls vary from free to €1.35 for connection plus 34 centimes per minute;

- 0899 79 – €1.35 for connection plus 34 centimes per minute.

Internet Access

There are a number of internet service providers (ISPs) in France, and the following websites can help you to choose the best provider for you.

🖳 *www.club-internet.fr*

🖳 *www.francenet.fr*

🖳 *www.illiclic.com* (operated by La Poste)

🖳 *www.freesurf.fr*

🖳 *www.wanadoo.fr* (operated by France Télécom and available in English)

🖳 *www.worldnet.fr*

The best way to get connected is to go to a public internet access provider (see below) and use this access to register an address and obtain the dial-up numbers, etc. so that you can then go online at home. Note that software may need to be installed in your computer. Alternatively, you can register with Wanadoo by phone (☎ 08 10 28 32 83), when you will be given all the access codes and phone numbers immediately.

Wanadoo offers a number of dial-up packages, which can work out cheaper than paying for access calls on a per minute basis if you spent more than a certain time online.

Public Internet Access

All France Télécom stores have internet access, as do many post offices. Public places that offer access usually require a telephone card.

Broadband

High-speed lines or broadband (*le haut-débit*) are gradually becoming more widely available, although not often in rural areas. However, the French government plans to have high speed lines available throughout the country, including rural areas, by 2007. To find out if broadband is currently available where you are, go to 💻 *www.francetelecom.fr* and on the front page click on '*Tout sur l'ADSL*', then click the red label/box, '*L'ADSL chez vous?*', enter your phone number and it will tell you straight away if high-speed lines are available to you.

There are various tariffs available for high-speed connections, for example Wanadoo and France Télécom offer ADSL packages, usually entailing a set fee plus a monthly payment. Offers are changing all the time and are frequently advertised on TV and on the relevant web sites. More information can be obtained from 💻 *www.francetelecom.fr* and 💻 *www.adsl-france.org*.

Useful Web Addresses

The following is a selection from the myriad websites accessible:

💻 *www.voila.fr* – A French search engine;

💻 *www.pagesjeunes.fr* – This site has the option at the bottom to convert the language to English.

💻 *www.meteoconsult.com* – Weather site. (Alternatively call ☎ 08 99 70 11 11 and press '1' for the weather forecast in English.)

💻 *www.service-public.fr* – This is the official gateway to the French civil service.

💻 *www.google.com* – Although this is an English-language search engine, when foreign web sites are located it gives you the option of translating the web page into English – the results are never less than entertaining!

Television & Radio

Whether your television (TV) set will work in France is dependent on which model you have. Most televisions bought in the UK in the last few years should work in France, as most now have the capability to pick up both Secam and PAL signals. If you buy a television in France, you may find that it's sold without a stand.

If you're learning French, watching French TV with subtitles is a good idea. If subtitles are available, they can be found on Teletext 888. If you have a TV guide, the programme may have a symbol of an ear to show that it has subtitles, which are generally for the hard of hearing but will do just as well for foreigners!

It's possible to get British television in France but a satellite dish is needed and you must ensure that you're aware of the legalities before proceeding. There are various British suppliers and installers of satellite who will give you all the information you need, including the following company, which has a comprehensive website:

> Big Dish Satellite
> Mouriol, Milhaguet, 87440 Marval   ☎ 05 55 78 72 98
> 🖳 *www.bigdishsat.com*

Licence

To watch TV in France you need a licence, costing €116.50 for colour and €74.31 for black and white. This fee covers all the television sets that you own in France, even if in different locations such as a caravan or holiday home. As in the UK, when a television set is purchased, the shop must inform the authorities and a television licence bill will duly arrive (unlike the UK, it takes several months!).

If you bring a British TV into France that's capable of receiving French programmes, you should notify the Centre Régional de la Redevance Audiovisuelle within 30 days.

> CRRA   ☎ 01 49 70 40 00
> 🖳 *www.service-public.fr*

Radio

There's a wide variety of local and national stations that can be received in the area, some of which are detailed below.

Station	FM Frequency	Description
ARL	98.1	Classical and current easy-listening music
Bergerac	95	A wide variety of current music
Bleu Gironde	100.1/100.4	A wide variety of current music
Chérie FM	89.9/102.7	Current easy-listening music
Culture	95.7/98/101.1	Talk radio and classical music
Europe 2	93.2/104.9/106.2	A wide variety of current music

FUN	98.3/103.3	Current chart music
Info	105.5	News and regional information.
Inter	94.5/106.4	Talk radio and classical music
Nostalgie	102.6	As the name suggests, music from the past
NRJ	98.1	A wide variety of classical and current music
Orion	87.6	'Golden oldies' but primarily French music
RFM	90.7	Current easy-listening music
RTL	97.3/103.8/107.2	A mix of talk radio and music
Sud Radio	95.5/103.8	A mix of talk radio and music

Domestic Services

Equipment & Tool Hire

To hire equipment or tools you generally need to take some identification, e.g. a household bill, and must pay a deposit, by cheque or debit card.

Entertainment

Cinemas

Some French cinemas show English-language films in their original version, i.e. in English with French subtitles. These are identified by the letters *VO* (*version originale*) next to the title. (*VF* indicates that a film has been dubbed into French.)

English Books

Libraries and book shops stocking books in English are listed in each chapter. Those with impaired vision may be interested in the following service:

The English Language Library for the
Blind, 35 rue Lemercier, 75107 Paris   ☎ 01 42 93 47 57
🖳 *www.ellb.online.fr*

Festivals

There are many annual festivals in this region, just a small selection of which are listed in this book. Dates vary each year, so just the month has been given. A *Fêtes en Périgord* brochure, giving precise dates of events in Dordogne, is available from tourist offices; there are no equivalent publications for Lot or Lot-et-Garonne.

Holidays

The official French public holidays (*jours fériés*) are listed below. Note, however, that when a holiday falls on a Saturday or Sunday, another day off isn't usually granted 'in lieu', but when a holiday falls on a Tuesday or Thursday, the day before or the day after may also be taken as a holiday – either officially or unofficially. Shops may close independently of each other on these days.

Date	Holiday	French
1st January	New Year's Day	Jour de l'An
March/April	Easter Monday (1)	Lundi de Pâques
1st May	Labour Day	Fête du Travail
8th May	VE Day	Fête de la Libération/Victoire 1945
May (2)	Ascension Day	Jour de l'Ascension
May/June (3)	Whit Monday	Pentecôte
14th July	Bastille Day	Fête Nationale
15th August	Assumption Day	Fête de l'Assomption
1st November	All Saints' Day	Toussaint
11th November	Armistice Day	Fête de l'Armistice
25th December	Christmas Day	Noël

Notes:
1. Good Friday isn't a public holiday in France.

2. Ascension Day is the sixth Thursday after Easter.

3. Whit Monday is the second Monday after Ascension Day.

Mardi Gras in February is allowed by some businesses as a staff holiday.

Video/DVD Hire

DVDs are widely available and are usually viewable in English, but check the back of the case before buying or renting: there will be a Union Jack and/or the words *Sous-titres* (sub-titles) and *Langues* (languages) with '*Anglais*' in the list that follows. Some video shops also hire out DVD players (*lecteurs*).

Medical Facilities & Services

Ambulances

Ambulances are operated privately in France. If an ambulance has been agreed or requested by a doctor or medical establishment, the cost can be reclaimed if you're registered with the French social security system. In the event of a medical emergency dial ☎ 15.

Doctors

French doctors and dentists have flexible working hours and doctors may have an 'open surgery' during the week, or even at certain times every day, when no appointment is necessary; you just go and wait your turn.

You don't need to register with a doctor or dentist when you arrive in France; simply call when you need an appointment. There's a charge each time you visit or they visit you (more expensive in the evenings) which is partially reclaimable if you're registered with French social security or if you're on holiday from the UK and have an E111 form. **Remember to keep all receipts, including those of any prescriptions and the labels from any medicines prescribed, to send with your claim.**

If you intend to be in France for a long period or indeed permanently, it's recommended to ask your UK doctor for a print-out of your medical record. He may not be able to give you copies of the actual written records, but should be willing to provide a print-out (although you may be charged – £50 or more), which you should take to a French doctor on your first visit.

An E111 is valid for a minimum of a year, but if it's more than a year old it may be harder to get the paperwork sorted out. They're free from post offices in the UK, so if you aren't living permanently in France it's advisable to renew yours regularly.

When you go to a doctor or dentist in France, he will give you a form with details of the treatment given, their details and reference number. Ensure that you give your British address if you intend to reclaim these costs with your E111. This form should be attached to your E111 and sent to the nearest Caisse Régionale Assurance Maladie (CRAM – see **Health Authority** on page 62).

Emergencies

In the event of an emergency, dial one of the following numbers:

Any medical emergency
SAMU (Service d'Aide Médical d'Urgence)   ☎ 15

Police (see also below)
Gendarmes   ☎ 17

Fire or accident not requiring medical help (see below)
Sapeurs-Pompiers   ☎ 18

The *SAMU* are often the first on the scene in the event of an accident. You should call the police first and they will contact the *SAMU*, or you can call them as well.

If you need to call any of the above numbers, you will be asked a series of questions. Below are examples of what you may be asked and a selection of possible responses (with English translations).

1. Your name and phone number:
    Quel est votre nom et numéro de téléphone?
    [Give your surname first, then your first name, then a contact telephone number]

2. The nature of accident or problem:
    Quelle est la nature de l'accident?
    Il/elle s'est écroulé(e) (S/he has collapsed/fainted)
    Il/elle est tombé(e) d'une échelle/un arbre (S/he has fallen off a ladder/tree)
    Il/elle a eu une crise cardiaque (S/he has had a heart attack)

3. Your exact address/position and how to get there:
    Quelle est votre adresse exacte et pouvez-vous me donner des directions?
    [Give the address/location using the following vocabulary]
    au carrefour (at the crossroads)
    au coin (on the corner)
    tournez à droite/gauche (turn right/left)
    tout droit (straight on)
    après/avant (after/before)
    sur votre gauche/droite (on the left/right

4. How many people are involved:
    Combien de personnes sont impliquées?
    une/deux/trois personnes (one/two/three people)

5. The condition of any injured parties:
    Quels sont les blessures?
    Il/elle est inconscient(e) (S/he is unconscious)
    Il/elle a une hémorragie (S/he is bleeding)
    Il/elle souffre beaucoup (S/he is in a lot of pain)
    Il/elle a une fracture de la jambe/du bras (S/he has broken a leg/arm)

6. What treatment has been given:
    Quel médicament a été préscrit?
    [Give name of medication] ·
    Aucun (None)
A number of other useful emergency numbers are listed below.

Electricity problems
Dordogne   ☎ 08 10 33 30 24
Lot   ☎ 08 10 33 30 46
Lot-et-Garonne   ☎ 08 10 33 30 47

Emotional crisis
        Counselling In France   ☎ 05 55 60 01 23
        💻 *www.counsellinginfrance.com*

        Samaritans   ☎ 01 47 23 80 80
        An English-language service available
        from 3 to 11pm daily.

Gas leak
        Gaz de France

Dordogne
Bergerac   ☎ 05 53 57 18 90
Périgueux   ☎ 05 53 08 13 41
Sarlat-la-Canéda ☎ 08 10 57 78 23
Lot   ☎ 08 10 04 60 46
Lot-et-Garonne ☎ 05 53 68 39 69

Lost or stolen bank cards
Banque
Populaire   ☎ 08 25 08 24 24
BNP Paribas   ☎ 08 25 03 24 24
Banque
Tarneaud   ☎ 08 25 00 59 59
Caisse
d'Epargne   ☎ 08 92 68 32 08
Crédit
Agricole   ☎ 08 00 81 08 12 (*includes Britline* – see page 49)
Crédit
Lyonnais   ☎ 08 21 80 90 90
Crédit Mutuel   ☎ 05 56 24 28 28
Société
Générale   ☎ 08 25 07 00 70

Pest control (e.g. termites)
        ☎ 08 00 13 31 34

Poisoning

	Centre Anti-Poisons
Bordeaux	☎ 05 56 96 40 80
Toulouse	☎ 05 61 77 74 47

Other emergency numbers are listed in the front of the yellow pages.

Fire Brigade

The fire brigade (*sapeurs-pompiers* or *pompiers*) have a high level of medical training and are one of the first on the scene of any accident, often carrying out medical procedures until the arrival of the *SAMU*. In rural areas, *pompiers* are often 'reserves' and are called to duty by a siren giving three short, very loud blasts.

You can also call the fire brigade if you have a bee or wasp swarm. In the summer, such swarms are common and the *pompiers* get very busy, but they will still usually come the same day, although it may be late! You pay them directly, around €30, for the service.

Health Authority

The Caisse Régional Assurance Maladie (CRAM) deals with medical claims and expenses. You must contact CRAM in order to join the French social security system. Before you can join this system you need to have applied for or be in possession of a residence permit (*titre de séjour*, more commonly known as a *carte de séjour*, although strictly this is just one type of *titre de séjour*). Ambiguous new regulations came into force in January 2004, which can be interpreted to mean that EU nationals no longer require a *titre de séjour*; you should apply for one nevertheless, as the application procedure ensures that you meet the criteria for residence.

CRAM representatives pay regular visits to certain towns (usually to the *mairie*), in which case you can meet them in person and ask any questions you may have. Otherwise, you will need to contact one of the CRAM offices listed in the relevant chapter.

Police

There are two main types of police in France: *police nationale* and *gendarmes*. The *police nationale* is under the control of the Interior Ministry and deals with 'general' crime, mostly in urban or semi-urban areas. They're most commonly seen in towns and are distinguished by the silver buttons on their uniforms. At night and in rain and fog they often wear white caps and capes.

The *gendarmerie nationale* is part of the army and under the control of the Ministry of Defence, although it's also at the service of the Interior Ministry. *Gendarmes* deal with serious crime on a national scale and all crime in rural areas where there's no *police* station. They're also responsible for motorway patrols, air safety, mountain rescue, etc. *Gendarmes* wear blue uniforms and traditional caps (*képis*) and have gold buttons on their uniforms. Gendarmes include police motorcyclists (*motards*), who patrol in pairs.

In addition to the above, most cities and medium-size towns have their own police force, *police municipale* or *corps urbain*, who deal mainly with petty crime, traffic offences and road accidents. They're based at the *mairie*. All French police are armed with guns.

Some of the smaller *gendarmeries* are being merged with others and a rural station may be open only limited hours, but the local number will always be put through to the station that's on duty.

Motoring

Accidents

In the event of an accident involving two or more cars, it's normal for the drivers to complete an accident report form (*constat à l'amiable*), which is provided by French insurance companies. This is completed by all drivers involved, who must agree (more or less) on what happened. You can write in English or any other language and it's important that you check the particulars (e.g. address) of the other driver(s) listed on the form against something official, such as their driving licence. Take care when ticking the relevant boxes that the form cannot be added to or changed later and be sure that you're happy that you understand what has been written by the other driver(s). A *constat à l'amiable* isn't mandatory, and you can refuse to complete one if the other driver(s) disagree with your interpretation of what happened.

Car Insurance

It isn't necessary to have an insurance 'green card' (although some insurance companies issue one as a matter of course), but you must notify your insurance company of your dates of travel. Insurance for British registered cars abroad is becoming more difficult, many British insurance companies cutting the length of time they're allowing a car to be abroad, so check carefully with your insurance company. If you're bringing your car to France permanently but cannot re-register it (e.g. because it's a lease car or has been modified), there are some French companies that will insure your car, but only for a maximum of 12 months. **However, you should read the small print, as cover may apply only for six or three months or even for one month.**

AGF Assurfinance
💻 *www.agf.fr*

AXA Assurance
💻 *www.axa.fr*

Azur Assurances
💻 *www.azur-assurances.fr*

GAN Assurances
💻 *www.gan.fr*

MAAF Assurances
💻 *www.maaf.fr*

Mutuel du Mans Assurances
💻 *www.mma.fr*

Europ Assistance, 1 promenade de la Bonnette, 92230 Gennevilliers   ☎ 01 41 85 85 85
Provides international breakdown cover, often included in car insurance policies.

Car Repairs & Service

Most privately owned petrol stations service and repair cars and some of the large chains, such as Shell and Esso, have a workshop attached. Even small towns will have a repair garage of some description. However, if your car is damaged, you must contact your insurer **before** having any repairs carried out, as the insurer may specify certain garages to carry out the repairs or insist that a loss-adjuster approve the cost of the repair.

Petrol Stations

Petrol stations in France are generally open much shorter hours than in the UK, although there are some that are manned 24 hours a day, where a British credit card can be used for payment. Otherwise, if a station has a '24/24' sign, this means that petrol can be bought using automated pumps that will only take a credit or debit card with a microchip and a four-digit code, such as French bank cards.

Dordogne

Bergerac	Elf, rue Docteur Vizerie	☎ 05 53 57 67 97
	Open every day 6am to 10.30pm.	
Périgueux	Total, 138 rue Pierre Sémard, Périgueux	☎ 05 53 05 97 97
	Open every day from 6am to 10pm.	

Lot

Cahors	Total, route Toulouse	☎ 05 65 35 11 26
	Open every day from 6am to 10pm.	
	Shell, 33 avenue du 7ème RI	☎ 05 65 35 21 00
	Open every day from 6am to 11pm.	

Lot-et-Garonne

Agen	Total, 131 avenue Jean Jaurès	☎ 05 53 48 42 00
	Open every day from 6am to 10pm.	
Marmande	Shell, 22 avenue Paul Gabarra	☎ 05 53 64 01 60
	Open every day from 6.30am to 9.45pm.	

Rules & Regulations

When driving in France, you must have the following in your car at all times:

● Vehicle registration document or, if you're driving a leased or hired car, a letter of authority and a VE103 Hired Vehicle Certificate from the leasing or hire company;

● Your driving licence;

● Vehicle insurance documents;

● A warning triangle;

● Spare bulbs.

It's also advisable to carry a fire extinguisher and a first-aid kit.

Note also the following general rules and regulations relating to driving in France:

● The wearing of seatbelts is compulsory and includes passengers in rear seats when seatbelts are fitted. You (or any of your passengers) can be fined up to €90 for not wearing a seatbelt. Children must be accommodated in approved child seats, and children under ten cannot ride in the front of a vehicle unless it has no back seat.

- Failure to dip your lights when following or approaching another vehicle can cost you up to €750 and a penalty point on your licence, if you have a French licence. (French licenses *permis de conduire* work in reverse, with points given with the licence that you can then lose.)

- French traffic lights usually have a small set of lights at eye level, which are handy if you can't see the main lights (there are rarely lights on the far side of a junction). If the amber light (either a normal round light or an arrow shape) is flashing, you may continue (in the direction indicated, if an arrow shape) but must observe any relevant priority signs. If you jump a red light, you can be fined €300 and earn four penalty points!

- Watch out for a triangular sign with a red border displaying a large black X. This means that you **don't** have priority at the next junction (which may not be a crossroads) but **must** give way to the right, however minor the joining road is.

- Always come to a complete stop at junctions when required to (i.e. by a STOP sign) and ensure that your front wheels are behind the white line. Failing to stop behind the line can cost you €750 and four licence points.

- **Beware of moped riders.** French people are allowed on mopeds from the age of 14, and many youngsters pull out and weave around traffic without looking or indicating; even French motorists give them an extremely wide berth when overtaking!

- The name sign as you enter a village or town marks the start of the urban speed limit (see below) and the name crossed through as you leave marks the end.

- Parking in towns with parking meters is often free between noon and 2pm (times vary).

- And finally, don't assume that a British licence plate will prevent you from being stopped. From autumn 2004, tickets for motoring offences such as illegal parking and speeding will be sent for payment to the country in which a car is registered.

Further details of French driving regulations can be found in ***Living and Working in France*** (see page 300).

Speed Limits

Speed limits in France vary according to road conditions, as shown below. When visibility is below 50m (165ft) for any reason (e.g. rain or fog), you must not exceed 50kph (32mph) on **any** road. Speeds shown are in kilometres per hour with miles-per-hour equivalents in brackets.

Type Of Road	Speed Limit	
	Dry Road	*Wet Road*
Motorway	130 (81)	110 (68)
Dual-Carriageway	110 (68)	90 (56)
Single-Carriageway	90 (56)	80 (50)
Town	50 (32)	50 (32)

Note: The above limits apply unless otherwise indicated.

If you're caught exceeding a speed limit by 40kph (25mph), your driving licence can be confiscated on the spot.

Pets

General Information

France is a nation of dog-lovers, although French people's attitude towards other pets and animals in general can be alarmingly indifferent (sometimes also to dogs). The following information may be of use to those importing a pet or buying a pet in France.

● Many restaurants will provide food and water for dogs, some even allowing dogs to be seated at the table! Hotels may provide a rate for pets to stay.

● It's common practice to have third party insurance in case your pet (or child!) bites someone or causes an accident; the majority of household insurance policies include this, but you should check.

● Dogs must be kept on leads in most public parks and gardens in France and there are large fines for dog owners who don't comply.

● There have been no reported cases of rabies in central or southern France for ten years, but if you intend to put a cat or a dog into kennels or a cattery, it must be given a rabies vaccination.

● Rural French dogs are generally kept more as guard dogs than as pets and often live outdoors. Vicious dogs are (usually) confined or chained, but in a small community other 'pet' dogs may be left to wander around the village or hamlet.

● In towns and cities, the use of 'poop scoops' is required and dedicated bins are provided in streets and parks. In Cahors, green bags are provided.

● Dogs aren't welcome on the majority of beaches and, if you're staying on a campsite, they must be vaccinated against rabies and wear a collar at all times.

● On trains, pets under 6kg (13lb) which can be carried in a bag are charged around €5, but larger ones must be on a lead and wear a muzzle and will be charged half the normal second-class fare.

● Some Mercure and Formule 1 hotels accept dogs (see page 46 for contact details).

Horse Dentists

Vets in France don't deal with horses' teeth and there are specific equine dentists, which are listed in the following chapters. You're advised to book a few weeks in advance and you will be included in their next circuit.

Horse Feed

The feed you need is obviously dependent on how your horses are used and what their current feeding regime is. In any case, until you've established your new suppliers, it's wise to bring over with you any specific feeds.

Your local agricultural Co-Op (look out for huge hoppers, sometimes in the middle of nowhere) will sell sacks of feed and often pony nuts. Some have started selling only 'high-performance' nuts, so check carefully. Maize and barley are often available.

A local farmer may be your best source of feed; grain is normally sold whole or as flour (*farine*), although some farmers will grind it for you. An alternative used locally for horses that have come from the UK is whole-grain barley soaked for 24 hours. Your local farmer will also be the best source of hay and straw. See also **Riding Equipment** on page 70.

Spillers export horse feeds to France; to find your nearest supplier visit Spillers' website at 💻 *www.spillers-france.com* or contact one of the following:

SA Sodiva, 7 rue de la Roberdière,
35000 Rennes   ☎ 02 99 59 87 05
🖳 *www.coopagr-bretagne.fr*

A. Vigala-Nord, rue du Canal, St Nicholas
les Arras, 62052 St Laurent Blangy   ☎ 03 21 60 40 40
✉ *savigala@nordnet.fr*

Identification

All dogs in France must be tattooed or microchipped with an identity number, enabling owners to quickly find lost pets and also preventing a rabies or other vaccination certificate from being used for more than one dog. Tattoos used to be done inside the ear but it may now be done inside the animal's back leg. The costs of the two procedures are similar, although charges aren't fixed and vary considerably according to the veterinary practice – between around €25 and €75 for tattooing and from €35 to €70 for microchipping.The numbers are kept in a central computer by SPA (see below). If you lose your pet, contact the nearest SPA office.

Pet Parlours

Although many dogs are used as guard dogs, there are many that are domestic pets, and a large number of 'pet parlours' (*salon de toilettage de chiens et chats*) are to be found in France.

Pet Travel

Pet Passport Scheme

The Department for Food, Agriculture and Rural Affairs (DEFRA) operates a 'pet passport' scheme (known as PETS) for the benefit of owners wishing to take their pets abroad and bring them back to the UK. Full details of the requirements for re-entry into the UK are available from the DEFRA helpline or website (☎ +44 (0)870-241 1710, 🖳 *www.defra.gov.uk*). The helpline is accessible from both England and France and the lines are open from 8.30am to 5pm (UK time) Mondays to Fridays. Alternatively, a company called Dogs Away offers a free eight-page booklet to guide you through the process (☎ +44 (0)20-8441 9311, 🖳 *www.dogsaway.co.uk*).

Crossing the Channel through the Tunnel reduces the possibility of stress for your pets, as you can remain with them. Some ferry companies may allow you to check your pet on the car deck during the crossing, but this isn't always easy and can make the pet more distressed when you leave it again.

If applying for a pet passport in France, always ensure that you have in your possession the *carte de tatouage* before you start the pet passport process, as unless you have this card, which has your name and address as the registered owner, the registration of the microchip (*puce*) will be refused, along with the rabies vaccination, blood test, etc.

Sea Crossings

Brittany Ferries   *UK* ☎ 0870-366 5333
Brittany Ferries issues a specimen copy of the certificate needed so that you can check that a French vet has the correct one. In an emergency, if a vet doesn't have a form, this copy can be used.

Eurotunnel   *UK* ☎ 0870-535 3535
The check-in desk for pets at Coquelles is to the right of the check-in lanes. Animals are checked in before entering the Eurotunnel site. A single journey costs £30 per animal; guide dogs for the disabled are free. You can book via the website but are advised to book by phone, as a limited number of pets are allowed per train.

Hoverspeed   *UK* ☎ 0870-240 8070
Each pet is charged £18 each way. Bookings aren't possible on line and must be made by phone.

Riding Equipment

Gamm Vert
🖥 *www.gammvert.fr*
These garden centres sell horse feed and some basic equipment, depending on the size of the store. The website gives both location and opening hours of your nearest store.

Décathalon
🖥 *www.decathlon.fr*
These large sports stores carry a wide selection of riding accessories and equipment, including the hire of clippers (*tondeuses*), which are available for half or full days.

SPA

The Société pour la Protection des Animaux (SPA) is an organisation similar to the RSPCA in the UK but it isn't a national scheme, so you must contact your departmental office with any complaints or questions. Details are included in the following chapters.

Veterinary Clinics

Most veterinary surgeries are open Mondays to Saturdays, usually closing for lunch. There are often open surgeries as well as appointments. Where a vet's name isn't given there's more than one vet at the surgery.

Many vets will deal with horses and other equines but generally those that are used for riding out rather than expensive eventing or competition horses.

Places To Visit

Beaches & Water Parks

Many towns and villages have a *plan d'eau*, which can be a lake or part of a river. It may be just for fishing and relaxing beside or there may be a beach, playground, crazy golf and more. Details of all such facilities are given in the following chapters.

Caves

The area is world-famous for its caves, where prehistoric paintings can be seen. When visiting any of the caves, you should wear sensible shoes and warm clothing, as the temperature inside is around 10°C (50°F) all year.

Churches

Churches of interest are signposted from main roads and motorways and can be easily identified, e.g. *Eglise XIVème Siècle* =14th century church.

Professional Services

Architects & Project Managers

As many architects also offer a project management and general building services, they have been listed under **Architects & Project Managers** in the **Tradesmen** sections.

Religion

Catholic Churches

Churches can be found in most communities, and services in the villages are generally held in rotation with other churches in the parish. Notices are displayed on church doors or just inside giving details of the forthcoming services. In some small villages, the church doesn't have regular services but is used only on special occasions once or twice a year.

Protestant Churches

For the purposes of this book, all branches of the Protestant Church have been included under this heading.

Restaurants

There are so many restaurants in the region that we've been able to give only a selection to get you started on your gastronomic voyage of discovery. It's usual for restaurants of all types to offer set menus (*menu*), which are dishes put together by the chef that complement each other and may change daily. In smaller restaurants, this may be all that's available, although there's usually a choice of two or three dishes for each course.

Routiers

These restaurants can be found on main roads and have a circular logo – half red, half blue. They're usually alongside lorry parking areas and provide meals for drivers which have a reputation for being good quality and good value, the restaurants themselves being clean and tidy. You may be seated canteen style and find yourself next to a 'trucker' but you will get a four-course meal, sometimes with wine included in the price (it's the coffee you have to pay extra for!). Prices vary, but around €10 is usual.

Rubbish & Recycling

Dustmen

The collection of household rubbish (*ramassage*) varies not only between departments but also within areas of each department. It may be collected once or twice a week, and there may be separate collections (e.g. weekly or fortnightly) for recyclable waste, which must be put in special bags (see **Recycling** on page 73).

In towns, you may find 'wheelie bins' in the street. If so, you're responsible for putting your rubbish sacks in the bins, which are then emptied once or twice a week. If there's more than one type of wheelie bin, the other(s) are for recycling (see **Recycling** on page 73).

Rural areas may also have wheelie bins, with one or two for each group of houses. If there are no bins, rubbish should be put in bin bags and left at the edge of the road, although you're advised to hang them up out of reach of marauding dogs, cats and wildlife; **dustmen won't go down drives or onto property**. Dustmen often come very early, so bags need to be put out the night before.

If collection day falls on a bank holiday, rubbish is generally collected the day **before** rather than the day after – or the collection may simply be cancelled.

The best way to find out what happens in your commune is to speak to your neighbours or enquire at the *mairie*.

In most areas, separate taxes are payable by homeowners for rubbish collection and many French people are fiercely protective of the services for which they pay. You're therefore strongly advised not to put rubbish into a wheelie bin if you're driving a car registered in another department; the same applies if you try to use a rubbish tip in a different department or even a different commune (see **Rubbish Tips** below).

Metal Collection

If the previous occupiers kindly left their old fridge or bedstead in the garden, your *mairie* should be able to put you in touch with your local 'rag and bone man' or arrange for them to be taken away. In some communes, there's a regular (e.g. quarterly) *récupération des objects encombrants*, the dates of which you should be advised in advance.

Recycling

The French are keen on recycling, but systems vary both regionally and locally, some areas having no facilities at all whilst others collect recyclable waste from outside your house. Whatever the system, the colour coding is always the same, as follows:

● **Blue** – Paper and card, including catalogues and junk mail, but not window envelopes;

● **Yellow** – Packaging, cans (including aerosol cans), tins, drinks cartons and plastic milk bottles but not plastic bags or the thin plastic that encloses junk mail or six-packs of bottles of water or other products;

● **Green** – All clear and coloured glass except drinking glasses and light bulbs; no corks or lids.

Here is a summary of some of the systems currently in place in this area:

● Blue and yellow categories put in green wheelie bins or bins with yellow lids at the roadside;

● Yellow bags for both blue and yellow categories. You may have to take the bags to the tip, or they may be collected from the roadside, in which case you simply leave them out alongside the wheelie bin for non-recyclable waste. Yellow bags are free and usually available from the *mairie*.

● A series of collection banks, usually for all three categories of waste, which may be cream with the relevant colour trim to distinguish their uses. They're often found by football pitches, in car parks or near the *mairie*.

There are many designs of kitchen bin in France that have two or three compartments for the different types of waste. Note that polystyrene cannot be recycled; if you have a large quantity, such as packaging from a household appliance, you can dispose of it at a tip (see below).

Batteries

Batteries can be recycled in most supermarkets, where you will find tall, clear Perspex/black containers on a chipboard plinth in the foyer or by customer services. Car batteries can be recycled at the rubbish tip (see below).

Clothes & Shoes

Recycling containers for clothes and shoes can often be found in supermarket car parks.

Printer Cartridges

Printer ink cartridges can also be recycled, sometimes in supermarket entrance foyers and sometimes at the *mairie* or library. Toner cartridges can be recycled at the rubbish tip.

Rubbish Tips

Every town and many large villages have a rubbish tip (*déchetterie*); even small communes may have a *décharge*, which is primarily for garden rubbish but may also be used for building rubble.

Déchetteries are clearly marked in towns and outlying areas by a symbol of a hand holding three arrows. Here you can dispose of large metal objects, such as bikes and cookers, as well as oil, glass, paper, clothes and batteries, although you may not be allowed to dispose of household rubbish bags, which should be put out for collection at your house.

Some rubbish tips have a maximum quantity of building rubble that they will accept each day from an individual and, if they suspect that you're a tradesman, they will refuse to allow you to deposit at all.

Some rubbish tips near the border with another department issue a pass to all residents who want to use the tip (available from your *mairie*). If you don't have a card and are driving a car registered in another department (or country), you may be asked where you live or even be prevented from using the tip at all.

Schools

If you're planning to put your children into French school, the first place to go is your *mairie*. They will give you details of the relevant school for your child's age, both private and state schools. The school week for junior and infant schools is generally Mondays, Tuesdays, Thursdays and Fridays. Some areas also have lessons on Wednesday mornings, as do most secondary schools (*collèges*). There's no school on Saturdays in this region and no school uniform.

Enrolment

To register your children at a school, you must go and see the head teacher and he will tell you whether there are places and the relevant start date. Take the following with you:

● Details of all vaccinations since birth;

● The name and address of his last school (if appropriate);

● A copy of his last school report and/or any results you have from any academic tests;

● Evidence of school insurance, which is compulsory in France (see below). At your first meeting, it will be sufficient to say that you've applied for the insurance.

● If your child previously attended a French school, the *Certificat de Radiation*, which is proof that all contact and dealings have terminated with the previous school. A closing report from a UK school may be accepted.

French schools don't usually provide stationery and can have a long list of stationery and equipment that you must provide, so ask for a copy.

Transport

There's a comprehensive network of school buses (*car/bus scolaire*), which collect children in rural areas. An application form for a bus pass can be obtained from the school or the *mairie* and you will need to provide two passport-size photographs. The cost, if any, depends on where you live, how many school-age children there are in the family and what schools they go to.

Holidays

Schools in France are divided into three groups for their holidays so that spring half term and Easter holidays are staggered, which prevents ski and other resorts from becoming overcrowded. Schools in Dordogne and Lot-et-Garonne are group C, while schools in Lot are group A. You may also find that there's no half-term break between the Easter and summer holidays. Calendars are distributed by a wide variety of organisations giving the school holiday dates for the three groups. If a school operates a four-day week, it will give you a list of holiday dates, which may vary by a day or two from the 'official' dates to make up the statutory hours per term.

Insurance

All children must have insurance to attend school in France. Insurance is provided by a number of companies, but Mutuelles d'Assurances Eléves (MAE) is the most popular. The most comprehensive cover is €24.00 and covers your child for all eventualities, both in and out of school and cover for use of all French medical facilities. Contact details for MAE are given below. Whichever insurer you use, you must provide the school with a certificate to prove that your child is covered.

	Mutuelles d'Assurances	☎ 08 20 00 00 70
	🖥 *www.mae.fr*	
	Central helpline open 9am to noon and 1 to 5.30pm Mondays to Fridays.	
Dordogne	17 rue 34ème Régiment Artillerie, Périgueux	☎ 05 53 53 20 19
Lot	Maison de l'Enseignement, 114 rue Denis Forestier, Cahors	☎ 05 65 35 29 36
Lot-et-Garonne	81 boulevard Carnot, Agen	☎ 05 53 68 29 28
	This office is open only from 9am to noon in the school holidays.	

Extra Tuition

If your child wants or needs extra help, but not structured lessons, it's worth contacting the local college, as it may be able to recommend a student who is happy to come to your house and spend time with your child going over class notes or lessons. Not only is this cheaper than a qualified teacher but a younger person may be less daunting for your children.

Shopping

General Information

Opening Hours

When available, the opening hours of various shops have been included, but they're liable to change and so it's advisable to check before travelling long distances to any specific shop.

Many small businesses are staffed only by the family and as a result you may find that the village shop or even the town co-op may close completely for two weeks while the proprietor goes on holiday.

Shop opening hours can change from summer to winter, particularly when school starts in September: Not only does the merchandise seem to change overnight, but shops that were open all day (*sans interruption*) and on Sunday mornings are suddenly closed for two hours at lunchtime and not open on Sundays at all. Other shops may change their lunchtime closure and close completely on Mondays.

The information in this section relates to shopping in general; details of shops in each department can be found in the following chapters.

Mobile Shops

In rural communities there are various mobile shops, all of which sound their horns loudly as they go through the village. These may include a bakery (*boulangerie*), a butcher's (*boucherie*), a grocery (*épicerie*) and a fishmonger's (*poissonnerie*).

Alcohol

There aren't as many off-licences (*caves*) in France as in England, as the hypermarkets and supermarkets sell the majority of alcoholic drinks. Some of the specialist shops listed under this heading sell table wine by the litre, usually starting at just over €1 per litre, but you must take your own container. Suitable containers with taps on can be bought at DIY stores or large supermarkets.

Bakers'

Bakeries (*boulangeries*) are usually small family-run businesses that close one day a week and often on Sunday afternoons. They also run delivery vans, going through local villages and hamlets from two to seven days a week, depending on the area.

British Groceries

Many supermarkets are now introducing some 'high demand' British produce to their international sections, e.g. Golden Syrup and HP Sauce. Stock varies with demand and the size of the shop, so keep a look out, especially in hypermarkets and popular tourist areas.

Expatdirect.co.uk   *UK* ☎ 07980-265553
💻 *www.expatdirect.co.uk*
Supplies British produce at supermarket prices: 30kg of goods delivered anywhere in France for £14.95.

Chemists'

Even small towns will have a chemist's (*pharmacie*) but they may be open limited hours, such as Tuesdays to Fridays and every other Saturday and Monday. Outside normal opening hours a notice should be displayed giving the address of the nearest duty chemist (*pharmacie de garde*). Alternatively, the *gendarmes* hold a list of duty chemists; dial ☎ 17 or the number of your local *gendarmerie*.

Chemists are trained to give first aid and can also carry out procedures such as taking blood pressure. They can be asked advice on many ailments and without a prescription can give a wider variety of medicines than are available over the counter in the UK. Chemists are also trained to distinguish between around 50 types of mushroom and toadstool and to identify local snakes in order to prescribe the correct antidote for poisoning.

DIY

There are many DIY (*bricolage*) stores in the region, most towns having at least one of the following:

Bricomarché	🖥 *www.bricomarche.com*
Castorama	🖥 *www.castorama.fr*
Mr Bricolage	🖥 *www.mr-bricolage.fr*
Weldom	🖥 *www.weldom.com*

Frozen Food

There are frozen food (*surgelés*) shops that deliver to homes and frozen food producers that only sell direct, orders being placed by phone, via the internet or with the driver. The two largest companies that both have shops and do home deliveries are:

Picard Surgelés	🖥 *www.picard.fr*
Thiriet Glaces	🖥 *www.thiriet.com*

Garden Centres

The most commonly found garden centres (*jardineries*) are Gamm Vert and Jardiland, the latter being a large store most commonly found on retail parks.

Gamm Vert	🖥 *www.gammvert.fr*
Jardiland	🖥 *www.jardiland.fr*

Key Cutting & Heel Bars

Key cutting kiosks and heel bars (*cordonneries*) may be found in a hypermarket complex, outside supermarkets or as independent stores in the high street.

Kitchens & Bathrooms

Specialist shops selling kitchen and bathroom furniture and fittings can often be found in large retail parks.

Markets

Some markets and fairs take place in the centre of towns and villages and can cause streets to be closed; as they're often situated on car parks, parking can become difficult. Food markets in France are well worth a visit if you haven't experienced them before (and aren't squeamish), but do check the prices, particularly at indoor markets, which are sometimes more expensive than you might expect.

Newsagents'

Many general newsagents' (*maison de la presse* or simply *presse*) sell British daily newspapers and even British magazines and paperbacks. They can order specific magazines or publications, such as the *TV* and *Radio Times*, on request.

Publications

Les Annonces du Lot, *Bonjour le 46*, *L'Oustal*, *le P'tit Bergeracois* and *Sud-Ouest* are just some of the local 'classified' newspapers, which include advertisements for local events, items for sale, cars, etc. They're free and can be found in *tabacs*, bakeries and other shops.

The two weekly newspapers listed below are designed and written for expatriates and can be delivered anywhere in the world. An annual subscription costs between £75 and £90.

The Guardian Weekly   UK ☎ 0870-066 0510
🖳 *www.guardian.co.uk*
Condenses the best of *The Guardian*,
The Observer, *Le Monde* and *The Washington
Post* and adds bespoke articles.

The Weekly Telegraph   UK ☎ 01454-642464
🖳 *www.expat.telegraph.co.uk*
Condenses the best of *The Daily* and *The
Sunday Telegraph* and adds bespoke articles.

Organic Food

Organic produce (*produits biologiques/bio*) is widely available in supermarkets and hypermarkets. Organic shops are becoming more popular but tend to appear and disappear rapidly.

Passport Photos

Kiosks can usually be found in the entrance to supermarkets and in hypermarket centres.

Post Offices

French post offices offer a wide range of facilities, including cash machines, internet access and automated postage machines that can operate in English.

Retail Parks

Retail parks tend to be on the outskirts of cities and large towns and in France there tends to be a hypermarket at the centre.

Second-Hand Goods

Brocantes come in all shapes and sizes and are a cross between an antique shop and a second-hand shop. You can find them in most towns and along main roads. *Brocantes* can be the source of some good bargains. *Dépôts-vente* (a cross between a pawnshop and a charity shop) are also a good source of second-hand goods. They sell on behalf of the public for a commission of around 20 per cent.

Supermarkets & Hypermarkets

French supermarkets advertise heavily on roadside hoardings, often giving directions and distance in minutes, but be aware that these directions can just stop, leaving you lost and apparently a great deal more than '5 mins' away from the store. They often advertise at the side of a competitor's store, when their store is actually in the next town.

The most common supermarkets in this region are listed below; the websites will give you the location of the store nearest to you.

Leclerc	💻 *www.e-leclerc.com*
Intermarché	💻 *www.intermarche.com*
Champion	💻 *www.champion.fr*
Super U	💻 *www.super-u.com*

Hypermarkets (*hypermarchés*) are one of the best sources of electrical goods and general household items. There doesn't seem to be the quantity of specialist electrical stores in France as there is in the UK and it's quite normal to buy your new washing machine from Géant or Auchan. Hypermarkets tend to be situated in a retail park on the outskirts of towns and cities and the buildings themselves are often small shopping precincts with a variety of shops and services.

Note the following general points regarding French supermarkets and hypermarkets:

● Very few supermarkets open on Sundays – occasionally on Sunday mornings but never in the afternoon – and no hypermarkets open on Sundays.

● Opening hours can change from summer to winter, with longer lunchtime closing and later evening opening in the summer.

● Larger stores may open all day Mondays to Fridays, others only on Fridays and Saturdays, closing for lunch the rest of the week, the smallest stores closing for lunch every day.

Swimming Pool Equipment

Once summer arrives all the supermarkets and DIY stores are stocked with pool equipment and accessories, from chlorine and pumps to covers and steps.

Sports

General information relating to certain sports is given below (in alphabetical order). A selection of the activities available in each department is provided in the following chapters; full details are available from tourist offices and *mairies*. Not surprisingly, large towns have the widest range of facilities.

Note that many 'physical' sports require a licence. The relevant club will have the forms and a medical may be required, which your doctor can carry out as a standard consultation.

Golf

The following website provides full details in English of all the clubs in the area as well as across France: 🖳 *www.golflounge.com/fr*.

Horse Riding

Local tourist offices have copies of *Topo Guides*, which give details of the routes in the area suitable for horse riding. Your local horse yard is the best place to enquire about competitions, as not all yards are competitive. Those that are will be involved in many events, both regional and local, throughout the year.

Snooker, Pool & Billiards

French billiards is a highly skilful (and, some say, tedious) game played with just three balls on a table without pockets. Snooker and pool are also widely played. Many bars and cafés have pool tables, and some also snooker and/or billiard tables.

Tourist Offices

Tourist offices hold details of local events throughout the year and are a good source of general information and local guide books. Details of relevant regional and departmental offices are given in the following chapters; opening hours are current but may change slightly from year to year. The Paris tourist office, listed below, can provide information on the whole of France

Office de Tourisme de Paris, 25 rue des
Pyramides, 75001 Paris   ☎ 08 92 68 30 00
🖳 *www.paris-touristoffice.com*

Tradesmen

Almost every commune has a tradesman (*artisan*) of some description, from carpenter (*menuisier*) or builder (*maçon*) to electrician (*électricien*) or plumber (*plombier*). One way to find out what local tradesmen there are is to look through the phone book in the residential listing for your commune; tradesmen will have their profession next to their name and address. The best way, however, is to ask at the *mairie*; it's likely that the *Maire* will even give you a personal introduction.

Using local French tradesman has the advantage that they know the materials they will be working with, are familiar with the systems in place in your property and, as they live locally, will have a reputation to maintain. The increasing influx of Britons to rural France means that more and more French artisans are working for and with the British, which in turn is making them more willing to communicate in a mixture of French and English, drawings and sign language. (see also **Translators & Teachers** below).

Registered builders in France have their work guaranteed for 10 years and must be fully insured to cover any accident or damage to themselves, you or your property. To check whether a tradesman is registered to work in France, go to ⌨ *www.cofacerating.fr*, click on the Union Jack at the top and go to 'For more information on ... companies"; this takes you to a form where you enter the tradesman's telephone number. If he's registered, the company information will appear; a big red cross indicates that he isn't registered.

Should you decide to use an un-registered tradesman – either French or British – you should be aware that, if there's an accident, you will be personally and financially liable; you will have no warranty on the work carried out and you won't be able to claim the low tax rate (5.5 per cent instead of 19.6 per cent) available until the end of 2005 for renovation work. You could have additional problems if you need to make an insurance claim involving the work (e.g. in the case of a flood or subsidence).

Note, however, that tradesmen's insurance doesn't cover them for all trades, but only for the skills for which they're registered; for example, your builder may offer to sort out your electrics, but he may not be registered as an electrician and hence not insured for that work.

Just as you would in the UK, ensure that you have got several quotes, if possible have seen some work already done and that you are happy with the tradesman.

Further details of finding and supervising builders in France can be found in *Renovating and Maintaining Your French Home* (see page 300).

Planning Permission

If you want to make any alterations to your home – even painting the window frames a different colour – you must first visit the *mairie*, as there are strict regulations (which vary from commune to commune) governing what can and cannot be done and a strict procedure that must be followed for certain types of work. This is too a complex subject to describe here. For full details, refer to *Renovating and Maintaining Your French Home* (see page 300).

Translators & Teachers

French teachers and translators in each department are listed under this heading in the following chapters. See also **Schools** on page 74.

Translation

If you have a small amount of text that you need translated, the Altavista website (⌨ *www.altavista.com*) can translate up to 150 words from a variety of different languages. This isn't an accurate translation and should never be relied on for legal or professional purposes, but it will give you the gist of the information. This and the Google site (🖥 *www.google.com*) can also translate websites.

Utilities

Electricity

In France electricity bills are in two parts: consumption and a monthly standing charge (*abonnement*). Electricity consumption is charged according to one of a range of tariffs. The standing charge is related to how much power (calculated in kilowatts or kW) you have available to you at any time: the more power you have available, the higher the standing charge. Your consumption charge is also related to the amount of power you have available, the charge per unit being higher the more power is available.

On the back of your electricity bill (*votre facture en détail*) it will say what your standing charge is per month (…*€/mois*). Under *montant à prélever* it will give you your existing allowance of kW at any one time, e.g. '*puissance 6kW, code 024*'. You will also find the cheap rate hours (*heures creuses*), which are usually from 1 to 7am and from noon to 2pm.

If you use more than the power available, the trip switch is triggered and you will be thrown into darkness and left to fumble for a torch. To prevent repeated 'tripping' of the system, you must ensure that your allowance of power is sufficient to cover your expected maximum power consumption at any one time (e.g. running the dishwasher, washing machine and cooker all at once), although this will cost you more.

An alternative is to install a piece of equipment called a *délesteur*, which is a tiny computer wired into your system: when the system is overloaded, it automatically switches off apparatus in order of priority (pre-determined by you, e.g. hot water tank, tumble drier, but not lights, alarm or plug sockets).

Like most other utility bills, electricity bills are normally issued bi-monthly in France. As your meter will be outside the property and accessible from the street (you mustn't block access to it), it will usually be read without your knowing it. If a reading hasn't been possible, your electricity bill will be estimated (indicated by an *E* alongside the figures). If the estimate is higher than the actual reading, you can take your bill to your local office (listed in subsequent chapters) and you will be sent an amended bill.

Gas

Gas (*gaz*) can be natural, butane or propane. If you aren't on mains gas (which is generally available only in larger towns and residential areas), you will need a tank (*citerne*), which provides propane gas, or bottles to provide butane. If you use gas only for cooking, bottles are sufficient; if you have gas central heating, a tank is essential. The main difference between natural and propane gas is that propane burns much hotter (take care when trying to simmer milk!) and appliances designed for natural gas will need to have the injectors changed to a smaller size. If the appliance is new, it should come with two sizes of injector (the larger size, for natural gas, is usually the one that comes fitted).

If there's already a tank at the property, you will be required to pay a deposit for it and, when it has been filled up, the price of a full tank of gas, irrespective of how much was left in it. The gas company will credit the previous owners with what was left in the tank. The deposit can be as much as €1,000 and a tank full of gas as much as €800, so you should take this into account when negotiating the price of the property. Instead of a deposit, you can chose to pay a monthly charge for the tank.

You can monitor your gas consumption using the gauge on a tank and re-order when it drops to the red line. You may find that the gas company will come automatically when they believe you should be due for a refill. Gas bottles don't have gauges but can simply be shaken to ascertain how much gas is left.

You don't always have to pay immediately when your tank is refilled. The driver may give you a delivery note stating the quantity delivered, the price per unit and the total due. If the bill is large, you may be able to send two cheques, one dated a month after the other, but check with your supplier first.

Water

Water in France is supplied by a variety of organisations, from national companies to individual communes – in the latter case with bills sent by the *mairie*.

Wood

To find a local supplier of firewood, ask a neighbour or at the *mairie*, as many farmers in the region supply suitable wood. When ordering wood, you need to specify how much you want in an arcane measure called a *stère*, which is roughly 0.6 cubic metres (many people erroneously believe it's one cubic metre) or 500kg of wood. You may also need to specify whether it's for burning now or in a few years and whether it's for a large open fire or a log burner. Wood for log burners is slightly more expensive, as it has to be cut smaller. You can of course order the longer length and cut your own for the log burner. Electric and petrol chainsaws (*tronçonneuses*) are available from all DIY stores from the autumn onwards and can also be hired from certain outlets. Depending on the age and type of wood, expect to pay around €20 to €25 per cubic metre.

Six cubic metres should be enough for a winter if you're only using fires and log burners for cold days or just evenings, for example. If fires are your only source of heating, you will need more, depending of course on how many fires you have and whether you have a wood-burning cooker.

Wood varies in suitability for use on an open fire. Good and unsuitable woods are listed below.

Good Woods

- Apple tree (*pommier*) – produces a good scent;

- Ash (*frêne*) – burns well and produces plenty of warmth whether green or brown, wet or dry;

- Beech (*hêtre*) – almost smokeless;

- Chestnut (*châtaignier*) – needs to be aged;

- Oak (*chêne*) – must be old and dry;

- Pear tree (*poirier*) – produces a good scent.

Unsuitable Woods

- Birch (*bouleau*) – bright and fast burning;

- Elm (*orme*) – doesn't burn well;

- Fir (*sapin*) – bright and fast burning;

- Poplar (*peuplier*) – fast burning and produces a bitter smoke.

Chimney Sweeps

It costs around €45 to have a chimney swept (*ramonage*). The chimney sweep (*ramoneur*) may ask you to sign a form that enables him to charge you a lower rate of VAT. Although you're no longer legally required to have your chimney swept regularly, if you have a chimney fire and are unable to produce a receipt showing that your chimney has been swept recently, you may have difficulty claiming on insurance (check your policy). If using a fire or log burner throughout the winter, you're recommended to have a chimney swept at least once a year anyway. Chimney sweeps are listed under **Tradesmen** in the following chapters.

2

Dordogne

This chapter provides details of facilities and services in the department of Dordogne (24). General information about each subject can be found in **Chapter 1**. All entries are arranged alphabetically by town, except where a service applies over a wide area, in which case it is listed at the beginning of the relevant section under 'General'. A map of Dordogne is shown below

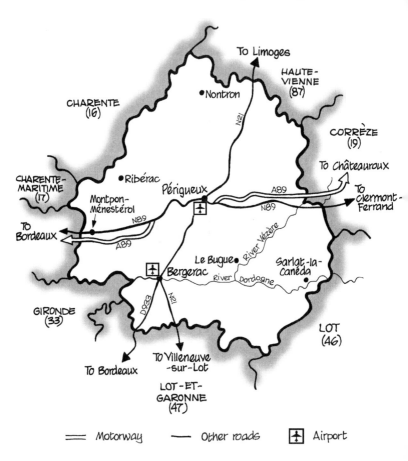

Accommodation

Camping

Bergerac   Camping Municipal de la Pelouse,
                  8bis rue Jean-Jacques Rousseau   ☎ 05 53 57 06 67
                  (ten minutes from the town centre on the banks of the
                  Dordogne river) A two-star campsite open all year.

Le Bugue	Le Rocher de la Granelle, route du Buisson	☎ 05 53 07 24 32

www.lagranelle.com
This three-star camp site is by the river and has a swimming pool and games room as well as mobile homes and caravans to rent. Open from May to September.

Montpon	Le Port Vieux, 1 rue de la Paix	☎ 05 53 80 30 98

By the river. Open May to September.

Nontron	Camping Municipal, Mas Viconteaux	☎ 05 53 56 02 04

(to the south of the town in the direction of Ribérac)
A two-star campsite, with a swimming pool open all year round.

Périgueux	Camping de Barnabé, rue des Bains, Boulazac	☎ 05 53 53 41 45

(east of Périgueux)
Situated on the bank of the river this campsite is open all year round.

Ribérac	Camping Municipal de La Dronne, route d'Angoulême	☎ 05 53 90 50 08

Beside the river, this campsite also has mobile homes to rent. Open June to mid-September.

Sarlat-la-Canéda	Le Caminel, route de Brive	☎ 05 53 59 37 16

Châteaux

Montiganac	Château de Puy Robert, route de Valojoulx	☎ 05 53 51 92 13

www.puyrobert.com
This four-star hotel is an elegant neo-Renaissance château with a restaurant offering high quality and imaginative cuisine. There's a swimming pool and outside dining. Double rooms from €114 to €151.

Hotels

Only the towns that have a limited number of hotels are listed here. Bergerac, Le Bugue, Périgueux and Ribérac all have a wide selection of hotels, including national chains such as those given on page 46.

General　　　*www.otedis.com*
This website has a comprehensive list of hotels, with prices and booking information

Various tourist office websites have details of hotel accommodation, including the following:

🖥 *www.perigord.com*
🖥 *www.bergerac-tourisme.com*

Montpon | Le Puits d'Or, 7 rue Carnot   ☎ 05 53 80 33 07
Pets are accepted at this hotel and rooms cost €35 per night.

Mussidan | Le Midi, 9 rue Villechanoux   ☎ 05 53 81 01 77
(just east of Montpon)
This hotel has a large outdoor pool and rooms cost from €45 to
€60 per night.

Nontron | Hôtel Pelisson, 3 place Alfred Agard   ☎ 05 53 56 11 22
In the town centre, this hotel has rooms from €43 to €52
per night.

Bars & Nightlife

Beaumont | Le Surier, Moulin de Surier   ☎ 05 53 57 81 43
Disco/club. Open Wednesdays to Sundays in July and August,
the rest of the year Fridays to Sundays.

Bergerac | Le Bataclan, Aéroport de Moumanière   ☎ 05 53 73 95 38
The 'Cosmopolitan Company', which is based at the airport,
puts on cabaret evenings complete with show girls throughout
the year at various venues across the region. Phone for details
or the current programme.

Bowling Bergeracois,
route de Bordeaux   ☎ 05 53 57 82 58
Ten lanes, video games and crazy golf.

Le Jumpy, rue de l'Alma   ☎ 05 53 23 37 77
This bar hosts shows and themed evenings, including karaoke.

La Poissonnerie,
7 rue Colonel de Chadois   ☎ 05 53 74 14 46
This music bar is open Tuesdays to Saturdays from 11am to
1am (3am on Fridays and Saturdays). Hot and cold snacks are
available at all hours and there are regular events all year
round, from jazz and Irish evenings to Cuban singers and
philosophical debates.

Le Rocksane, 14 bis rue Pozzi   ☎ 05 53 63 03 70
Rock and general concert venue in the centre of town.

Le Roxane, route d'Agen   ☎ 05 53 73 83 87
Nightclub open Sundays to Wednesdays.

Le Windsor, route de Bordeaux   ☎ 05 53 23 64 00
This is one of the largest discos in France and comprises four
clubs, a restaurant and a pub open from 8.30pm. The complex
is open Thursday (free entry) Friday and Saturday evenings,
Sunday afternoons and all day on bank holidays.

Biras   Le Brantôme, route d'Angoulême,
Le Riz   ☎ 05 53 35 26 83
(ten minutes north of Périgueux)
Karaoke every Friday and a dinner and show on Saturdays.

Brantôme   L'Auberge du Hussard,
6 rue Georges Saumade   ☎ 05 53 05 54 23
This bar has the ambiance of an old bistro with décor, posters
and furniture from the past and over 40 beers. Open 3pm to
11pm every day in the summer but only weekends out of
season.

L'Eyzies   Le Pesca Lune, Tursac   ☎ 05 53 06 85 85
(north-east of Le Bugue, following the river Vézère)
Despite its location within a renovated farm building, this bar
has a very international feel. There are Mexican frescoes on
the walls, tropical cocktails and Oriental, Latin and Andalusian
music in the background. At the weekends there's a variety of
live acts such as oriental dancing and Cuban or
Brazilian bands.

Fougueyrolles   Roller Disco   ☎ 05 53 74 60 33
(directly south of Montpon on the D708)
Fridays and Saturdays 9pm to midnight, Sundays 2 to 7pm.

Montpon   Discobus
This bus travels around the area of Montpon and the western
Dordogne on Friday and Saturday evenings. Venues are
advertised locally.

Le Marignan,
place des Trois Frères Laplagne   ☎ 05 53 82 63 61
(set back in the left hand corner as you face the fountain)
Bar with table football and pool.

Le Pizou, Le Tackouk   ☎ 05 53 81 81 81
(directly west of Montpon on the D10)
This venue holds a tea dance every Thursday from 2.30pm and
on Friday and Saturday evenings becomes a club with a disco
from 10.30pm to 5am.

Nontron   Le Club, route de Périgueux   ☎ 05 54 56 00 65
🖳 *www.clubing.fr.st*

Périgueux   Barrio Gotico, 3 rue de la Sagesse   ☎ 05 53 05 07 33
There are three contemporary bars and a restaurant offering
international cuisine at this venue. Open Tuesdays to
Saturdays from 7pm to 2am.

Etap Hôtel, 33 rue Président Wilson   ☎ 05 53 05 53 82
This hotel holds dinner dances and concerts.

Le Privilège, 223 route d'Angoulême   ☎ 05 53 53 70 18
Disco open Thursdays to Saturdays.

Le Feeling Club Cabaret,
160 avenue Maréchal Juin   ☎ 05 53 03 71 52
Bar/club with disco and live shows, open Mondays to
Saturdays 4pm to 2am.

Le Mello, 46 rue de la Sagesse   ☎ 05 53 08 53 97
Music bar with jazz, blues, soul, R 'n' B, concerts and themed
evenings.

Le Réservoir, 192 route d'Angoulême   ☎ 05 53 06 12 73
🖥 *www.le-reservoir.org*
Concert and band venue.

Toqués de Bière, 38 rue Pierre Sémard   ☎ 05 53 08 13 39
Crêperie with an Irish theme, bottled beers and darts club.
Open Mondays to Saturdays from 5pm.

Ribérac   La Gavotte, 21ter place de Gaulle   ☎ 05 53 91 63 11
There are regular concerts during the summer and occasional
concerts out of season at this crêperie.

Café des Colonnes,
17 place du Général de Gaulle   ☎ 05 53 90 01 39
This colonial-style cafe is open until 1am at the weekend.

Sarlat-la-Canéda Le Pub, Hôtel de Gérard,
1 passage du Barry   ☎ 05 53 59 57 98
(in the centre of the old town, access via rue Fénelon)
This piano bar hosts various other musical evenings and has a
large selection of bottled beers, whiskies and cocktails. There's
a summer terrace and it's open every day all year round from
5pm to 2am.

Le Griot, route de Souillac   ☎ 05 53 28 13 10
(2km north-east of the town centre)
This club has dancing and shows. Open all year Fridays to
Sundays and bank holidays.

Siorac-en-Périgord	Le Lucky, le Port	☎ 05 53 31 61 55
	Club/bar open Tuesdays to Sundays in the summer; Fridays, Saturdays and bank holidays the rest of the year.	

Business Services

Computer Services

General	Euro Laptops, Le Castelat, Gourdon	☎ 05 65 37 63 45
	🖳 *www.gourdonnet.com*	
	Software, hardware, upgrades, new computers and help with all aspects of setting up and using your computer by a British-qualified IT trainer, who serves the whole area.	
	PJS Informatique, Le Pereyrous, Musclat	☎ 05 65 37 06 24
	🖳 *www.pgsinformatique.com*	
	Peter Smith runs this business dealing with computer repairs, upgrades, web design and training sessions, covering Cahors, Gourdon, Sarlat-la-Canéda and Souillac.	
Bergerac	ADM Informatique, 15bis rue Mounet Sully	☎ 05 53 57 49 58
	🖳 *www.adm24.com*	
	Repairs, accessories, training and sales, both new and second-hand.	
Eymet	MCD Informatique, 3 place Gambetta	☎ 05 53 23 65 45
	✉ *dean@mcd-informatique.co*m	
	(south of Bergerac on the border of Dordogne and Lot-et-Garonne)	
	This shop has bilingual staff who undertake computer sales and service, repairs, maintenance, website set-up and internet connection.	
Périgueux	Info 2000, 26 rue Président Wilson	☎ 05 53 35 95 40
	🖳 *www.aquinet.com*	
	Repairs, maintenance, telephone assistance and training.	

Employment Agencies

The main offices of the national employment agency, ANPE, are as follows:

Bergerac	16 rue Petit Sol	☎ 05 53 63 77 77
Périgueux	1 rue Littré	☎ 05 53 02 62 62

Communications

Fixed Telephones

General   France Télécom: Dial 1014 or go to
                    💻 *www.francetelecom.fr*
                    Local shops are listed below.

Bergerac   25 rue Colonel Chadois
                    Mondays 2 to 6.30pm, Tuesdays, Thursdays and Fridays
                    9.30am to 12.30pm and 1.30 to 6.30pm, Wednesdays and
                    Saturdays 9.30am to 6.30pm.

Périgueux   1 rue Taillefer
                    Mondays to Saturdays 9.30am to 6.30pm.

Sarlat-la-Canéda 41 avenue Gambetta
                    Mondays 2 to 6pm, Tuesdays to Fridays 9.15am to 12.15pm
                    and 2 to 6pm, Saturdays 9.15am to 12.30pm and 2 to 5pm.

Internet Access

Bergerac   La Poste, 36 rue de la Résistance   ☎ 05 53 63 50 00
                    Mondays to Fridays 8.30am to 6.30pm and Saturdays 8.30am
                    to noon.

                    Espace Culturel, 7 rue de la Résistance   ☎ 05 53 22 24 40
                    Mondays 2 to 7pm, Tuesdays to Saturdays 10am to 7pm.

Le Bugue   Office de Tourisme, Porte de la Vézère,
                    rue Jardin Public   ☎ 05 53 07 20 48
                    💻 *www.perigord.com/bugue*
                    April to October, Mondays to Saturdays 9.30am to 12.30pm
                    and 2.30 to 6.30pm, Sundays and bank holidays 10am to 1pm;
                    July and August, every day 9am to 1pm and 3 to 7pm;
                    November to March, Tuesdays to Saturdays 9.30am to
                    12.30pm and 2.30 to 6.30pm.

Montpon   Bibliothèque, rue de Verdun   ☎ 05 53 82 30 54
                    Mondays and Thursdays 2 to 6pm, Wednesdays 9am to noon
                    and 2 to 6pm, Saturdays 9am to noon and 2 to 5pm.

Nontron   Cyberspace,
                    place des Droits de l'Homme   ☎ 05 53 56 17 51
                    Mondays, Tuesdays, Thursdays and Fridays 10am to noon and
                    2 to 8pm, Wednesdays and Saturdays 2 to 10pm and
                    Sundays 3 to 7pm.

Périgueux   Net Runner, 11 rue Victor Hugo   ☎ 05 53 53 64 31
                    Open every day noon to midnight (school holidays
                    2pm to midnight).

Arena Games, 13 rue des Farges   ☎ 05 53 53 75 21
(in the centre of the town near the tourist office)
Mondays to Fridays 11am to midnight, Saturdays and Sundays
2pm to 2am, school holidays every day 2pm to midnight.

Ribérac   There's a booth outside Intermarché on route Mussidan.

Sarlat-la-Canéda La Taverne du Web,
17 avenue Gambetta   ☎ 05 53 30 80 77
Mondays to Thursdays noon to 6pm, Fridays and Saturdays
noon to 10pm, Sundays 2 to 7pm. English spoken.

Cyber Espace, 13 avenue Gambetta   ☎ 05 53 31 22 37
Tuesdays 5 to 8pm, Wednesdays 9am to noon and 1.30 to
8pm, Thursdays 5 to 8pm, Fridays 1.30 to 9.30pm, Saturdays
9am to 1pm and 2.30 to 8.30pm.

Mobile Telephones

All France Télécom shops (see above) sell mobile phones, as do the following:

Bergerac   Espace SFR, 27 rue de la Résistance   ☎ 05 53 23 50 40
Mondays to Saturdays 10am to 7pm (closed Mondays,
Wednesdays and Thursdays noon to 2pm).

Espace SFR Centre Cial,
La Cavaille Nord   ☎ 05 53 27 45 51
(in the Leclerc shopping centre)
Mondays to Saturdays 9.30am to 8pm.

Montpon   Odyssée Télécom, 61 rue Thiers   ☎ 05 53 80 24 84
Tuesdays to Saturdays 9.30am to noon and 2 to 7pm.

Nontron   Moving Phones, rue de Verdun   ☎ 05 53 56 82 96
Open Tuesdays to Saturdays.

Périgueux   Odyssée Télécom, 225 route
d'Angoulême   ☎ 05 53 46 71 95
Open Tuesdays to Saturdays.

Bouygues Télécom, 3 place Bugeaud   ☎ 05 53 06 72 36
(at the bottom of the boulevard to the right of Monoprix)
Open Tuesdays to Saturdays.

Ribérac   Moving Phone,
23bis place Général de Gaulle   ☎ 05 53 90 48 65
Tuesdays to Fridays 9am to noon and 2.30 to 7pm, Saturdays
9am to noon and 2.30 to 6pm.

Domestic Services

Crèches & Nurseries

Bergerac	Les Mômes, 24 rue Saïl d'Escola	☎ 05 53 27 31 33

Crèche and nursery for infants from two-and-a-half months to six years old.

Périgueux	Crèche Municipale et Halte-Garderie des Arènes, 34 rue de Strasbourg	☎ 05 53 08 04 29
	Crèche Municipale et Halte-Garderie Câlins Câlines, chemin de Saltgourde	☎ 05 53 53 55 79

Equipment & Tool Hire

Boulazac	Loxam, ZI avenue Henry Deluc	☎ 05 53 09 45 11

🖳 *www.loxam.fr*
(east of Périgueux)

Le Buisson-de-Cadouin	A. Zamperini, route Cabans	☎ 05 53 74 19 08

🖳 *www.az-vente-location.com*
(near Le Bugue)

Trélissac	Daudou Matériel, avenue Firmin Bouvier, ZI Boulazac	☎ 05 53 09 47 00

🖳 *www.betonniere.biz*
(east of Périgueux)
A variety of equipment from cement mixers to lawn mowers.

Fancy Dress Hire

Bergerac	JF Lagrange, 4bis rue St Louis	☎ 05 53 57 00 51
St Laurent-des-Vignes	Espace Fête Regain, Le Paillet (just south of Bergerac)	☎ 05 53 58 22 73

Garden Services

General	Julian Urrutia, Bergerac	☎ 05 53 57 98 69

All aspects of tree surgery handled and a mobile sawmill to turn trunks into beams and planks. Fluent English spoken. Covers the whole of the department.

	Lorenti's, l'Ancienne Gare, Monbahus	☎ 05 53 71 40 31

Landscaping, maintenance and garden design. English spoken. Covers southern Dordogne.

Condat-sur-	Hemelin Espaces Verts, La Bechade	☎ 05 53 50 89 47

Vézère   🖳 *www.hamelinespacesverts.com*
                    (east of Périgueux close to the border with Corrèze)
                    Garden design and year-round maintenance.

Périgueux   Dominique Périer, 11 place Faidherbe   ☎ 05 53 53 89 04
                    Garden design and maintenance.

Launderettes

Bergerac   Le Lavomatic, place Gambetta   ☎ 06 64 39 13 27
                    Open every day.

Le Bugue   Laverie, 9 avenue de La Libération
                    (opposite the Crédit Agricole bank)
                    Open every day 6am to 10pm.

Montpon   Lav'Matic 2000, 43 rue Thiers   ☎ 05 53 82 35 71
                    (on the main road going through the centre of town)
                    Open every day 7am to 9pm.

Périgueux   La Lavandière, 61 rue Gambetta   ☎ 05 53 09 57 76
                    (in the town centre, east of the train station)
                    Open every day 8am to 9pm.

Sarlat-la-Canéda La Croix Rouge
                    (set back in the parade of shops alongside the
                    Champion supermarket)

Septic Tank Services

Agonac   Périgord Assainissement, Le Lyonnet   ☎ 05 53 08 72 87

Bergerac   Assainissement Lissague,
                    2 rue Paul Petit   ☎ 05 53 58 65 33

Montazeau   Vidanges Rapides du Vélinois,
                    Le Viradis   ☎ 05 53 57 97 25

Sarlat-la-Canéda Sanitra Fourrier, Eyrard   ☎ 05 53 59 02 66

Entertainment

This section isn't intended to be a definitive guide but gives a wide range
of ideas for the department. Prices and opening hours were correct at the
time of publication, but it's best to check before travelling long distances.

Cinemas

Bergerac   Le Cyrano, place de la République   ☎ 05 53 74 53 10
                    (opposite the tourist office)

| Montpon | Le Lascaux, rue Wilson (behind the Espace Culturel) | ☎ 05 53 82 12 64 |

Montpon — Le Lascaux, rue Wilson
(behind the Espace Culturel) — ☎ 05 53 82 12 64

Nontron — Cinéma Louis Dellac,
place des Droits de l'Homme — ☎ 05 53 56 18 93

Périgueux — CGR Montaigne, boulevard Montaigne ☎ 05 53 08 10 07
programme details ☎ 08 36 68 04 45

Ribérac — Cinéma Max Linder,
rue des Mobiles de Coulmiers — ☎ 05 53 90 29 08

Sarlat-la-Canéda Le Rex, avenue Thiers — ☎ 05 53 31 04 39

English Books

Meyrals — Association Culturelle Internationale
de Périgord, Carmensac Haut — ☎ 05 53 30 30 23
✉ *emboiling@wanadoo.fr*
(west of Sarlat-la-Canéda, signposted from the D48 between
St Cyprien and Les Eyzies)
This is an English library open Monday afternoons from 2 to
4pm and Wednesday mornings from 10am to noon (hours may
be extended in the future). You need to be a member of the
Association Culturelle Internationale de Périgord to use the
library. Membership costs €20 per year for a family or €15 per
person. There's an additional library membership fee of €15 per
family or €10 per person.

Montcuq — Chimera, 13 rue Faubourg St Privat — ☎ 05 65 22 97 01
(south-west of Cahors)
This shop is run by a British lady and deals in second-hand
English and French books.

Souillac — O'Learys, 2 avenue Jean Jaurès — ☎ 05 65 37 09 42
(east of Sarlat-la-Canéda)
This library operates a book exchange system.

There are English-language books at all the following public libraries:

	Mon	Tue	Wed	Thu	Fri	Sat
Bergerac place Bellegarde ☎ 05 53 57 67 66	closed	1.30–6.00	10.00–6.00	1.30–6.00	1.30–6.00	10.00–12.00 1.00–6.00
Le Bugue rue Jardin Public ☎ 05 53 07 59 08	3.00–6.00	9.00–12.00 2.30–6.00	9.00–12.00 2.30–6.00	9.00–12.00 2.30–6.00	10.00–12.00	2.30–5.00

Nontron rue de Verdun ☎ 05 53 56 22 36	closed	10.00–12.00 1.30–6.30	10.00–12.00 1.00–6.00	10.00–12.00 1.30–6.30	10.00–12.00 1.30–6.30	9.00–12.00
Périgueux 12 ave Georges Pompidou ☎ 05 53 45 65 45	closed	11.00–6.00	11.00–6.00	11.00–6.00	11.00–6.00	10.00–5.00
Ribérac rue de la République ☎ 05 53 92 52 20	closed	1.30–6.30	10.00–12.00 1.30–6.30	1.30–5.30	9.00–12.00 1.30–6.30	3.00–6.00
Sarlat-la-Canéda rue de la République ☎ 05 53 31 11 66	2.00–6.00	2.00–7.00	10.00–6.00	closed	2.00–6.00	10.00–5.00

Festivals

There are many festivals in this department, and just a small selection is detailed here. A *Fêtes en Périgord* brochure, available from tourist offices, gives details of festivals throughout the department. Festivals are annual unless otherwise stated.

May	Sarlat-la-Canéda Festival Rock de Sarlat	☎ 05 53 31 45 45
May/June	Sarlat-la-Canéda Ringuetta A celebration of traditional games and toys every other year on the May/June Pentecôte holiday.	☎ 05 53 31 45 45
July	Ribérac World Music Festival A variety of concerts and shows over five days towards the end of the month.	☎ 05 53 92 52 30
	St Pantaly d'Excideuil African Festival (north-east of Périgueux) The first weekend in July, with up to four concerts each evening.	☎ 05 53 62 48 30
July/August	Périgueux Various jazz concerts in the streets on Tuesdays.	☎ 05 53 53 10 63
	Sarlat-la-Canéda Festival des Jeux du Théâtre	☎ 05 53 31 45 45

⌨ *www.festival-theatre-sarlat.com*
There has been a summer games festival in the town at the
end of July and beginning of August since 1952.

Sarlat-la-Canéda
Festival du Périgord Noir   ☎ 05 53 31 45 45
A series of classical music concerts.

Sarlat-la-Canéda
Salon National d'Art Photographique   ☎ 05 53 31 45 45
National photographic exhibition.

August   Le Bugue
                Grandes Fêtes de la St Louis   ☎ 05 53 07 20 48
                Comprises a *brocante* (car boot/jumble/second-hand sale),
                fireworks display and a big fair on the last day.

                Périgueux
                Mimos, Festival International du Mime ☎ 05 53 53 10 63

August/   Périgueux
September   Sinfonia – Festival International de
                Musique Baroque   ☎ 05 53 53 10 63

September   Sarlat-la-Canéda
                Concours Dessine-Moi   ☎ 05 53 31 45 45
                An art competition on the second Sunday of the month.

October   Montpon
                La Foire à l'Ancienne   ☎ 05 53 82 23 77
                A fair featuring local producers and artisans on the last Sunday.

November   Sarlat-la-Canéda
                Festival du Film   ☎ 05 53 31 45 45
                This is held at the beginning of the month.

Theatres

Bergerac   Centre Culturel Municipal et d'Arts
                Appliqués, place Gambetta   ☎ 05 53 57 71 51

Montpon   Espace Culturel Antoine de St Exupéry,
                rue Verdun   ☎ 05 53 82 30 54
                Full programme of events available from the tourist office.

Périgueux   Théâtre d'Odysée,
                esplanade du Théâtre   ☎ 05 53 53 18 71

                Théâtre le Palace, 15 rue Bodin   ☎ 05 53 05 94 60

Video & DVD Hire

Bergerac   Empire Vidéo, 1 rue de la Bargironnette ☎ 05 53 61 75 43
                  Mondays to Saturdays 10am to 12.30pm and 2 to 9pm,
                  Saturdays until 10pm.

Montpon   Saint Seiya, 11 rue Thiers   ☎ 05 53 80 65 20
                  (on the main street through the centre of town)
                  Mondays and Tuesdays 2 to 8pm, Wednesdays, Thursdays
                  and Sundays 3 to 7pm, Fridays and Saturdays 3 to 8pm.

                  There's also a 24-hour dispenser for both DVDs and
                  videos next to Intermarché.

Nontron   Video Games, 6 rue de Verdun   ☎ 05 53 60 35 00
                  (just up from the main square in the centre of the town)
                  Mondays 2.30 to 7pm, Tuesdays to Saturdays 10.30am to
                  12.15pm and 2.30 to 7.15pm. DVD and videos for hire as well
                  as video and DVD players. Exchange and sale of cassettes for
                  a variety of games consoles.

Périgueux   Vidéo Futur, 21 rue Gambetta   ☎ 05 53 04 17 82
                  (on the roundabout at Place Roosevelt, east of the railway
                  station)
                  Mondays to Saturdays 10.30am to 12.30pm and 3 to 8pm.

Ribérac   Vidéo Club, 121 rue du 26 Mars 1944   ☎ 05 53 90 85 03
                  Mondays to Saturdays 10am to 12.30pm and 3 to 8pm.
                  There's also a 24-hour video and DVD dispenser.

Sarlat-la-Canéda Votre Ecran, 35 avenue Gambetta   ☎ 05 53 31 10 79
                  Open every day for DVD and video hire.

Leisure Activities

This section isn't intended to be a definitive guide but gives a wide range
of ideas for the department. Prices and opening hours were correct at the
time of publication, but it's best to check before travelling long distances.

Art Classes

Belvès   ☎ 05 53 29 63 76
                  (east of Sarlat-la-Canéda)
                  Drawing classes in a French/English group. Beginners to
                  experts in maximum groups of four.

Bergerac   Bergerac Accueille, Maison des
                  Associations, Place Jules Ferry   ☎ 05 53 61 82 26
                  Adult classes for painting on silk and porcelain, drawing and
                  other types of painting.

Montpon	Ombres et Couleurs, Ecole Primaire, rue de Verdun	☎ 05 53 80 15 45

Courses Tuesday, Wednesday and Friday evenings. Contact Mr Micoine.

Nontron	Art & Création	☎ 05 53 56 03 99

Contact Mme de Rauglaudre.

Périgueux	Centre Culturel de la Visitation, rue Littré	☎ 05 53 53 55 17

A variety of art classes, including 'Clair de Lune', which is a group producing cartoons and comic strips.

Ribérac	Arts Plastiques, Centre Culturel, rue Gambetta	☎ 05 53 91 36 28

Various art courses, including watercolours. For details of children's workshops contact Mr Peyronneau (☎ 05 53 90 11 57).

	Centre Culturel	☎ 05 53 90 51 23

Silk painting. Contact Mme Davin.

	Club du Temps Libre	☎ 05 53 90 32 06

Painting on porcelain.

Sarlat-la-Canéda	Atelier Arts Plastiques, 32 rue Lachambeaudie	☎ 05 53 59 43 60

Workshops held throughout the week, including watercolours, sculpture, drawing and pastels.

Ballooning

La Roque-Gageac	Montgolfière du Périgord, St Donat	☎ 05 53 28 18 58

🖥 *www.perigordballons.com*
(south of Sarlat-la-Canéda)
Flights available all year, subject to weather conditions.

Bike Hire

Bergerac	Périgord Cycles, 11 place Gambetta	☎ 05 53 57 07 19

Open all year 8am (Saturdays 9am) to noon and 2 to 7pm.

Montagrier	Centre VTT, allée des Marronniers	☎ 05 53 90 13 25

(east of Ribérac)
Mountain bike hire.

Ribérac	Cycle Cums, 35 rue du 26 Mars 1944	☎ 05 53 90 33 23

	Cycle Senrens, 19 rue Jean Moulin	☎ 05 53 90 02 41

Sarlat-la-Canéda Base VTT du Périgord Noir,
                  Centre Commercial Pré de Cordy   ☎ 05 53 59 67 70
                  (south-east of the town)

Boat, Train & Wagon Rides

Boat Trips

Bergerac   Périgord Gabares, quai Salvette   ☎ 05 53 24 58 80
One hour cruises aboard traditional boats to learn the history of
the river or the history of the old town or just to enjoy the
scenery. Available every day from Easter to November.

Creysse   Gabares du Port de Creysse,
          Port de Creysse   ☎ 05 53 23 20 45
Cruises from 2 to 6pm and dinner cruises at 12.30pm and
7.30pm, Easter to November. Navigate the waterways aboard
authentic old craft. Dinner cruises need to be booked 48 hours
in advance.

Le Roque-   Gabares Norbert   ☎ 05 53 29 40 44
Gageac   🖳 www.norbert.fr
Travel down the Dordogne aboard traditional boats, which will
take you past five of the most beautiful châteaux in the valley.
One hour trips departing between 10am and 6pm from the
beginning of April until the first Sunday in November
(afternoons only in October).

Mauzac   Les Gabares de Mauzac, Port Gabarier   ☎ 05 53 23 90 36
         🖳 www.gabare.fr
River cruises that operate all year on a circuit on the 'Cingle de
Trémolat' (a section of the Dordogne) lasting one hour.
Sightseeing and themed cruises available.

St Martial   Promenade en Gabare   ☎ 05 53 80 35 77
d'Artenset Take the time to travel along the gentle river Isle on a traditional
flat-bottomed boat, a cruise of around one-and-a-half hours.
From May to September on Sundays and bank holidays at 4pm;
July and August every day at 3pm, 4.30pm and 6pm.

Train Rides

Bergerac   Autorail Espérance   ☎ 05 53 59 55 39
In July and August there are daily trips from Mondays to
Saturdays between Bergerac and Sarlat, some journeys
including tastings of regional specialities.

Wagon Rides

Mazeyrolles   Le Périgord en Calèche   ☎ 05 53 29 98 99
              🖳 www.perigord-en-caleche.com

A calèche is a type of horse-drawn cart or carriage. These can be hired for day trips through the forest – with a driver, who provides a meal at lunchtime and a tasting of *foie gras* and a local drink on the way back.

Vaux-en-Périgord	Babette et Philippe, la Métairie du Roc	☎ 05 53 24 32 57

💻 *www.equitation-en-perigord.com*
From April to September you can hire horse-drawn wagons for three to seven days. You're given instruction for the horse and wagon and accompanied for the first few miles. Each night you stay at pre-arranged accommodation. Covered wagons can take up to six people, more open wagons four people.

Boules/Pétanque

Bergerac	Petite Boule de Naillac, 25 rue du 26ème RI	☎ 05 53 74 60 25

Montpon	Pétanque Montponnaise	☎ 06 78 92 10 05

(off avenue Georges Pompidou, just after the gendarmerie in the direction of Libourne)
Every day from 2.30 to 7.30pm.

Nontron	La Boule Nontronnaise	☎ 05 53 56 29 04

Contact Mr Chauvet.

Périgueux	Entente Périgueux Pétanque, Maison des Sportifs, 10bis rue Louis Blanc	☎ 05 53 53 06 72

This organisation will give you details of your nearest pétanque club.

Ribérac   There's a large boulodrome on rue du Stade, just north of the town centre and alongside the tennis courts and sports stadium.

Sarlat-la-Canéda There's a boulodrome at Place de la Libération and a covered boules ground at Place Roger Lapébie.

Bridge

Bergerac	Bergerac Bridge Club, Gymnase Aragon, Allée des Grands Ducs	☎ 05 53 63 13 95

Montpon	Bridge Club de Montpon, Foyer Municipal, rue Henri Laborde	

Meetings every Friday evening.

Nontron	Bridge Club du Nontronnaise	☎ 05 53 60 92 81

Contact Mr Gardette.

Périgueux   Club de Bridge de Périgueux,
                   3 boulevard Lakanal   ☎ 05 53 53 43 80

Ribérac   Club de Bridge   ☎ 05 53 90 04 49
                   Contact Mr Lesueur for details.

Sarlat-la-Canéda   Périgord Noir Top Bridge Evasion,
                   Hôtel St Albert, 10 place Pasteur   ☎ 05 53 31 55 55

                   Sarlat Bridge, Le Colombier   ☎ 05 53 31 18 59
                   Held at the old hospital (le Colombier) in room Favelelli on
                   Mondays 2 to 6pm, Tuesdays and Fridays 8.15pm to midnight
                   and Saturdays 2 to 6pm.

Children's Activity Clubs

Bergerac   14 rue Eugène Fromentin   ☎ 05 53 74 06 67
                   Gym for infants from two years old.

Montpon   Les Ateliers d'Eveil Culturel,
                   la Bibliothèque, rue de Verdun   ☎ 05 53 82 30 54
                   Workshops and activities organised for 6 to 16-year-olds on
                   Wednesday afternoons in term time.

                   Copains d'Eté, Copains d'Idées   ☎ 05 53 82 30 54
                   Summer activities arranged for three to six-year-olds and 6 to
                   14-year-olds.

Périgueux   Actions Jeunes,
                   7 place du Marché au Bois   ☎ 05 53 09 60 60
                   A programme of events and activities organised for 12 to 16-
                   year-olds.

Ribérac   Centre de Loisirs, Ecole Jules Ferry,
                   rue Pierre Serbat   ☎ 05 53 90 01 48
                   Activities organised during the school holidays for 4 to
                   12-year-olds.

Circus Skills

Périgueux   Ini Cirque, rue Clermont des Piles   ☎ 06 19 56 50 83

Pressignac-Vicq   The Magic Rock Circus, La Fourquerie ☎ 05 53 61 88 07
                   Minimum age five.

Sarlat-la-Canéda   Ecole de Cirque, 32 rue Lachambeaudie ☎ 05 53 59 43 60
                   Circus school for youngsters aged six and upwards.

Crazy Golf

Le Bugue   Planète Mini-Golf, Le Port   ☎ 05 53 07 10 74
                  (beside the river by the swimming pool)

Dancing

Bergerac   Club Bergeracois de Danse de Salon,
                  23 rue Davout   ☎ 05 53 57 64 22
                  Traditional dance (waltz, tango, etc.).

Le Bugue   Energy Danse   ☎ 05 53 07 15 39

                  Section Danse du Foyer Rural   ☎ 05 53 29 21 26
                  Ballet and contemporary dance.

Montpon   Ecole de Danse, rue du Général Leclerc ☎ 05 53 81 99 52
                  (in the building next to the swimming pool)
                  Ballet for children and adults.

Nontron   Association Sissonne, Ecole de Danse   ☎ 05 53 56 17 57
                  Contact Mme Mousnier.

Périgueux   Studio 2, 7 rue Bodin   ☎ 05 53 09 40 54

                  Veronique Danse, 18 rue Thiers   ☎ 05 53 53 23 29

Ribérac   Ecole de Danse Entrechats,
                  41 rue Couleau   ☎ 05 53 90 58 22
                  Ballet, modern and jazz for all age groups from four years old.

                  Les Petits Danseurs Périgord Sud Charente,
                  Salle No.1, Palais de Justice,
                  rue du Palais   ☎ 05 45 98 50 85
                  Ballet classes from eight years old.

Sarlat-la-Canéda Centre de Danse et d'Expression,
                  17 boulevard Eugène le Roy   ☎ 05 53 59 13 22
                  Dance, music, mime and relaxation classes.

                  Annie Vanherzeele   ☎ 05 53 59 33 42
                  Oriental dance classes.

St Martin-de-   Salsa classes at the Salle des Fêtes ☎ 05 53 91 36 28
Ribérac   (just south of Ribérac)
                  Every Monday at 8pm.

Dog Clubs

Périgueux   Société Canine de la Dordogne,
                  24 rue de Cronstadt   ☎ 05 53 35 31 46

Pineuilh	Club de Chien de la Vallée de la Dordogne, Résidence des Sables, 1 rue du Marais ☎ 05 57 41 92 02 (east of Bergerac, just south of Port Sainte Foye)

Drama

Bergerac	'La Gargouille', Théâtre Populaire du Périgord, Salle le P'tit Chat Noir, Les Vaures ☎ 05 53 22 54 76
	Les Amateurs, 57 rue Sully Prudhomme ☎ 05 53 57 26 76 🖳 www.alma-inter.com/amateurs
	'Rue Merline', 16 rue des Conférences ☎ 05 53 22 48 73 ✉ christart24@wanadoo.fr Theatrical workshops in French for foreigners.
Nontron	Les Troubadours Nontronnais ☎ 05 53 56 03 55 Theatrical and cultural events.
Périgueux	Foyer Laïque Section Théâtre, 803 rue Raymond Raudier ☎ 05 53 09 85 43
Ribérac	Centre Culturel, rue Gambetta ☎ 05 53 08 16 10 Theatrical workshops. Contact Mr Romary.
Sarlat-la-Canéda	Amis du Théâtre de Sarlat et du Périgord Noir, Ancien Théâtre, rue Tourny Workshops, courses and shows. Meetings every Monday evening.
	Les Tréteaux du Matin, 3 rue Emmanuel Lasserre ☎ 05 53 31 63 38 Workshops on Wednesdays for school-age children and on Tuesday evenings and at weekends for adults.

Gyms & Health Clubs

Bergerac	Espace Gym, 23 rue Professeur Testut ☎ 05 53 57 73 29 Gym with cardio machines and free weights. Hours may vary, but generally open Mondays to Fridays until 10pm and Saturday mornings, closing for lunch Mondays to Thursdays.
Périgueux	Amazonia, 12ter rue des Prés ☎ 05 53 53 25 21 🖳 www.amazonia.tm.fr Gym with cardio machines and fitness classes, open every day from 6am to 11pm.

Sarlat-la-Canéda Evasion Fitness Club Sarladais,
avenue Edmond Rostand ☎ 05 53 31 03 46
Weights, gym, health club and aerobic classes. Open
Mondays, Tuesdays, Thursdays and Fridays 10am to 8pm,
Wednesdays noon to 8pm, Saturdays 10am to 5pm.

Karting & Quad Bikes

Badefols-sur-   Rêv'Quads, Les Bö-Bains ☎ 05 53 73 52 52
Dordogne   💻 *www.bo-bains.com*
(directly east of Bergerac)
Open all year. Participants must be over 16 and have a
motorbike licence.

Fougueyrolles   Pro Glisse, Le Vieux Château ☎ 05 53 74 60 33
(west of Bergerac)

Javerlhac   TGEC Karting, Beaumont, Teyjat ☎ 05 53 56 36 11
(north of Nonton)

La Douze   Garden Karting, Les Martinies Hautes ☎ 05 53 35 28 55
500m outdoor karting track. Individuals, groups and lessons.
There's a shaded terrace for spectators and a small restaurant.

Nontron   Association Sportive de Karting
Nontron ☎ 05 53 09 71 31

Sarlat-la-Canéda Association Sportive de Karting de
Sarlat ☎ 05 53 59 02 52
Contact Mr Rouge.

Kite Flying

Bergerac   Nez au Vent Cerf-Volant Club,
13 rue Maurice de Vlaminck ☎ 05 53 57 82 49

Model Clubs

Neuvic   Club Aéromodelisme,
22 rue de la Providence ☎ 05 53 91 37 39
(south-east of Ribérac, south-west of Périgueux)
Contact Mr Tallet.

Périgueux   Modèle Yacht Club de Périgueux, Maison
des Sportifs, 10bis rue Louis Blanc ☎ 05 53 04 15 38

Ribérac   Aéro Club Jean Mermoz,
Aérodrome de Ribérac ☎ 05 53 90 10 41
Contact Mr Galluret.

Music

Bergerac	Club Stella, 2 rue Bertrand de Born	☎ 06 62 19 23 56

Overlook, la Rock School,
14bis rue Pozzi ☎ 05 53 63 03 70

Le Bugue Ecole de Musique ☎ 06 88 61 43 30

Montpon Ecole Nationale de Musique de la Dordogne,
Espace Culturel Antoine de
St Exupéry, rue de Verdun ☎ 05 53 8043 69
Introduction to music and lessons for five-year-olds to adults.
Lessons held at the Ecole Primaire, rue de Verdun. Instruments
taught include drums, piano, saxophone, flute, guitar and violin.

Nontron Ecole de Musique ☎ 05 53 60 93 46
Contact Mr Lemoine.

Périgueux Jazzogène, Centre Culturel de la
Visitation, rue Littré ☎ 05 53 09 83 80
Improvisation and jazz workshops every Saturday 5.30 to
7.30pm. For more information telephone after 7pm.

Ecole Municipale Britten,
3 rue de Varsovie ☎ 05 53 09 49 46

Ribérac Ecole de Musique, 20 rue du 26 Mars ☎ 05 53 90 26 51
Wind instruments and the piano.

Sarlat-la-Canéda Ecole Nationale de Musique du
Sarladais, 35 rue de Cahors ☎ 05 53 31 22 44
Lessons on Tuesday afternoons and Wednesday mornings and
afternoons during term time.

Académie de Piano,
107 avenue de Selves ☎ 05 53 59 55 32
Piano courses, including classical to jazz, for children and
adults.

Photography

Bergerac Photo Club de Bergerac, Maison des
Associations, place Jules Ferry ☎ 05 53 57 10 33

Montpon Photo Club Montponnais,
13 rue Foix de Candalle ☎ 05 53 80 70 70
Contact Mr Liados.

Nontron	Club Photo de Nontron Contact Mr Poinet.	☎ 05 53 56 00 8?
Périgueux	Photo Ciné Club SNCF de Périgueux, 19 rue Pierre Semard	☎ 05 53 06 27 7?
Sarlat-la-Canéda	Photo Club, 2 rue Lachambeaudie	☎ 05 53 59 43 6(

Pottery

| Ribérac | Atelier de Poterie, Centre Culturel | ☎ 05 53 92 52 3(|

Scouts & Guides

Bergerac	Scouts de France, 28 rue Nungesser et Coli	☎ 05 53 27 02 8(
Lamonzie- Montastruc	Guides de France, Monsacou ✉ jmaillou@club-internet.fr	☎ 05 53 23 36 48
Périgueux	Guides de France, Presbytère St Georges, 44 rue Béranger	☎ 05 53 08 16 67
	Scouts de France Périgueux Trélissac Contact Mr Glénisson.	☎ 05 53 35 12 71

Social Groups

| General | Bilingual Club | ☎ 05 53 46 77 47 |

Meetings across Dordogne, including outings, golf days, etc. to help integrate English-speaking newcomers into French life. Contact Mr Waldemar Kaminski.

Bergerac	Dordogne Ladies Club International, 14 rue Alain Fournier ✉ maureenenfrance@wanadoo.fr	
	Table Ronde Française, 34 boulevard Victor Hugo The French Round Table.	☎ 05 53 58 54 54
Meyrals	Association Culturelle Internationale de Périgord, Carmensac Haut ✉ emboiling@wanadoo.fr	☎ 05 53 30 30 23

(west of Sarlat-la-Canéda, signposted from the D48 between St Cyprien and Les Eyzies)
This is an organisation aimed at assisting the integration of foreigners into the area and to help towards a better understanding between cultures. Contact Emma Boiling for more information.

Nontron   Foyer Socio Educatif, 'La Ruche'   ☎ 05 53 60 83 30
                   Exchange group between France and Britain and between
                   France and Germany. Contact Mme Mouhot.

St Martial-
d'Artenset-   (on the N89 east of Montpon)
le-Bourg   An English-speaking group meets in the bar here every Friday
                   morning and the owner of the bar speaks very good English.

Rotary Clubs

Bergerac   Rotary Club de Bergerac, La Flambée,
                   153 avenue Pasteur   ☎ 05 53 57 52 33

Nontron   Rotary Club de Nontron   ☎ 05 50 32 15 02
                   Contact Mr Francis-Mathieu.

Sarlat-la-Canéda   Rotary Club de Sarlat, Hôtel Montaigne,
                   10 place Pasteur   ☎ 05 53 31 55 55

St Laurent-   Rotary Club Bergerac Cyrano   ☎ 05 53 27 40 10
des-Vignes   Meetings held at hotel/restaurant Le Mylord, route de Bordeaux.

Spas

St Avit   La Baignerie, 2 les Petits Briands   ☎ 05 57 46 57 41
St Nazaire   (directly west of Bergerac)
                   A small private spa that can be hired for 75-minute sessions
                   between 9am and 7.30pm every day (9pm at weekends).
                   There's a small pool, a Turkish bath and a sauna (for a
                   maximum of four people). English spoken.

Stamp Collecting

Bergerac   Association Philatélique Bergerac-
                   Périgord, place Jules Ferry   ☎ 05 53 58 75 25

Montpon   Amicale Philatélique et Cartophile   ☎ 05 53 80 34 97
                   Contact Mr Laur.

Nontron   Association Culturelle et Philatélique
                   Haut Périgord   ☎ 05 55 03 61 24
                   Contact Mr Bremard.

Périgueux   Amicale Philatélique de la Dordogne   ☎ 05 53 08 46 58
                   Contact Mr Moniotte for details of meetings.

Sarlat-la-Canéda   Association Philatélique   ☎ 05 53 59 33 56
                   Contact Mr Plasroques.

Tree Climbing

Carsac-Aillac   Indian Forest Périgord,
Le Manoir de la Feuillade   ☎ 05 53 31 22 22
💻 *www.perigord.com/manoir.la.feuillade*
Explore the tree canopy via rope ladders, bridges and aerial
runways. Full safety equipment provided. Open every day
9.30am to 7.30pm (closed if raining).

St Vincent-   Airparc Périgord, Port d'Enveaux   ☎ 05 53 29 18 43
de-Cosse   Tree-top adventures on three different courses. Allow around
two hours. Adults and children. There's also a restaurant/bar
and canoes for hire.

Vintage Cars

Périgueux   Périgord Auto Rétro, Maison des
Sportifs, 1bis rue Louis Blanc   ☎ 05 53 53 06 72

Sarlat-la-Canéda Véhicules Anciens du Sarladais   ☎ 05 53 28 64 61
Exchanges of ideas and spares, restoration, shows and
outings. Contact Mr Cloup.

Walking & Rambling

Bergerac   Club Stella, 25 boulevard Henri Sicard   ☎ 05 53 58 33 48

USB Section Randonnée Pédestre   ☎ 05 53 73 15 12
This is the local section of the Aquitaine walking organisation.
Contact Chantal Delarue for details of local walks.

Le Bugue   Objectif 42   ☎ 05 53 03 92 60
This is the local walking group. Contact Mr Guy Melin.

The tourist office has booklets giving routes of varying
lengths near the town.

Montpon   There are 14 walks around Montpon from 5 to 30km (3 to
18mi). A free guide is available from the tourist office
giving details of the routes.

Périgueux   La Randonnée Pédestre en Aquitaine,
46 rue Kléber   ☎ 05 53 45 51 21
This office is open Mondays to Fridays 9am to 12.30pm and
1.30 to 5pm and has details of walks and walking groups in the
department.

Ribérac   Accompanied walks are organised every Wednesday
from mid-June to mid-September. Details from the tourist
office (☎ 05 53 90 03 10).

Detailed guides of walks around Ribérac and the forest are on sale at the tourist office.

Wine Courses

Bergerac	Wine School, La Maison des Vins de Bergerac 🖳 *www.vins-bergerac.fr* Wine courses are held on Wednesday mornings from mid-June to the end of August.	☎ 05 53 63 57 57

Yoga

Bergerac	Attitude, 22 rue Diderot	☎ 05 53 74 84 10
	Atlante, Maison des Associations, Salle No.5, place Jules Ferry	☎ 06 03 50 78 18
Le Bugue	Classes throughout the year.	☎ 05 53 35 42 15
Lusignac	Maria Bos, La Roussie (directly north of Ribérac)	☎ 05 53 90 36 08
Périgueux	CSL Ardant du Picq, 50 rue Ludovic Trarieux	☎ 05 53 08 50 00
	Cercle de Yoga Périgourdin, 22 rue Carnot	☎ 05 53 53 34 98

Medical Facilities & Services

Ambulances

In the event of a medical emergency dial ☎ 15.

Bergerac	☎ 05 53 74 55 55
Le Bugue	☎ 05 53 07 10 70
Montpon	☎ 05 53 80 32 19
Nontron	☎ 05 53 56 06 90
Périgueux	☎ 05 53 81 03 98
Ribérac	☎ 05 53 90 07 72
Sarlat-la-Canéda	☎ 05 53 31 12 54

Chiropractors

Eymet	Simon Pullen, 18 boulevard National (Eymet is on the southern border of Dordogne) This is an English-speaking chiropractor.	☎ 05 53 23 32 21

Doctors

English-speakers may like to contact the following doctors:

Bergerac	Dr Blondeau, 4 place Deux Conils	☎ 05 53 23 50 55
Le Bugue	Cabinet Médical, avenue de la Libération	☎ 05 53 07 26 87
Montpon	Dr Roye, 51 rue Thiers	☎ 05 53 80 33 95
Nontron	Dr Chraibi, avenue Jules Ferry	☎ 05 53 56 03 03
Périgueux	Dr Lamonzie, 6 rue Clarté	☎ 05 53 08 56 98
Ribérac	Maison Médicale, 1 avenue de Royan	☎ 05 53 90 19 00
Sarlat-la-Canéda	Dr Barret, 19 rue Cordeliers	☎ 05 53 30 86 00

Dentists

English-speakers may like to contact the following dentists:

Bergerac	Dr Escarment, 10 cours Alsace Lorraine	☎ 05 53 27 01 22
Le Bugue	Cabinet Dentaire, avenue de la Libération	☎ 05 53 07 26 87
Montpon	Cabinet Dentaire, 6 rue Pont	☎ 05 53 80 38 87
Périgueux	Dr Tocanne, 18 rue Prés Wilson	☎ 05 53 53 32 74
Ribérac	Dr Lavaud, 8 rue Achille Simon	☎ 05 53 91 26 18
Sarlat-la-Canéda	Dr Laporte, 60 avenue Thiers	☎ 05 53 59 14 76

Gendarmeries

Bergerac	9 avenue Président Wilson	☎ 05 53 74 70 00
Le Bugue	place Farge	☎ 05 53 03 83 95
Montpon	rue St Roch	☎ 05 53 80 85 30
Nontron	rue Maîtres des Forges	☎ 05 53 60 82 30
Périgueux	boulevard Bertran de Born	☎ 05 53 02 71 17

| Ribérac | rue André Malraux | ☎ 05 53 92 00 17 |
| Sarlat-la-Canéda | place Salvador Allende | ☎ 05 53 31 71 10 |

Health Authority

| General | CRAM Aquitaine, 80 avenue de la Jallère, Bordeaux | ☎ 05 56 11 64 13 |

💻 *www.cram-aquitaine.fr*
This is the regional office.

| Bergerac | 2 boulevard 8 Mai 1945 | ☎ 05 53 61 77 74 |

Le Bugue   Mairie, place Hôtel de Ville
There's a representative at the *mairie* from 1.30 to 4.30pm on the second Friday of each month. No appointment necessary.

Montpon   Ancien Collège   ☎ 05 53 45 40 60
There's a representative here from 8.30am to noon on the first Wednesday of each month (no appointment necessary) and from 1 to 4pm on the third Friday of each month (by appointment).

Nontron   Point Multi-Services, place Paul Bert   ☎ 05 53 45 40 60
There's a representative here from 9am to noon on the second and fourth Wednesday of each month (no appointment needed) and from 1 to 4pm on the second Wednesday of each month (by appointment).

Périgueux   11 rue Louis Blanc   ☎ 05 53 45 40 60
This is the head office for Dordogne. Open Monday to Friday 8am to 5pm. No appointment necessary.

Ribérac   Centre Médico-Social   ☎ 05 53 45 40 60
There's a representative here from 1.30 to 4.30pm on the second Thursday of each month (no appointment necessary) and from 1.30 to 4.30pm on the fourth Thursday of each month (by appointment).

Sarlat-la-Canéda Centre Socio Culture   ☎ 05 53 45 40 60
There's a representative here from 9am to noon on the second Tuesday of each month and from 9am to noon and 1 to 4pm on the fourth Tuesday of each month (no appointment necessary) as well as from 9am to noon and 1 to 4pm on the fourth Thursday of the month (by appointment).

Hospitals

| Bergerac | Centre Hospitalier Samuel Pozzi, 9 avenue Prof. Albert Calmette | ☎ 05 53 63 88 88 |

| Périgueux | Centre Hospitalier Périgueux, 80 avenue Georges Pompidou | ☎ 05 53 07 70 00 |
| Ribérac | Hôpital de Ribérac, rue Jean Moulin | ☎ 05 53 92 55 55 |

This hospital doesn't have an emergency department.

| Sarlat-la-Canéda | Centre Hospitalier Jean Leclaire, Le Pouget, rue Jean Leclaire | ☎ 05 53 31 75 75 |

Motoring

Breakers' Yards

| Nanthiat | Nanthiat Auto Casse, La Lande (just east of Thivers) | ☎ 05 53 62 52 80 |
| St Nexans | Jean-Claude Rameau, Les Farguettes (east of Bergerac airport) | ☎ 05 53 24 34 19 |

Car Dealers

Bergerac	Alfa Romeo, Garage Chadourne, 49 boulevard Victor Hugo	☎ 05 53 57 97 50
	Audi/VW, Garage Alary, route de Bordeaux	☎ 05 53 74 54 84
	BMW, Garage Alary P. Autos, ZA Vallade Nord	☎ 05 53 57 43 95
	Citroën, Cazes SA, route Bordeaux	☎ 05 53 74 44 44
	Daewoo, Daniel Beaupuy, 20 boulevard Joseph Santraille	☎ 05 53 57 01 03
	Fiat, Garage de Naillac, 39 avenue Général de Gaulle	☎ 05 53 57 18 97
	Ford, Dordogne Autos, route de Bordeaux, St Laurent-des-Vignes	☎ 05 53 73 80 52
	Honda, F David, 73 avenue Paul Doumer	☎ 05 53 22 65 57
	Hyundi, F David, 73 avenue Paul Doumer	☎ 05 53 22 65 57

Lancia, Garage de Naillac,
39 avenue Général de Gaulle   ☎ 05 53 57 18 97

Mercedes-Benz, Verrouil Sarl, Le Bridet,
ZI Valade   ☎ 05 53 22 21 11

Mitsubishi, F. David,
73 avenue Paul Doumer   ☎ 05 53 22 65 57

Nissan, Garage Saint Marc, route Eymet ☎ 05 53 57 71 80

Peugeot, Géraud Concess,
117 rue Clairat   ☎ 05 53 22 28 28

Renault, Bergerac Autos,
route de Périgueux   ☎ 05 53 63 65 65

Rover, Garage Saint Marc, route Eymet   ☎ 05 53 57 71 80

Toyota, Verrouil Sarl, Le Bridet,
ZI Valade   ☎ 05 53 22 21 11

Vauxhall/Opel, Auto Service Bergerac,
33 avenue Général de Gaulle   ☎ 05 53 63 14 00

Le Bugue   Peugeot, Bruneteau Bernard,
route du Buisson   ☎ 05 53 07 26 72

Renault, Garage ESA Chevaux,
84 route Paris   ☎ 05 53 08 60 60

Montpon   Audi, Jean Lagarde,
54 avenue Georges Pompidou   ☎ 05 53 80 41 21

Citroën, Montpon Autos,
1 avenue Georges Pompidou   ☎ 05 53 80 31 00

Peugeot, Garage Bonnet,
51 avenue Jean Moulin   ☎ 05 53 80 85 55

Renault, Garage Fougère,
1 avenue André Malraux   ☎ 05 53 80 32 07

VW, Jean Lagarde,
54 avenue Georges Pompidou   ☎ 05 53 80 41 21

Nontron	Citroën, Garage Limousin, 4 avenue Yvon Delbos	☎ 05 53 56 01 42
	Peugeot, Lalay-Prédignac, ZA La Margot, route Piégut	☎ 05 53 56 00 21
	Vauxhall/Opel, Garage Allary, 14 route Piégut	☎ 05 53 56 01 03
Périgueux	Alfa/Lancia, Rebiere, 228 avenue Michel Grandou	☎ 05 53 08 09 44
	Audi, Garage Lagarde, route d'Images, Trélissac	☎ 05 53 02 35 50
	BMW, Claude Madronet, Rond Point de l'Agora, Boulazac	☎ 05 53 45 44 00
	Citroën, Garage Deluc, route de Limoges, Trélissac	☎ 05 53 02 70 10
	Daewoo, Claud's Autos, ZAE Marsac	☎ 05 53 03 37 70
	Fiat, Rebière, 2 28 avenue Michel Grandou	☎ 05 53 35 76 20
	Ford, Dordogne Autos, ZAC du Landry, Boulazac	☎ 05 53 45 46 56
	Honda, Garage F David, 157 avenue Maréchal Juin	☎ 05 53 35 64 10
	Mercedes, Magot SA, 192 route de Lyon	☎ 05 53 02 34 34
	Mini, Claud Madronet, Rond Point de l'Agora, Boulazac	☎ 05 53 45 44 00
	Mitsubishi, BD Auto, 156 route de Bordeaux	☎ 05 53 35 64 12
	Nissan, Pradier et Fils, 5 rue Antoine Gadaud	☎ 05 53 53 85 85
	Peugeot, Garage Reynet, 8 rue Clermont Pile	☎ 05 53 53 34 88

Renault, SARDA, route de Limoges,
Trélissac ☎ 05 53 02 41 41

Seat, Franc Auto,
219 route d'Angoulême ☎ 05 53 08 16 27

Subaru, F David,
157 avenue Maréchal Juin ☎ 05 53 04 00 20

Suzuki, Garage F. David,
157 avenue Maréchal Juin ☎ 05 53 04 00 20

Toyota, Magot SA, 203 route de Lyon ☎ 05 53 06 40 40

Vauxhall/Opel, Agora Autos,
230 avenue Michel Grandou ☎ 05 53 35 76 40

VW, Garage Lagarde, route de Limoges,
Trélissac ☎ 05 53 02 35 50

Ribérac   Alfa/Lancia, Gilles Dumon,
route de Périgueux ☎ 05 53 90 00 83

Citroën, Garage Lafargue,
21 rue Jean Moulin ☎ 05 53 90 05 38

Fiat, Gilles Dumon, route de Périgueux ☎ 05 53 90 00 83

Ford, Garage Raymond,
rue André Cheminade ☎ 05 53 90 06 85

Peugeot, JF Bittard,
20 avenue de Verdun ☎ 05 53 90 01 09

Renault, C Duresse,
route de Mussidan ☎ 05 53 90 19 19

Vauxhall/Opel, Daniel Edely,
rue André Cheminade ☎ 05 53 90 49 78

Sarlat-la-Canéda Alfa Romeo, Garage Mora, Rivaux ☎ 05 53 59 19 71

Audi, Garage Lagarde,
12bis avenue Aristide Briand ☎ 05 53 31 18 02

Citroën, Sarlat Autos Salive,
avenue Dordogne ☎ 05 53 31 47 00

Ford, Ford Auto Service,
avenue Dordogne ☎ 05 53 59 05 23

Mazda, Garage Delpech, le Pontet ☎ 05 53 59 63 02

Peugeot, Grand Garage de la Dordogne,
Pré Cordy ☎ 05 53 28 68 68

Renault, Garage Robert,
33 avenue Thiers ☎ 05 53 31 78 00

Seat, Garage de la Canéda, Giragne Est ☎ 05 53 59 44 48

Vauxhall/Opel, Delpech, le Pontet ☎ 05 53 59 63 02

VW, Garage Lagarde,
12bis avenue Aristide Briand ☎ 05 53 31 18 02

Tyre/Exhaust Centres

Bergerac   Feu Vert, avenue Paul Doumer ☎ 05 53 61 17 18

Montpon   Soubzmaigne, route de Bordeaux ☎ 05 53 80 37 21

Nontron   Point S CPN, 2 boulevard Gambetta ☎ 05 53 60 81 40

Périgueux   Speedy, 8 rue Arsault ☎ 05 53 35 48 21

Ribérac   Périgord Pneus, ZI Chaumes ☎ 05 53 90 05 06

Sarlat-la-Canéda Soubzmaigne, 36 avenue de Selves ☎ 05 53 59 00 33

Pets

Dog Training

Les Landes   Centre d'Education Canine,
St Martial de Valette ☎ 05 53 60 96 72
(in the north of the department, west of Nontron)

Ribérac   Club d'Education Canine,
28 chemin d'Engauthier ☎ 05 53 90 16 87
Training sessions Saturdays 2 to 6pm. Telephone enquiries
after 8pm.

Salon Yves Massoubre, La Bassetie   ☎ 05 53 54 75 38
🖳 *www.massoubre-yves.com*
(south of Périgueux)
Individual dog training for all breeds.

Farriers

General   Rodolphe Bagouet, Gouts Rossignol   ☎ 06 16 45 55 39
(north-east Dordogne)

Stéphane Marty, Foncène,
Cénac et St Julien   ☎ 05 53 28 95 25
(south-east Dordogne)

Horse Dentists

Vets don't deal with teeth rasping and there are specialist equine dentists.
You need to telephone in advance to be booked onto the next circuit.

General   Christian Frémy, 19 boulevard Horizon,
Penne d'Agenais   ☎ 05 53 41 73 78
(east of Villeneuve-sur-Lot)

Kennels & Catteries

Creysse   Pension et Toilettage La Roque,
21 La Roque   ☎ 05 53 23 46 14
(east of Bergerac)
Kennels and cattery.

Périgueux   Géraldine Nuret, Lac Lagraule,
Champcevinel   ☎ 05 53 08 84 90
(north of Périgueux in the woods near Cornille, signposted
'*chenil*')
Kennels only.

Pet Parlours

Bergerac   Toilettage 7.8.9., 9 rue Fénelon   ☎ 05 53 58 31 43

Le Bugue   Toilettage F Nougaillon,
81 rue de Paris   ☎ 05 53 54 73 33

Montpon   Au Look du Chien, rue Thiers   ☎ 05 53 81 10 70
(on the main road through the centre of town)
Open Tuesdays to Saturdays.

Nontron   Le Look Canin, 5 rue Brune   ☎ 05 53 56 45 99

Périgueux	Masala Toilettage, 121 avenue Michel Grandou	☎ 05 53 54 31 24

(on the main road going out of town towards Trélissac)
Open Tuesdays to Saturdays.

Ribérac	Le Youki, 3 rue Jean Moulin	☎ 05 53 90 57 14

Sarlat-la-Canéda	Au Confort du Chien, 1 rue Pierre Brossolette	☎ 05 53 59 07 76

Riding Equipment

Nontron	CWD, Chemin Fontaine de Fanny (west of the town)	☎ 05 53 60 72 70

SPA

Bergerac	Head office: place Jules Ferry Kennels: route de Sainte Alvère	☎ 05 53 27 26 67 ☎ 05 53 27 03 79

Périgueux	SPA Périgueux, 1 route Bordeaux, Marsac sur l'Isle (just west of the town)	☎ 05 53 04 16 54

Veterinary Clinics

Bergerac	Clinic Vétérinaire, 8 boulevard Beausoleil (north of the town centre)	☎ 05 53 74 43 90

Le Bugue	Nougaillon-Gauchot, 83 rue Paris	☎ 05 53 07 22 04

Montpon	Dr Williams, RN89, route de Bordeaux This vet speaks very good English.	☎ 05 53 80 28 78

Nontron	Clinic Vétérinaire, 8 rue Chatenet	☎ 05 53 56 00 83

Périgueux	Clinic Vétérinaire, 51 rue Gabriel Lacueille	☎ 05 53 53 49 49

Ribérac	Clinic Vétérinaire, 8 rue des Mobiles de Coulmiers Dr Bonvalet at this practice speaks English.	☎ 05 53 90 26 90

Sarlat-la-Canéda	Gauchot Nougaillon, rue Louison Bobet	☎ 05 53 29 34 30

(on the west side of town near the Champion supermarket)

Places To Visit

This section isn't intended to be a definitive guide but gives a wide range of ideas for the department. Prices and opening hours were correct at the time of publication, but it's best to check before travelling long distances.

Animal Parks & Aquariums

Creysse   Musée Aquarium de la Rivière
Dordogne, Port de Creysse   ☎ 05 53 23 34 97
A collection of fish native to the Dordogne, including migrating fish such as salmon and sturgeon. There's a museum of river fishing covering pre-historic times to the present day. Open from Easter to the end of October 10am to noon and 2 to 6pm (July and August till 7pm).

Le Bugue   Aquarium du Perigord Noir,
route du Camping Municipal   ☎ 05 53 07 10 74
🖥 *www.parc-aquarium.com*
Europe's largest private aquarium, with immense tanks, some of which are entered by divers to swim with the fish. The whole area is visitor-friendly, being on one level with rest benches. There's a souvenir shop, bar and snack food restaurant. Open every day: mid-February to the end of March and October to mid-November, 10am to 5pm; April, May and September 10am to 6pm; June 10am to 7pm; July and August 9am to 7pm. Adults €8.20, children between 4 and 15 €5.80.

Elevage de Sangliers, Mortemart   ☎ 05 53 03 21 30
This wild boar breeding centre offers guided tours at 3pm every day from 15th June to 15th September, Sundays only (plus Wednesdays in the school holidays) the rest of the year. Unaccompanied visits from 10am to 7pm all year round. Allow around an hour for a visit, 90 minutes for a guided tour.

Jacquou Parc, La Menuse   ☎ 05 53 54 15 57
(on the D710)
Animal park including sheep, birds, cattle and donkeys. Rides and other attractions. Open every day in the Easter holidays 10am to 6pm and then Sundays 10am to 6pm until the summer holidays; July to August every day 10am to 7pm; September Sundays only 10am to 6pm.

Montazeau   Parc Animalier de Montazeau   ☎ 05 53 61 29 84
🖥 *www.parcanimalier.fr.fm*
(south of Montpon)
A park with wild animals, such as kangaroos, boar and black swans, and some domestic breeds, such as donkeys and goats. There's also a nursery for newborn animals. Open every Wednesday, Saturday and Sunday 2 to 7pm (daily in the school holidays).

St Martial- d'Artenset	Elevage de Grands Cervidés, Le Raymondeau	☎ 05 53 82 23 76

A 'natural' breeding centre for deer. Open to the public at 5pm Tuesdays, Thursdays, Saturdays, Sundays and bank holidays from mid-June to the end of August.

Beaches & Water Parks

Many towns and villages have a *plan d'eau*, which can be a lake or riverside location. It may be just for fishing and picnics or there may be facilities such as a beach, playground and crazy golf.

Bergerac	Aqua Park Junior Land, route de Bordeaux	☎ 05 53 58 33 00

This park has four swimming pools, water chutes and direct access to the Dordogne river for canoes. There are mountain bikes to hire, mini motorbikes and quads, beach volleyball, table tennis and archery. Pools are lit in the evenings. Open every day from May to September from 10am to 11pm.

Groléjac	Plan d'Eau de Groléjac	☎ 05 53 59 48 70

A 15ha (37-acre) park with a beach, lifeguard, playground and picnic areas, drinks and parking. Windsurfing, pedalos and canoes available in peak season. Open June to mid-September. Admission €2 (under-sevens free).

La Jemaye	Les Etangs de la Jemaye (south-west of Périgueux)	☎ 05 53 06 80 17

This is a large lake in the middle of the Double forest with a leisure area including a beach, playground, picnic area, toilets and various cycle and footpaths.

Lanquais	Etang du Ligal	☎ 05 53 57 43 36

Beach and lifeguard, water slide, pedalos and shaded picnic area. Open July and August.

Le Bugue	Les Etangs du Bos, Audrix	☎ 05 53 54 74 60

(five minutes from Le Bugue in the direction of Gouffre)
Natural lakes covering 7ha (17 acres). Facilities include a boules court, trampolines and a play area for young children, picnic area, snack bar and swimming, with a lifeguard in the summer. The leisure park has pedalos, fishing, swimming and four water chutes.

Montpon	Base de Loisirs de Chandos	☎ 05 53 82 23 77

A lake with a sandy beach, playground, water slide, snack restaurant and lifeguards in July and August.

Parcoul	Le Paradou, D674	☎ 05 53 91 42 78

💻 *www.leparadou24.fr*
(in the Double forest by the river Dronne, west of Ribérac)

This water park has a lake for swimming, pedalos and fishing, water toboggans, trampolines, crazy golf, cafe, bar and a mini train. Open every day from 15th June to 15th September.

Sigoulès Base de Loisirs de Pomport Siguoulès ☎ 05 53 58 81 94
Beach, bathing and lifeguards in July and August.

Vergt Lac de Neufond ☎ 05 53 54 93 90
Beach open June to September.

Villefranche-de-Lonchat Lac de Gurson ☎ 05 53 80 77 57
💻 *www.lac-de-gurson.com*
Sixty-three hectares (155 acres) of open space and leisure lake, with a water slide, pedalos, games and a beach with lifeguards.

St Paul-de-Serre Plan d'Eau du Rosier ☎ 05 53 04 52 69
A 42ha (100-acre) leisure park and a 9ha (22-acre) lake. There's a beach with a lifeguard, a water toboggan, table tennis, volleyball, trampolines and bouncy castle, jet skis and quad bikes for hire and crazy golf, paint ball, pedalos, restaurant and picnic area.

Caves

Le Bugue Gouffre de Proumeyssac, Audrix ☎ 05 53 07 27 47
💻 *www.perigord.com/proumeyssac*
Called the 'Cristal Cathedral', this cave is the largest of its kind in the Périgord area – an immense underground vault, whose walls are decorated with a multitude of crystallisations. Light plays off the walls to the accompaniment of music during the 45-minute guided tour. Audio translation equipment is available. Before the entry tunnel was dug, entrance was in groups of three via a type of basket raised and lowered by a horse – a method that's still available! Outside there's a playground, picnic area and bar. Open February, November and December 2 to 5pm; March, April, September and October 9.30am to noon and 2 to 5.30pm; May and June 9.30am to 6.30pm; July and August 9am to 7pm. Adults €7.60, children €5.

Grotte de Bara-Bahau ☎ 05 53 07 44 58
This cave was discovered in 1951 and has pre-historic art and evidence of the bears that lived there 35,000 years ago. Guided tours last around 35 minutes. Open February to June 10am to noon and 2 to 5.30pm; July and August 9.30am to 7pm; September to December 10am to noon and 2 to 5pm.

Les Eyzies Cap Blanc, Les Eyzies en Périgord ☎ 05 53 59 21 74
Only a few kilometres from Les Eyzies, this prehistoric centre reveals another aspect of prehistoric art. Open every day May to October.

Grottes du Roc de Cazelle,
route de Sarlat　　　　　　　☎ 05 53 59 46 09
🖳 *www.rocdecazelle.com*
Caves and underground passages, cliff paths and prehistoric
dwellings. Open every day: December and January 11am to
5pm; February to April, October and November 10am to 6pm;
May, June and September 10am to 7pm; July and August
10am to 8pm.

Les Eyzies-de-
Tayac

Grand Roc & Les Abris de
Laugerie Basse　　　　　　　☎ 05 53 06 92 70
🖳 *www.grandroc.com*
This cave has guided tours in English lasting around 30
minutes. The cliff face that is now known as the 'Prehistoric
Shelter of Laugerie Basse' has been inhabited by man for over
15,000 years. Both sites are open 10am to 6pm and 9.30am to
7pm in high season. Entry to both the Grand Roc and the
Prehistoric Shelter costs €9 for adults, €4.50 for children.
No dogs.

Peyzac-le-
Moustier

La Roque St Christope　　　　☎ 05 53 50 70 45
🖳 *www.roque-st-christophe.com*
The oldest and largest prehistoric cave site in Western Europe.
This cliff dominates the Vézère valley for 900m at five levels,
with 100 caves that housed up to 1,000 people in pre-historical
times. Open November to February 11am to 5pm; March and
October 10am to 6pm; April to June and September 10am to
6.30pm; July and August 10am to 7pm. English guide books
available. Adults €6, children €4.

Villars

Grottes de Villars　　　　　　☎ 05 53 54 82 36
🖳 *www.grotte-villars.com*
These caves were discovered in 1953 by the local pot-holing
club and 13km (8mi) of passages have so far been mapped.
Along with calcite flows and needle-fine stalactites there are
pre-historic paintings from the Magdalenian period and
numerous stalagmites. Above ground there's a cafe and
playground. Open every day: October 2 to 6.30pm; April to
June and September 10am to noon and 2 to 7pm; July and
August 10am to 7.30pm.

Châteaux

Bourdeilles

Château de Bourdeilles　　　　☎ 05 53 03 73 36
(north-east of Ribérac)
This château is a furnished example of a feudal fortress and
Renaissance palace, including 15th to 19th century furniture.
Closed for the first three weeks of January and Tuesdays
out of season.

Castelnaud-la-

Château de Castelnaud　　　　☎ 05 53 31 30 00

Chapelle	(south-east of Le Bugue in the south-east corner of the department) This is a feudal château offering magnificent views of the Dordogne valley and housing a collection of weapons and armour from the 13th to 17th centuries, furniture and life-size war machines. Open every day of the year: February to April and October to mid-November 10am to 6pm; May, June and September 10am to 7pm; July and August 9am to 8pm; mid-November to the end of January 2 to 5pm; Christmas school holidays 10am to 5pm.
Jumilhac	Château de Jumilhac ☎ 05 53 52 42 97 The château has a Renaissance roof and 17th century drawing room, while in the grounds are gold-themed gardens, a maze and rose gardens. Guided tours in English. Open all year round: 1st June to 30th September 10am to 7pm; July and August 9.30am to 11.30pm; remainder of the year Saturdays, Sundays and bank holidays 2 to 6.30pm.
Lanquais	Château de Lanquais ☎ 05 53 61 24 24 (15 km east of Bergerac towards Sarlat-la-Canéda) This château has rooms, from kitchens to salons, furnished in a variety of styles: from medieval to Renaissance. Open April to October daily except Tuesdays 2.30 to 6pm; May, June and September daily except Tuesdays 10.30 to noon and 2.30 to 6.30pm; July and August every day 10am to 7pm.
Monbazillac	Château de Monbazillac ☎ 05 53 63 65 06 💻 *www.château-monbazillac.com* (just south of Bergerac airport) This château holds permanent and temporary exhibitions and has a wine shop on rue de Marsan with tastings of the local sweet wine. Guided tours and unaccompanied visits of the château and gardens all year round.
Mussidan	Château-de-Montréal, Issac, ☎ 05 53 81 11 03 This château was built between the 12th and 17th centuries and is still lived in. It has beautiful rooms, an impressive library and an underground passage. Open July to September 10am to noon and 2.30 to 6.30pm; March to June and October by appointment.
St Leon-sur-Vézère	Château de Chabans, Côte de Jor ☎ 05 53 51 70 60 An important private collection of stained glass is housed here as well as tapestries, embroidery and other works of art. The courtyard, park and gardens are open to visitors and there's a shaded picnic area and tea rooms. Guided tours available. Open May, June and September every day 2 to 7pm; July and August daily 2 to 8pm; October Sundays only 2 to 6pm. Adults €6.80, under 15s free.

Ste Mondane   Château de Fénelon   ☎ 05 53 29 81 4?
(between Sarlat-la-Canéda and Souillac on the D703)
This is a furnished château with wonderful views over the
Dordogne valley. Open every day: November to February 2 to
5pm; March to June and September to October 10am to noon
and 2 to 6pm; July and August 9.30am to 7pm.

Miscellaneous

Bergerac   La Maison des Vins de Bergerac,
1 rue des Récollets   ☎ 05 53 63 57 55
💻 *www*.vins-bergerac.fr
A tour of the 17th century building and its cloisters ends in the
wine cellars, where you can taste the local wines. Closed
January. Open mid-June to August daily 10am to 7pm; the
remainder of the year Tuesdays to Saturdays 10.30am to
12.30pm and 2 to 6pm.

Couze St Front Moulin à Papier de la Rouzique
en Périgord   ☎ 05 53 24 36 16
This paper mill, which houses a varied collection of watermarks
and rare documents, has been in use since the 15th century.
Hand-made writing and art paper is on sale at the shop. The
mill is open every day from 1st April to 15th October from 2 to
6.30pm (July and August 10am to 7pm).

Nontron   La Coutellerie Nontronnaise,
place Paul Bert   ☎ 05 53 56 01 55

La Coutellerie (shop) 33 rue Carnot   ☎ 05 53 60 33 76
The knife workshops of Nontron are the oldest in France,
knives having been made here since 1653. Each piece is
produced by hand and is unique to these workshops. You can
see knives being made from Mondays to Saturdays 9am to
noon and 1.30 to 6pm. The shop is open Mondays to
Saturdays 9.15am to noon and 2 to 7pm. Free entry.

St Capraise-de- Ascenseur à Poissons de Tuilières   ☎ 05 53 73 54 00
Lalinde   A hydro-electric dam on the Dordogne river, with a fish lift and eel
trap.

Tursac   La Madeleine, Vallée de la Vézère   ☎ 05 53 06 92 49
💻 *www.site-de-la-madeleine.com*
A medieval troglodyte village that has been carefully preserved.
Open out of season 10am to 6pm, high season 9.30am to 7pm.

Préhisto Parc, Vallée de la Vézère   ☎ 05 53 50 73 19
Commemorates the life of Neanderthal man. Open every day:
March to June 10am to 6pm; July and August 9.30am to
7.30pm; September to mid-November 10am to 6pm.

Museums & Galleries

Bergerac
Musée du Tabac, 10 rue Ancien Pont   ☎ 05 53 63 04 13
This tobacco museum is the only one of its kind in Europe and is open Tuesdays to Fridays 10am to noon and 2 to 6pm all year round; mid-March to mid-November additionally Saturday and Sunday afternoons 2 to 6pm (July and August also Monday afternoons 2 to 4pm).

Cendrieux
Musée Napoléon,
Château de la Pommerie   ☎ 05 53 03 24 03
🖳 *www.musee-napoleon.com*
More than 500 objects, paintings and sculptures displayed by descendants of the Bonaparte family. The château itself is a historic monument. Open every day 1st June to15th September 3 to 6pm (July and August 10.30am to12.30pm and 2.30pm to 6.30pm).

Couze St Front
Ecomusée du Papier,
Moulin de la Rouzique   ☎ 05 53 24 36 16
The mill was restored and opened as a museum in 1991 and now houses a rich collection of watermarked paper and machines that are used for demonstrations of paper-making. Open April to mid-October 2 to 6.30pm (July and August 10am to 7pm).

Groléjac
Moulin à Huile de Noix   ☎ 05 65 41 48 70
(on the D704 between Sarlat and Gourdon)
Watermill producing walnut oil. Free entry and tastings. Open spring to autumn.

Hautefort
Musée de la Médecine,
l'Ancien Hospice   ☎ 05 53 50 40 27
Situated in the old Hospice of Hautefort, this museum comprises various rooms tracing the history of medicine, a chapel and a garden with medicinal plants. Open every day from April to mid-October. Guided tours available.

Le Bugue
Musée de Paléontologie et Maison de la
Vie Sauvage, 9 rue de la République   ☎ 05 53 08 28 10
This museum houses a collection of fossils from various parts of the world, but the majority were found locally, showing that the sea stretched as far as Périgord 80 million years ago. There are also preserved birds and mammals from all over Europe, showing how they adapted to their surroundings.

Mussidan
Musée André Voulgre   ☎ 05 53 81 23 55
Museum of Périgord art, crafts and traditions. Open weekends from March to November and every day from June to mid-September.

Nontron   Musée des Jouets   ☎ 05 53 56 25 5(
                   A collection of puppets and toys, including fire engines,
                   aeroplanes and soldiers, as well as puzzles and games. Open
                   mid-April to June and September weekends, bank holidays and
                   school holidays 2.30 to 5.30pm; July and August every day
                   10.30am to 1pm and 2.30 to 6pm.

Périgueux   Musée Militaire du Périgord,
                   32 rue des Farges   ☎ 05 53 53 47 36
                   An exceptional collection of over 13,000 pieces of military
                   weaponry from the Middle Ages to the time of the Resistance.
                   Open 1st May to 30th September Mondays to Saturdays 1 to
                   6pm; October to December Mondays to Saturdays 2 to 6pm;
                   January to March Wednesdays and Saturdays 2 to 6pm.
                   Closed bank holidays.

                   Musée du Périgord, 22 cours Tourny   ☎ 05 53 06 40 70
                   The oldest museum in Dordogne, within an ancient building
                   that was originally a convent and later a prison. Collections
                   include pre-historic, Roman, Middle Ages, Renaissance,
                   African and fine arts. Open Wednesdays to Sundays all year:
                   April to September weekdays from 11am to 6pm, weekends 1
                   to 6pm; October to December weekdays 10am to 5pm,
                   weekends 1 to 6pm. Closed on bank holidays. Adults €3.50,
                   under 18s free.

Pomport   Musée Automobile, Château de Sanxet ☎ 05 53 58 37 46
                   (south-west of Bergerac)
                   A private collection of 23 rare cars. The owner will share with
                   you his passions for classic cars and Bordeaux wine. Open
                   every day from 9am to 7.30pm.

Port Sainte Foy   Musée de la Batellerie,
                   Maison du Fleuve   ☎ 05 53 61 30 50
                   This museum commemorates the history of trade on the river
                   Dordogne, including traditional flat-bottomed boats for carrying
                   wine barrels, model boats and a history of the wine of Montréal.

Parks, Gardens & Forests

General   Parc Naturel Régional Périgord-
                   Limousin   ☎ 05 53 60 34 65
                   Situated between Angoulême, Limoges and Périgueux, the
                   regional park constitutes a naturally preserved land rich in
                   heritage. There's plenty to be seen here all year round, with
                   natural sites such as marshlands, peat bogs, lakes and chalk
                   meadows, and wildlife including otters, pond terrapin and
                   dippers. The park also hosts numerous events – mushroom,
                   wood and chestnut fairs, a brass band festival and a
                   turkey fair – and is headquarters of the French
                   Conker Federation.

Carlux	Jardins de Cadiot	☎ 05 53 29 81 05

Gardens and terraces on 2ha (5 acres) with thousands of plant varieties and ten colour-themed areas. Open every day from 1st May to 31st October, 10am to 7pm.

Fôret de la Double	Maison Forestière	☎ 05 53 06 80 17

(south-west of Périgueux)
An extensive forest with many nature trails, paths for walking and cycling and a bird observatory. Visit the Maison Forestière for maps, advice and more information.

Le Bugue	Les Jardins d'Arborie	☎ 05 53 08 42 74

🖳 *www.jardins-arborie.com*
Floral displays from five continents with ancient Bonsai and 2,000 cacti and tropical plants.

Le Buisson-de-Cadouin	Jardin de Plan Buisson, rue Montaigne	☎ 05 53 22 01 03

(a few kilometres due south of Le Bugue)
An unusual landscaped garden with more than 200 varieties of bamboo and nearly 180 different types of grass, most of which are on sale at the adjoining nursery. Open mid-July to the third week of August 10am to 7pm, closed March to mid-April, the rest of the year by appointment.

Salignac	Les Jardins du Manoir l'Eyrignac	☎ 05 53 28 99 71

(north-east of Sarlat-la-Canéda)
The gardens of Eyrignac Manor are considered to be among the most beautiful in France and are unique in the originality of their design. They were laid out in the 18th century and transformed in the 19th century to an English design, as was the fashion of the time. The gardens have been restored with devotion and skill to the original layout, including water effects with five fountains. There's a restaurant on site and a one-hour guided tour available. Dogs admitted if kept on a lead.
Open every day of the year: 1st October to 31st March 10.30am to 12.30pm and 2.30pm to dusk; April and May 10am to 12.30pm and 2 to 7pm; June to September 9.30am to 7pm.

Terrasson	Les Jardins de l'Imaginaire, place du Foirail	☎ 05 53 50 86 82

🖳 *www.ot-terrasson.com*
Spacious gardens covering 6ha (15 acres), including a modern garden with unique water displays, a large rose garden and a display of over 5,000 irises. Open from April to mid-October. Closed Tuesdays except in July and August.

Vézac	Les Jardins de Marqueyssac	☎ 05 53 31 36 36

🖳 *www.marqueyssac.com*
(south-west of Sarlat-la-Canéda)

These gardens are a listed site and offer shaded walks through
a maze of 150,000 hand-pruned box trees past waterfalls and
waterways with a magnificent view over the Dordogne valley. A
horse drawn carriage (*barouche*) brings you from the château
to the tearoom and terrace. On Thursday evenings in July and
August the gardens are open until midnight, with the paths
beautifully lit. Open every day of the year: mid-November to
January 2 to 5pm; February to April and October to mid-
November 10am to 6pm; May, June and September 10am to
7pm; July and August 9am to 8pm.

Regional Produce

Beauregard et Bassac	Chez Suzon (north-east of Bergerac) Duck and goose breeder for *foie gras* and related products. Open every day throughout the year from 10am to noon and 2.30 to 6pm.	☎ 05 53 63 13 62
Eygurande	Les Vergers du Petit Laurent Locally grown fruit, apple juice and jam. Open every day from 10am to 5pm.	☎ 05 53 90 82 85
Montcaret	Fromagerie Van der Horst 🖳 *www.vdh-fromages.flappie.nl* (directly west of Bergerac) This cheese producer is open every day until 7.30pm (closed Sunday lunchtimes).	☎ 05 53 58 62 38
Montpon	Jean Lecomte, Domaine de Jarrauty Sale of Périgord wine and visits to the wine-making facilities on request.	☎ 05 53 80 31 74
Nojals et Clottes	Rucher du Grand Salers (on the southern border of the department, south-west of Bergerac) A honey producer. Visit the beehives and taste the honey. Open Tuesdays to Saturdays 3 to 7pm.	☎ 05 53 22 45 30
St Barthélémy-de-Bellegarde	Les Vergers de la Grange This local producer is open 2.30 to 6.30pm Mondays to Saturdays for the sale of fruit, honey, nuts and apple juice.	☎ 05 53 80 36 10
Ste Foy-de-Longas	La Truffière de la Bergerie (east of Bergerac) This truffle producer is open throughout the year.	☎ 05 53 22 72 39
Sorges	Ferme Andrevias, RN21 Open during the week to visit the breeding centre for the geese. July and August open until 6pm Tuesday and Thursday.	☎ 05 53 05 02 42

L'Ecomusée de la Truffe   ☎ 05 53 05 90 11
Truffles and their production, the secrets of the 'black diamond',
the markets and the gastronomy. The visit takes around an
hour and there's a shop on site. Open every day mid-June to
October 9.30am to noon and 2.30 to 6pm, closed Mondays the
rest of the year. Adults €4, children €2.

Towns & Villages

Bergerac   Office de Tourisme   ☎ 05 53 57 03 11
Bergerac is the capital of 'Périgord Pourpre' and has many
streets full of half-timbered buildings. The tourist office
organises guided tours around the town in July and August on
Mondays, Tuesdays and Thursdays, departing at 11.30am.

Eymet   Office de Tourisme   ☎ 05 53 23 75 95
On the southern border of the department, this town centre has
an enclosed square with a fountain in the middle and a variety
of shops and restaurants in the arcades surrounding it. Eymet
is a walled town that was built in 1270 and you can explore the
narrow streets and 15th and 16th century houses at your
leisure or with a guide from the tourist office during July
and August.

Le Bugue   Le Village du Bournat   ☎ 05 53 08 41 99
A village that takes you back in time, including a fun fair,
windmill, working craftsmen and farming demonstrations.
English-speaking guide available. Allow from two hours to all
day for the visit. Open mid-February to mid-November:
February to April and October and November 10am to 5pm;
May to September 10am to 7pm. Pets welcome. July and
August adults €12, rest of the year €8.70, Children €6 all year.

Professional Services

The following offices have an English-speaking professional.

Accountants

Bergerac   Groupe La Brégère,
                29 avenue Marceau Feyry   ☎ 05 53 57 29 84

Périgueux   Mr Bourlioux, 5 place Hoche   ☎ 05 53 08 88 88

Solicitors & Notaires

Bergerac   Maître Baubau,
                34 boulevard Victor Hugo   ☎ 05 53 74 50 50

Périgueux   Nectoux-Vaubourgoin,
                11 avenue Georges Pompidou   ☎ 05 53 06 83 00

Religion

Anglican Services In English

Chancelade
(west of Périgueux)
Services on the second Sunday of each month at 4pm.

Chapdeuil
(in the north-west of the department, west of Brantôme)
Services on the first and third Sundays of each month
at 10.30am.

Limeuil
(just south-west of Le Bugue)
Services every Sunday at 10.30am.

Ribérac
Services on the second Wednesday of the month at 11am and
on the fourth Sunday of the month at 4pm.

For details of the English services of the Aquitaine Chaplaincy and to receive its monthly newsletter, contact the Revd Michael Selman, 1 Lotissement de la Caussade, Floirac (☎ 05 56 40 05 12).

Protestant Churches

Selected churches are listed below.

Bergerac
Eglise Evangélique Libre, 5 rue Durou   ☎ 05 53 73 37 79

Eglise Réformée,
16 rue du Docteur Simounet   ☎ 05 53 57 02 79

Périgueux
Assemblée de Dieu, 141bis route Lyon   ☎ 05 53 04 44 00

Eglise Evangélique Libre de Périgueux,
4 rue Conseil   ☎ 05 53 08 98 98

Eglise Evangélique du Renouveau,
8 cours Fénelon   ☎ 05 53 35 24 01

Eglise Réformée,
20bis rue Antoine Gadaud   ☎ 05 53 53 09 83

Restaurants

Bergerac
There are many restaurants in the old quarter of Bergerac
north of the river, including some of the following:

Le Bistrot du Gourmet,
109 rue d'Argençon   ☎ 05 53 74 24 82
Open every day both lunchtime and evenings with a €10 lunch
menu Mondays to Fridays.

Buffalo Grill, route Bordeaux   ☎ 05 53 74 60 36
(on the Leclerc retail park south-west of the town)
Steak house-style restaurant open 11am to 11pm every day.

Au Bureau, 9 rue de la Résistance   ☎ 05 53 74 81 72
This bar/brasserie has an €11.20 set menu Monday to Friday
lunchtimes, including Welsh and Mexican dishes.

La Mama, place Malbec   ☎ 05 53 58 68 84
There are no set menus at this Italian restaurant, open
Tuesdays to Saturdays.

Le Mandarin, 10 rue Berggren   ☎ 05 53 63 16 58
Chinese, Vietnamese and Thai cuisine in the centre of town.
€10 lunch menu, other set menus from €11. Open Tuesdays
to Sundays.

McDonald's,
11 parc Commercial La Cavaille   ☎ 05 53 23 26 36
(on the retail park south-west of the town)

Le Millésime,
12 rue du Colonel de Chadois   ☎ 05 53 74 25 41
(off rue de la Résistance, near the tourist office)
€13 to €15 set menus available lunchtimes Tuesdays to
Fridays, €18.50 to €30 set menus in the evenings plus à la
carte. Closed Sundays and all day Mondays.

Le Nautic, 12 Promenade Pierre Loti   ☎ 05 53 57 03 27
Seafood a speciality in this traditional restaurant beside the
Dordogne. Set menus from €17 to €31. Closed all day
Mondays and Sunday and Tuesday evenings.

Le Perroquet, place Malbec   ☎ 05 53 57 18 95
(just to the east of the town centre)
A Parisian-style brasserie with service until 10.30pm. Set
menus from €11 to €25. Closed Sundays.

La Petite Taverne,
13 boulevard Montaigne   ☎ 05 53 63 25 65
🖥 *www.la.petite.taverne.com*
(just north of Eglise Notre Dame in the centre of town)
€10 set lunch menu, evening set menus range from €16 to
€33. Closed Tuesdays.

La Scala, 27 rue des Conferences   ☎ 05 53 22 72 10
Italian and regional cuisine. €10 set menu at lunchtimes, plus
€13.50 to €17 menus. Service from 11am to 11pm every day.
Closed November to March.

Le Saigon, 19 place des Deux Conils   ☎ 05 53 58 00 27
Vietnamese cuisine and take-away. €10.50 set menu
at lunchtime.

La Sauvagine, 18 rue Eugène Leroy   ☎ 05 53 57 06 97
Seafood a speciality, with gastronomic cuisine using regional
produce. Set menus from €12.20 to €30. Closed Sunday
evenings and all day Mondays as well as the first two
weeks in July.

Le Sud, 19 rue de l'Ancien Pont   ☎ 05 53 27 26 81
Moroccan cuisine with a shaded terrace and €12.50 lunchtime
menu Tuesdays to Fridays. Closed Mondays.

Le Bugue   Asiatique le Pha, 25 rue Jardin Public   ☎ 05 53 08 96 96
Asian cuisine, including take-away. No set menus.
Closed Mondays.

L'Abreuvoir, 31 Grand' Rue/
Place des Ors   ☎ 05 53 03 45 45
The only restaurant in the old part of Le Bugue, with a shaded
terrace. The cuisine is based on local produce. Menus from
€19 to €33.

Le Colibri, 40 rue de Paris   ☎ 05 53 07 24 55
Restaurant and *crêperie* with Périgord specialties. Open every
day (until 2am in the summer), but closed November to Easter.

Le Cygne, rue Cingle   ☎ 05 53 07 17 77
Fine cuisine and elegant surroundings in an old bourgeois
house. Menus from €13.50 to €32 plus *à la carte*. Closed
Friday lunchtimes, Sunday evenings, all day Mondays and the
first two weeks in January and October.

Les Fontenilles, 10 route Campagne   ☎ 05 53 07 24 97
Original and creative cuisine, with set menus from €11 to €22
and *à la carte* menu. Closed December. Animals accepted and
English spoken.

Les Marronniers, place de la Gare   ☎ 05 53 07 22 54
Regional specialities with set menus from €10 to €24 and *à la
carte*. Closed 20th December to 2nd January.

Le Parc, route de Limeuil   ☎ 05 53 04 10 00
In an exceptional setting by a lake amid parkland with dining on
a covered terrace.

Le Pergola, 16 avenue Libération   ☎ 05 53 54 18 05
Italian cuisine, regional menus, take-away and a shaded
terrace in the summer. Set menus from €15 and pizzas
from €7.

Le Relais Bugouis,
15 avenue de la Libération   ☎ 05 53 04 84 15
Périgourdine specialities, traditional cuisine and take-away.
Open all year round with menus from €10 to €29, snacks
available in the summer and an air-conditioned dining room.

Royal Vézère, place de l'Hôtel de Ville   ☎ 05 53 07 20 01
This restaurant is within a three-star hotel and offers formal
dining with menus from €25 to €58.

Hôtel du Château, Campagne   ☎ 05 53 07 23 50
(just east of Le Bugue, facing the Château de Campagne)
Traditional and original cuisine with set menus from €18 to €46.
Closed the last two weeks of October.

Montpon   Auberge de l'Ecade, route de Coutras   ☎ 05 53 80 28 64
Gastronomic cuisine and take-away to order. Weekday
lunchtimes set menu €13.50, evening set menus €24 to €43.
Closed Monday and Tuesday evenings and all day
Wednesdays.

La Pizzabella, 21 avenue Jean Moulin   ☎ 05 53 82 31 22
This is a pizza take-away on the main road. Open Tuesdays
to Sundays.

Le Puits d'Or, 7 rue Carnot   ☎ 05 53 80 33 07
Shaded terrace in the summer and open fire in the dining room
in the winter. €11 lunchtime menu Mondays to Fridays plus €19
to €28 set menus and *à la carte* menu.

Le Romain, 42 le Bourg, Ménestérol   ☎ 05 53 80 16 55
Traditional cuisine. Open lunchtimes and evenings, closed
Wednesdays.

Nontron   Le Pelisson, 3 avenue Alfred Agard   ☎ 05 53 56 11 22
(at the top of the square in the centre of town)
Set menus from €21 to €36.

Périgueux   Le 8, 8 rue de la Clarté   ☎ 05 53 35 15 15
€14 to €18.50 lunchtime menus, €24 to €34 set menus in the
evenings. Closed Sundays and Mondays.

Auberge de Savoie, 19 rue Aubergerie   ☎ 05 53 09 58 32
Open every day, lunch and evenings with raclettes
and fondues.

Au Bien Bon, 15 rue des Places   ☎ 05 53 09 69 91
€10 lunchtime menu during the week and *à la carte* menu in
the evenings.

Au Bouchon, 12 rue de la Sagesse   ☎ 05 53 46 69 75
Traditional bistro in the pedestrian quarter. Shaded outside
seating in the summer. €14 to €17 lunchtime menus. Closed
Saturday lunchtimes and all day Sundays and Mondays.

**Buffalo Grill, ZAC de l'Agora,
Boulazac**   ☎ 05 53 07 86 15
(on the retail park east of Périgueux)
Steak house-style restaurant open every day until 11pm.

Le Canard Laqué, rue de Lammay   ☎ 05 53 09 15 61
Chinese restaurant with a €10 set menu at lunchtime and other
set menus from €14 to €24. Closed Sunday evenings.

Les Coupoles, 7 rue de la Clarté   ☎ 05 53 08 22 97
Italian restaurant open Tuesdays to Saturdays. €13 set menu
and *à la carte*.

Del Arte, la Feuilleraie   ☎ 05 53 03 83 25
(on the Leclerc complex east of Périgueux)
Pizza and pasta restaurant open every lunchtime and evening.

Le Grain de Sel, 7 rue des Farges   ☎ 05 53 53 45 22
Regional cuisine using local produce. €10 to €13 lunchtime
menus Tuesdays to Fridays, €18 to €26 set menus in the
evenings plus *à la carte* menu. Closed Sundays and Mondays.

Helliniko, 6 rue de la Clarté   ☎ 05 53 09 60 69
Although not a restaurant, this Greek delicatessen has
prepared foods for take-away such as moussaka.

Hercule Poireau, 2 rue de la Nation   ☎ 05 53 08 90 76
(in a small side street opposite the church in the centre of town)
Gastronomic cuisine served in a vaulted dining room. Set
menus from €18 to €45. English spoken.

Le Maharaja, 3 rue Denfert Rochereau ☎ 05 53 53 88 82
Indian restaurant with take-way service. €10.55 set menu
Monday to Friday lunchtimes plus €18 to €29 menus and
à la carte.

McDonald's, La Feuilleraie   ☎ 05 53 35 11 96
(on the retail park on the east of town)

**McDonald's, avenue Louis Suder,
Marsac-sur-l'Isle**   ☎ 05 53 54 89 33
(on the retail park west of Périgueux)

Le Pataterie, 17 rue St Front   ☎ 05 53 09 58 09
A 'spud u like' style restaurant, with €8.50 and €9.50 lunchtime
menus, others up to €16.50.

Pizzeria l'Olivio, rue des Places   ☎ 05 53 09 63 88
Outside seating in the summer. €9.50 to €16 set menus.
Closed Sundays.

La Taula, rue Denfert Rochereau   ☎ 05 53 35 40 02
€16 lunchtime set menu, plus €16 to €28 set menus. Closed
Sundays and Mondays.

L'Univers, 3 rue Eguillerie   ☎ 05 53 53 34 79
Fish is a speciality, including fresh lobster and hot oysters.

Ribérac   Café des Colonnes,
17 place du Général de Gaulle   ☎ 05 53 90 01 39
This colonial-style cafe was established in 1832 and, although
open all day, serves meals only at lunchtime.

Le Cheval Blanc, rue du 26 Mars 1944   ☎ 05 53 90 46 28
(on the main road as you enter the town from the north)
Monday to Friday lunchtime menu at €10 with other set menus
up to €24 plus *à la carte* menu.

Le Citronnier, 3 place Nationale   ☎ 05 53 90 22 72
Seafood a speciality. Open Tuesday lunchtimes to Friday
evenings, Saturday evenings and Sunday lunchtimes. Set
menus from €18 to €26.

Le Commerce, 8 rue Gambetta   ☎ 05 53 91 28 59
€11 set menu at lunchtime and other set menus from
€16.50 to €26.

La Gavotte, 21 ter place de Gaulle   ☎ 05 53 91 63 11
There are no set menus at this restaurant.

Hôtel de France, 3 rue Marc Dufraisse   ☎ 05 53 90 00 64
(in a side street off place de Gaulle)
€23 set menu.

Le Midi, 35 place Nationale   ☎ 05 53 90 02 96
Mainly snacks; no set menus. Open Mondays to Saturdays.

St Laurent-des-   Le Mylord,
Vignes   1 route de Bordeaux Castang   ☎ 05 53 27 40 10
(5km south-west of Bergerac)
Traditional cuisine using local produce. An 18th century house,
with an outside dining terrace, a formal restaurant and a

separate bistro. Set menus in the bistro range from €13.50 to €25 and in the formal restaurant from €32 to €46. Open every day.

Ste Alvère   Le Provençal, 15 rue de La République   ☎ 05 53 74 34 63
(just north-west of Le Bugue)
Set menus from €16 to €30. Open every evening except Thursdays from 7pm and Saturday and Sunday lunchtimes. Booking required at weekends.

Sarlat-la-Canéda Auberge de Mirandol,
7 rue des Consuls   ☎ 05 53 29 53 89
Outside seating in a small cobbled street and set menus from €13 to €29.
Auberge de la Salamandre,
6 rue des Consuls   ☎ 05 53 31 04 41
(on a cobbled side street in the old quarter)
Set menus from €13 to €22 plus à la carte menu.

Au Bon Chabrol, 2 rue des Armes   ☎ 05 53 59 15 56
Set menus from €10 to €21.50. Open every day in the summer; rest of the year closed Sunday evenings and all day Mondays.

Hôtel de la Madeleine,
1 place de la Petite Rigaudie   ☎ 05 53 59 10 41
🖳 www.hoteldelamadeleine-sarlat.com
Set menus from €25 to €43. Open July and August every day both lunchtime and evening. Closed mid-November to mid-March. Rest of the year, closed Monday and Tuesday lunchtimes.

Le Jardin des Consuls,
4 rue des Consuls   ☎ 05 53 59 18 77
Traditional Périgord cuisine, including a vegetarian menu. Set menus from €13 to €22. Outside and inside dining, closed all day Mondays.

Pizzeria Pinocchio,
5 place de la Petite Rigaudie   ☎ 05 53 30 41 19
A small pizza restaurant overlooking the small gardens in the centre of town. No set menus. Out of season closed Sunday and Monday lunchtimes and all day Thursdays.

Pizzeria Romane, 3 Côte de Toulouse   ☎ 05 53 59 23 88
No set menus. Open Tuesdays to Saturdays.

Les Quatre Saisons, Côte de Toulouse   ☎ 05 53 29 48 59
(up a steep narrow alley off rue de la République)

Set menus from €18 to €50. Closed Thursday lunchtimes and
all day Wednesdays.

Vergt   Le Marsala, 68 Grand' Rue   ☎ 05 53 03 70 57
             Indian restaurant with no set menus. Open Tuesdays to
             Sundays noon to 2pm and 7 to 9pm (also Mondays in July
             and August).

             Restaurant du Parc, Logis de France,
             place Marty   ☎ 05 53 54 90 50
             Set menus from €15 to €30 and *à la carte* menu. Closed Friday
             and Sunday evenings and Saturday lunchtimes.

Rubbish & Recycling

Metal Collection

Boulazac   Sirmet, avenue Benoît Frachon   ☎ 05 53 05 16 29
             (on the east side of Périgueux)

St Aubin-de- Jean-Luc Artaso, Le Pouch   ☎ 05 53 24 30 51
Lanquais   (east of Bergerac)

Shopping

When available, the opening hours of shops have been included in the
listings below, but opening times are liable to change; you're therefore
recommended to check by telephone before travelling long distances to
any specific shop.

Alcohol

Bergerac   Cave Delperier, 11 rue Junien Rabier   ☎ 05 53 63 08 85
             Wine sold by the litre. Open Tuesdays, Saturdays
             and Sundays.

Le Bugue   Julien de Savignac,
             avenue de la Libération   ☎ 05 53 07 10 31
             Mondays to Saturdays 9.15am to 12.15pm and 3 to 7pm,
             Sundays 10am to 12.15pm (July and August open all day).
             Wine-tasting courses held and English spoken.

Montpon   Cave Montponnaise,
             48 avenue Jean Moulin   ☎ 05 53 82 41 58
             (on the eastern outskirts of town in an old petrol station)
             Wine sold by the litre.

| Périgueux | Curvier de France, 156 rue Michel Grandou, Trélissac ☎ 05 53 06 39 90 (on the eastern side of the town on the road to the retail park) Wine sold by the litre. |

Périgueux Curvier de France, 156 rue Michel
Grandou, Trélissac ☎ 05 53 06 39 90
(on the eastern side of the town on the road to the retail park)
Wine sold by the litre.

Ribérac Cave, place Nationale ☎ 05 53 90 91 79
Wine sold by the litre. Open Tuesdays to Saturdays 7.30am to
12.30pm and Sunday mornings. This store also sells some
organic produce, fruit and vegetables.

Sarlat-la-Canéda Cave du Gouyat, route de Brive ☎ 05 53 29 97 55
(alongside the Champion supermarket)

Architectural Antiques

Beaumont SPID Services, La Taillade ☎ 05 53 22 31 13
🖳 *www.spid-24.com*
(east of Bergerac)

British Groceries

Chalais Le Petit Atelier, avenue de la Gare ☎ 05 45 98 07 84
✉ *lepetitatlier@tiscali.fr*
(just over the northern border into Charente,
opposite Intermarché)
English groceries and books. Summer: Mondays, Wednesdays
to Saturdays 9.15am to noon and 2.30 to 6pm. Winter:
Mondays, Fridays and Saturdays 9am to noon and 2.30 to
6pm, Wednesdays and Thursdays 9am to noon.

Champagnac- The English Panier, rue André Lamaud ☎ 05 53 03 21 97
de-Bélair (south of Nontron)
Currently open Mondays to Fridays 9am to 12.15pm but the
hours may be extended.

Eymet The English Shop, 22 rue du Temple ☎ 05 53 23 79 39
(south of Bergerac on the border of Dordogne and
Lot-et-Garonne)
Traditional British groceries, including bacon, sausages and
cheese, as well as gifts and books. Open Tuesdays to
Saturdays 9.30am to 6.30pm and Sundays 9.30am
to 12.30pm.

Marsac-sur-l'Isle Best of British, boulevard de l'Horizon
🖳 *www.bestofbritish.fr*
(west of Périgueux)
Open Tuesdays to Saturdays 10am to1pm and 2 to 6pm. This
shop is opening in the spring of 2004 and the phone number
will be available on the website once it's open.

Building Materials

Bergerac   VM Matériaux Boissiere,
                    ZI rue Denis Papin   ☎ 05 53 63 77 00
                    🖳 *www.vm-materiaux.fr*

Le Bugue   Delprat Ets, quart de la Gare   ☎ 05 53 07 21 60

Montpon   Matériaux Lacombe, route Bordeaux   ☎ 05 53 80 33 02

Nontron   Paul Matériaux, 24 route Piégut   ☎ 05 53 56 18 99
                    🖳 *www.paul-materiaux.com*

Périgueux   Brico Dépot, route de Limoges,
                    Trélissac   ☎ 05 53 05 62 50
                    (on the retail park on the east side of Périgueux)
                    Mondays to Fridays 7am to noon and 2 to 7.30pm,
                    Saturdays 7am to 7.30pm.

Ribérac   Pinault Aquitaine, ZI Chaumes   ☎ 05 53 92 40 60
                    (north-east of the town)

Sarlat-la-Canéda   Philip Sarl, Brande   ☎ 05 53 59 31 40
                    (on the western outskirts of the town near the
                    Champion supermarket)

Caravans & Camper Vans

Marsac-sur-l'Isle   Caracol Loisirs, avenue Louis Suder   ☎ 05 53 04 73 73
                    🖳 *www.caracolloisirs.fr*
                    (west of Périgueux)
                    Repairs and sale of new and second-hand caravans
                    and camper vans.

Department Stores

Périgueux   Nouvelles Galeries,
                    7 rue de la République   ☎ 05 53 08 24 24
                    Mondays 2 to 7pm, Tuesdays to Saturdays 9.30am to 7pm.

DIY

Bergerac   Mr Bricolage, route Bordeaux   ☎ 05 53 23 39 90
                    (on the retail park on the west side of town)

Le Bugue   Bricomarché, route Buisson   ☎ 05 53 04 87 72
                    DIY, gardening and building supplies.

Montpon   Briconautes Rousseau,
                    route Ste Foy la Grande   ☎ 05 53 82 05 98
                    🖳 *www.les-briconautes.com*

| Nontron | Bricomarché, 6 avenue Jules Ferry | ☎ 05 53 56 64 94 |

| Périgueux | Bricomarché, avenue Georges Pompidou, Trélissac | ☎ 05 53 54 43 61 |
(on the eastern outskirts of Périgueux)

| | Mr Bricolage, Centre Carrefour, Boulazac | ☎ 05 53 09 50 64 |
(on the Carrefour retail park on the east side of Périgueux)

| Ribérac | Bricomarché, route Mussidan | ☎ 05 53 90 00 91 |

| Sarlat-la-Canéda | Brico Plaisance, avenue Dordogne | ☎ 05 53 59 28 80 |

Fabrics

| Bergerac | Mondial Tissus, Centre Cial la Cavaille | ☎ 05 53 61 88 13 |

| Périgueux | Compagnie Française, 10 rue de la République | ☎ 05 53 35 45 80 |

| Sarlat-la-Canéda | Le Marché aux Tissues, Pré de Cordy | ☎ 05 53 29 54 99 |
(on the south-east outskirts of the town)

Frozen Food

| Bergerac | Thiriet, 9 rue Ferdinand de Labatut, route de Bordeaux | ☎ 05 53 73 04 49 |

| Périgueux | Picard, 107 avenue Maréchal Juin | ☎ 05 53 09 87 13 |
Sundays 9.30am to 12.30pm and Mondays 3 to 7.30pm,
Tuesdays to Saturdays 9.30am to 12.30pm and
2.30 to 7.30pm.

Garden Centres

| Bergerac | Pepinières du Marais, 67 route de Bordeaux | ☎ 05 53 74 06 62 |

| | Brico Bati Jardi Leclerc, rue Emile Counord | ☎ 05 53 57 75 36 |

| Montpon | Hervé Rousseau, 21 rue Maréchal Foch | ☎ 05 53 80 34 07 |

| Nontron | France Rurale, 20 route Piégut | ☎ 05 53 56 57 95 |

Périgueux	Point Vert, rue de la Prairie, boulevard de l'Industrie, Marsac-sur-l'Isle	☎ 05 53 54 57 15

Périgueux   Point Vert, rue de la Prairie, boulevard
               de l'Industrie, Marsac-sur-l'Isle   ☎ 05 53 54 57 15
               (on the retail park west of Périgueux)
               Mondays 2 to 7pm, Tuesdays to Saturdays 8.30am to noon
               and 2 to 7pm.

               Jardiland, route de Limoges, Trélissac   ☎ 05 53 02 43 70
               (on the retail park east of Périgueux)
               Mondays to Saturdays 9.30am to noon and 2 to 7pm, Sundays
               10am to 12.15pm and 2.15 to 7pm.

Ribérac   Gamm Vert, rue André Cheminade   ☎ 05 53 90 43 92
               Mondays to Saturdays 9am to 12.30pm and 2 to 7pm.

Sarlat-la-Canéda La Jardinerie Paysage, Prés de Cordy   ☎ 05 53 31 02 44
               (on the retail park east of the town)

Hypermarkets

Bergerac   Leclerc, La Cavaille, route Bordeaux   ☎ 05 53 63 68 68
               (south of the river going south-west out of the town)
               Mondays to Thursdays 9am to 8pm, Fridays 9am to 8.30pm
               and Saturdays 8.30am to 7.30pm.

Périgueux   Carrefour, avenue Jacques Duclos,
               Boulazac   ☎ 05 53 35 89 00
               (just to the east of the town)
               Mondays to Saturdays 8.30am to 8.30pm (Fridays until 9pm).
               Inside the complex is an optician's, brasserie, dry cleaner;s,
               hairdresser;s and various clothes shops.

               Leclerc, La Feuilleraie, Trélissac   ☎ 05 53 35 75 75
               (east of the town)
               There is a jeweller's, chemist's, cafe and travel agent's within
               this complex. Mondays to Saturdays 8.30am to 8.30pm
               (Fridays until 9pm).

Kitchens & Bathrooms

Specialist kitchen and bathroom shops can often be found on the large
retail parks (see page 150).

Bergerac   Schmidt, route de Bordeaux,
               La Cavaille   ☎ 05 53 73 03 56

Montpon   L'Atelier Cuisine, rue Thiers   ☎ 05 53 80 46 76
               (on the main road through the centre of town)
               Open Tuesdays to Saturdays.

Périgueux	Hygena, 235 avenue Michel Grandou, Trélissac (on the retail park east of Périgueux)	☎ 05 53 03 76 44
Sarlat-la-Canéda	Cuisines Joël Perié, route de Souillac 🖥 *www.perie-meubles.com*	☎ 05 53 59 32 85

Markets

Bergerac   Markets all year round on Wednesday mornings and all day Saturdays.

There's a brocante (second-hand/antiques market) in the streets of the old town on the first Sunday of each month.

Truffle and *foie gras* market on Saturday mornings in November and December.

In July and August there are evening markets every Friday.

Beynac   Monday and Wednesday market.

Brantôme   Ordinary markets Tuesday and Friday mornings and a *foie gras* market every Tuesday morning from December to March.

Domme   Thursday morning market.

Eymet   Regular market on Thursdays, with additional markets in July and August on Sunday mornings and Tuesday evenings.

Lalinde   Thursday mornings.

Le Bugue   Tuesday and Saturday mornings, with a flower fair in April. Evening markets on Fridays in the summer.

Le Buisson   Friday morning market and in the summer an evening market on Fridays as well.

Monpazier   Thursday mornings.

Montignac   Wednesday and Saturday mornings.

Montpon   Wednesday mornings.

Mussidan   Saturday mornings.

Nontron   Saturday mornings.

Périgueux	Every day, the main markets being held on Wednesday mornings and all day Saturdays. The regular markets include truffles and *foie gras* in November and December and nuts in October and November.
	Evening markets on Wednesdays in July and August.
Ribérac	Friday mornings all year, with additional market on Tuesday mornings May to September.
	The nut and *foie gras* markets are held on Friday mornings November to March and truffle markets on Friday mornings mid-December to mid-February.
Ste Alvère	Mondays all year with a truffle market every Monday from December to February.
Sarlat-la-Canéda	From Easter to 1st November and during the Christmas holidays every day until 2pm at Sainte Marie. In July and August this market is open until 8pm every Friday.
	From 1st November to Easter on Tuesdays, Wednesdays, Fridays and weekends until 1pm at Sainte Marie.
	All-day markets all year round on Saturdays in the Cité Médiévale and place de la Grande Rigaudie.
	Saturday morning market in winter at place de la Mairie for *foie gras*, a nut market October and November and a truffle market November to March.
Thiviers	Saturday mornings.
Vergt	Friday mornings.

Organic Food

Bergerac	La Vie Claire, 65 rue Docteur Roux Mondays 2 to 7pm, Tuesdays to Saturdays 9am to 7pm.	☎ 05 53 57 96 57
Périgueux	Le Grain d'Or, 7 rue Salinière	☎ 05 53 53 17 73
	La Vie Claire, 15 rue Limogeanne Tuesdays to Saturdays.	☎ 05 53 53 43 32
Ribérac	Croq'Santé, 84 rue 26 Mars 1944	☎ 05 53 91 42 49
Sarlat-la-Canéda	Bio Star, 23 avenue Gambetta 🖳 *www.biocoop.fr*	☎ 05 53 59 53 03

Retail Parks

Bergerac   Les Rives de la Dordogne
                (south-west of the town)
                Shops include:

- BUT – general furniture and household accessories;

- Conforama – furniture, household appliances and electrical goods;

- Gifi – general furniture and household accessories;

- Gemo – clothes;

- Guy Patrice Tissus – fabrics;

- Intersport – sports goods;

- Leclerc – hypermarket;

- Literie 24 – beds;

- Mr Bricolage – DIY;

- Zenith – lighting.

Périgueux   La Feuilleraie
                (east of the town at Trélissac, spreading into Boulazac)
                Stores include:

- Aubert – baby clothes and goods;

- Brico-Dépot – building materials;

- Carrefour – hypermarket;

- Casa – gifts and household furnishings;

- Conforama – furniture, household appliances and electrical goods;

- Décathlon – sports goods;

- Gifi – general furniture and household accessories;

- Go Sport – sports goods;

- Hygena – kitchens;

- Jardiland – large garden centre;

- Leclerc – hypermarket;

- McDonald's – restaurant;

- Music Galaxie – music;

- Vulco – tyre and exhaust centre;

- Yamaha – motor bike centre;

- Zenith – lighting.

To the west of Périgueux is another retail park.
Stores include:

- Art de l'Eau – swimming pools;

- Brico Loisir – DIY;

- Connexion – electrical goods;

- McDonald's – restaurant;

- Monsieur Meuble – furniture;

- Point Vert – garden centre;

- Schmidt – kitchens;

- St Maclou – paint, decorating materials and carpets.

Second-Hand Goods

Bergerac	CBA, Rond Point, route de Marmande Open afternoons Tuesdays to Sundays. Brocante Hergat, Le Rooy Open Mondays to Saturdays.	☎ 05 53 63 12 67 ☎ 05 53 73 31 49
Le Bugue	Marie Brassier, route Périgueux No set hours so advisable to phone in advance.	☎ 05 53 07 11 12
Montpon	Brocante J. Meunier, rue Thiers (on the main road going through town)	☎ 06 53 26 65 60
Périgueux	Antiquités M. Saillard, 73 rue Combe des Dames 🖥 *www.ateliers-perigord.com*	☎ 05 53 53 90 57
Ribérac	Ribérac Antiquités, route d'Angoulême 🖥 *www.riberac-antiquites.com*	☎ 05 53 90 25 16
Sarlat-la-Canéda	Antiquités de la Vieille Ville, rue Lakanal	☎ 05 53 31 11 52

Sports Goods

Bergerac   Intersport, 40 rue de la Résistance   ☎ 05 53 74 51 11
                    (on the Leclerc complex)
                    Mondays to Fridays 9.30am to 12.30pm and 2 to 7.30pm,
                    Saturdays 9.30am to 7.30pm.

Montpon   Twinner, avenue Georges Pompidou   ☎ 05 53 80 72 72
                    (off the roundabout in the west of the town, to the left of
                    Intermarché supermarket)
                    Mondays to Saturdays 9am to 7.30pm.

Périgueux   Intersport, rue Cropt Basse,
                    Marsac-sur-l'Isle   ☎ 05 53 02 74 50
                    (on the Auchan complex)

Sarlat-la-Canéda Sport 2000, 33 avenue Dordogne   ☎ 05 53 30 80 61

Swimming Pool Equipment

General   Pool Serve, Domipech, Prayssas   ☎ 05 53 95 98 62
                    This company is run by a UK qualified pool engineer and
                    builds, refurbishes and maintains pools from its base in
                    Lot-et-Garonne.

Bergerac   Hydro Sud,
                    48 avenue Président Wilson   ☎ 05 53 57 02 83
                    Traditional construction as well as pool kits, saunas,
                    consumables, accessories and maintenance.

Condat-sur-   Hemelin Espace Verts, La Bechade   ☎ 05 53 50 89 47
Vézère   🖥 *www.hamelinespacesverts.com*
                    (east of Périgueux on the border with Corrèze)
                    Design, installation and maintenance of swimming pools.

Périgueux   Art de L'Eau, boulevard Avenir,
                    Marsac-sur-l'Isle   ☎ 05 53 08 28 99
                    (on the retail park west of Périgueux)

Sarlat-la-Canéda Everblue Piscines, route Montignac   ☎ 05 53 30 26 90
                    (west of the town near the Champion supermarket)

Sports

The following is just a selection of the activities available, the large towns
having a wide range of sports facilities. Full details are available from the
tourist office or the *mairie*.

Aerial Sports

Bergerac	Aéroclub de Bergerac, Aérodrome de Roumanière	☎ 05 53 57 31 36
	🖥 *www.aeroclub-de-bergerac.fr.fm*	
	Ecole de Parachutisme, Aérodrome de Roumanière	☎ 05 53 57 15 24
	🖥 *www.multimania.com/parachutisme24* Parachuting. Contact Bruno Roquet.	
Périgueux	Centre de Vol à Voile du Périgord, Aérodrome de Périgueux	☎ 05 53 04 02 03
	Gliders and microlights. An active club with courses and training, open every weekend and all week in the Easter and summer holidays. Minimum age 14.	
	Association Sportive Aéronautique de Périgueux, Aérodrome de Périgueux-Bassillac, Bassillac	☎ 05 53 54 41 19
Ribérac	Aéro Club Jean Mermoz, Aérodrome de Ribérac	☎ 05 53 90 10 41
	Contact Mr Galluret.	
Sarlat-la-Canéda	Aéro Club du Sarladais, Aérodrome, Domme	☎ 05 53 28 32 95
	Flying school, introductory flights and model planes.	

American Football

Bergerac	Stade Gaston Simounet, 30 rue Anatole France	☎ 05 53 63 55 95

Archery

La Force	Première Compagnie d'Arc du Périgord	☎ 05 53 58 01 24
	(just west of Bergerac) Contact the *Mairie* at La Force for more information.	
Nontron	Les Archers du Haut Périgord	☎ 06 71 20 79 74
	Contact Mr Delage.	
Périgueux	Compagnie d'Arc de Périgueux	☎ 05 53 06 13 52
	Contact Mr Desjeux for venue and meeting times.	
Ribérac	Les Archers de l'Etoile	☎ 05 53 91 37 39

Sarlat-la-Canéda   Sarlat Olympic Club Tir à l'Arc   ☎ 05 53 59 06 37
                   Contact Mr Drouard.

Badminton

Bergerac   Bergerac Objectif Badminton,
                   12 impasse Guilhem   ☎ 05 53 57 11 18
                   Minimum age 12.

Montpon   Badminton Club Montponnais,
                   Ancien Gymnase, rue Foix de Candalle ☎ 06 09 40 17 06
                   Leisure and competitions. Mondays 1 to 5pm,
                   Mondays and Thursdays 8 to 10pm and Saturdays
                   10am to 2pm.

Nontron   Badminton Club Nontronnais   ☎ 05 53 56 01 22
                   Contact Mr Baglione.

Sarlat-la-Canéda   Badminton Club du Sarladais   ☎ 05 53 30 31 66
                   Contact Mr Cuizinaud.

Canoeing & Kayaking

Bergerac   Aqua Park Junior Land,
                   route de Bordeaux   ☎ 05 53 58 33 00
                   Canoes for two adults and one child, from €8 for an hour. 6 to
                   15km (4 to 11mi) descents available, €25 to €41.

Groléjac   Explorando, le Pas de la Lande   ☎ 05 53 59 04 90
                   🖳 *www.canoedordogne.com*
                   Canoes for two to four people, descend at your own pace
                   between 9.30am and 4pm. English spoken.

Le Bugue   Canoeric, route de Camping Municipal ☎ 05 53 03 51 99
                   (next to the aquarium, with shaded free parking)

Périgueux   Association Loisirs Périgueux,
                   Moulin Sainte Claire   ☎ 05 53 04 24 08

Ribérac   Ribérac Randonnées, Camping
                   Municipal, route d'Angoulême   ☎ 05 53 90 50 08
                   Lessons and canoe hire June to September.

Clay Pigeon Shooting

Bergerac   Association Sportive Poudrerie,
                   boulevard Charles Garraud   ☎ 05 53 57 75 73
                   Minimum age 16.

▼ *Les Eyzies, Dordogne*

▲ *Restaurant, Limeuil, Dordogne*

▼ Marmande, Lot-et-Garonne

▲ *Le Bugue, Dordogne*

▶

Limeuil, Dordogne

▶ *La Rogue-Gageac,*
Dordogne

▲ *Chemin d'Halage, Lot*

▲ *Geese, Le Bugue*

▲ *Cailadelles, Lot-et-Garonne*

▶ *Restaurant sign,*
Figeac

◀ *Cahors, Lot*

▲ *Near Monflanquin, Lot-et-Garonne*

▲ *Village du Bournat, Le Bugue*

▲ *St Cirq-Lapopie, Lot*

◀

Brantome, Dordogne

Villeneuve-sur-Lot, Lot-et-Garonne

▲ *Boules, Le Bugue*

▲ *Les Eyzies, Dordogne*

▲ *Village du Bournat,*
Le Bugue

◄ *Chateau de Bonaguil,*
Lot-et-Garonne

Climbing

Bergerac	Association Sportive Poudrerie, boulevard Charles Garraud	☎ 05 53 27 18 22

Mountaineering and rock climbing. Minimum age six.

Lalinde	Base de Loisirs de la Guillou	☎ 05 53 61 02 91

✉ *laguillou@wanadoo.fr*
(on the river Dordogne, east of Bergerac)

Périgueux	Groupe Périgourdin Amis de la Montagne, 4 rue du Guesclin	☎ 05 53 35 51 24

Sarlat-la-Canéda	Escalade, 32 rue Lachambeaudie	☎ 05 53 59 43 60

Climbing and canyoning.

Cycling

Bergerac	Association Sportive Poudrerie, boulevard Charles Garraud	☎ 05 53 63 63 63

Le Bugue	Vélo Club Buguois	☎ 05 53 04 89 48

Montagrier	Centre VTT, allée des Marronniers	☎ 05 53 90 13 25

(east of Ribérac)
Mountain bike hire and route maps.

Montpon   In July and August there are cycle rides every Tuesday morning, accompanied and unaccompanied, meeting at 9am in front of the tourist office, place Clémenceau. The routes are around 10km (6.5mi).
L'Association du Cyclotourisme organises accompanied rides once a month out of season. Meetings on Tuesdays at 2pm in front of the tourist office.

Le Cyclotourisme de Montpon	☎ 05 53 80 39 30

Rides on Thursdays and Sundays all year, from 35 to 60km. Depart from Rue Foix de Candalle. October to May at 2pm, June to September 9.30am.

Nontron	Rayon Vert VTT	☎ 05 55 78 77 78

Dates of rides are publicised on a notice board on the front of the Hôtel de France bar. For more information contact Alistair Hay on the above number.

Périgueux	Club Velocio Périgourdin, Maison des Sportifs, 10bis rue Louis Blanc	☎ 05 53 53 06 72

Ribérac   Club Cyclotouriste Ribéracois   ☎ 05 53 90 28 49
                   For all age groups, regular rides departing from the
                   Palais de Justice, rue du Palais every Sunday
                   morning at 8.30am.

Sarlat-la-Canéda   There's a cycle path around Sarlat, Carsac-Aillac and Groléjac
                   accessible from the D704 north-east of Sarlat.

                   Union Cycliste Sarladaise   ☎ 05 53 31 53 31
                   The main office for this cycle club is at the Mairie.

Diving

Bergerac   Cyrano Plongée Bergerac,
                   16 rue Mergier   ☎ 05 53 22 38 66
                   Diving club for 16-year-olds and over.

Fencing

Bergerac   Cercle d'Escrime 'Les Cadets',
                   11 rue Valette   ☎ 05 53 57 03 92
                   💻 www.cadetsbergerac.free.fr

Nontron   Les Lames Nontronnaises   ☎ 05 53 46 31 22
                   Contact Mme Roussarie.

Périgueux   Périgueux Epée,
                   13 rue Talleyrand Périgord   ☎ 05 53 09 37 32

Sarlat-la-Canéda   Escrime, Salle d'Armes,
                   2 avenue Aristide Briand   ☎ 05 53 28 57 91

Fishing

Maps are available from fishing shops and tourist offices showing local
fishing waters. There's also information on species found in the area, prices
of fishing permits and dates of the fishing season. If there's a lake locally,
permits will be on sale in nearby *tabacs* and fishing shops and at the *mairie*.

Bergerac   Bergerac Pêche, place du Foirail   ☎ 05 53 61 93 09
                   Open Mondays to Saturdays 9am to noon and 2 to 7pm. Full
                   details of local fishing lakes and waterways available and
                   fishing permits can be purchased here.

                   Gaule Bergeracoise, Pont Robert   ☎ 05 53 61 17 50
                   Local fishing club.

La Jemaye   Les Etangs de la Jemaye   ☎ 05 53 06 80 17
                   (south-west of Périgueux)

This is a large lake in the middle of the Double forest with a leisure area and designated areas for fishing.

Montpon   The river Isle, which runs alongside Montpon, is a Class 2 fishing area and permits can be bought at Denost Chasse Pêche, 79 route de Bordeaux and the *tabac* at 60 rue Thiers.

Nontron   La Gaule Nontronnaise   ☎ 05 53 56 05 05
The local fishing club at Nontron. Contact Mr Barre.

Local lakes, all of which require fishing permits, are:
Etangs du Merle   ☎ 06 80 65 60 35
Champs Romain   ☎ 05 53 56 93 61
Miallet
A 77ha (190-acre) artificial lake.

Ribérac   The river Dronne is suitable for fishing, and annual or holiday fishing licences can be bought at the fishing shop at 13 rue Jean Moulin or the bar at 137 rue du 26 Mars 1944.

Sarlat-la-Canéda   Club Mouche Sarladais   ☎ 05 53 59 46 97
Fly fishing.

Golf

Marsac-sur-l'Isle   Golf Public de Périgueux   ☎ 05 53 53 02 35
🖥 *www.golfdeperigueux.fr*
18 holes, 5,933m, par 71. Equipment and golf carts for hire and a restaurant in the clubhouse. Green fees €25 to €35 for 18 holes. Discounts for couples and under 21s.

Monestier   Château des Vigiers   ☎ 05 53 61 50 33
18 holes, 6,003m, par 72. Golf carts, open and covered driving range, pro shop, bar and two restaurants. Green fees from €31.25 to €49.

Mouleydier   Golf Club Château les Merles   ☎ 05 53 63 13 42
9 holes, 2,549m, par 35. Small driving range and putting green, pro shop and bar, as well as a croquet lawn, tennis court and swimming pool. Closed Tuesdays in winter. Green fees €15.25 all year round.

St Felix-de-   Domaine de la Marterie   ☎ 05 53 05 61 00
Reilhac   🖥 *www.marterie.fr*
Currently 9 holes, 3,031m, par 37 but soon to be an 18-hole course, 6,100m, par 73. Clubhouse, bar and restaurant in an

18th century house. Covered driving range, golf carts and equipment for hire. Green fees €26 to €36. Discounts for couples and children. Website available in English.

Siorac-en-
Périgord
Golf de Lolivarie   ☎ 05 53 30 22 69
9 holes, 2,751m, par 35. Practice green, covered driving range, pro shop and bar. Golf carts for hire. Green fees €22 all year round.

Horse Riding

Bergerac   Les Veyllaux, Saint Germain et Mons   ☎ 05 53 58 15 78
💻 *www.bergerac-horse-club.com*
Courses, individual lessons and stabling.

Le Bugue   Arc en Ciel, Ferme du Peyrat,
Campagne   ☎ 05 53 07 23 66
Lessons and hacks, ponies and horses.

Montpon   Le Centre Equestre 'Les 4 Vents',
route de Vélines   ☎ 05 53 82 31 94
Riding lessons, jumping, dressage and hacks.

St Laurent-des- Le Centre Equestre de Beauperier   ☎ 05 53 81 70 43
Hommes   (between Montpon, Ribérac and Mussidan)
Open all year with a covered ménage, dressage area and cross country course. Riding school, hacks in the forest and pony club. English spoken.

Périgueux   La Cravache de Trélissac,
Espace Liberté F. Grandou   ☎ 05 53 08 14 58
(on the east side of Périgueux)

Villetoureix   La Bride du Welsh Poney-Club   ☎ 05 53 90 03 53
(just north-east of Ribérac)

Jetskiing

Fougueyrolles   Pro Glisse, Le Vieux Château   ☎ 05 53 74 60 33
(due south of Montpon on the D708)

Judo

Bergerac   Association Sportive Poudrerie,
boulevard Charles Garraud   ☎ 05 53 24 04 17

Le Bugue   Judo Club Buguois   ☎ 05 53 29 32 67
Phone for venues and dates.

Montpon   Judo Club Montponnais,
rue Foix de Candalle   ☎ 05 53 80 31 90

Tuesday and Friday evenings 5 to 8.30pm. Contact Mr
Gimenez for further information.

Nontron   Judo Club Nontronnais   ☎ 05 53 56 00 83
                      Contact Mr Ladrat.

Périgueux   Judo Club de Périgueux, Salle Omnisports
                      du Toulon, route d'Angoulême   ☎ 05 53 53 88 60

Ribérac   Salle des Arts Martiaux   ☎ 05 53 92 57 27
                      Courses for children and adults on Friday evenings.
                      For more information contact Mr Aubry out of
                      office hours.

Sarlat-la-Canéda Judo Jujitsu Sarlandais   ☎ 05 53 28 91 12
                      Contact Mr Besse.

Motorcycle Riding

Bergerac   Aqua Park Junior Land,
                      route de Bordeaux   ☎ 05 53 58 33 00
                      Mini-motorbikes and mini-quads for children, €8 for
                      half a day.

                      Moto Club Bergeracois,
                      3 rue Prosper Faugère   ☎ 05 53 27 13 18
                      Motor bike club.

Chanterac   'Ride On' Grégory Rousseau   ☎ 05 53 81 85 70
                      Individual and group lessons in motocross
                      and supercross.

Nontron   Moto Club du Périgord Vert   ☎ 05 53 56 62 11
                      Contact Mr Mousnier.

Périgueux   Moto Passion Périgueux, Maison des
                      Sportifs, 10bis rue Louis Blanc   ☎ 05 53 53 06 72

Ribérac   Les Manges Bitumes   ☎ 06 30 41 30 29
                      Contact Mr Bocquier.

Sarlat-la-Canéda Association Circuit Automobile de
                      Bonnet   ☎ 06 85 41 03 24

                      Moto Club Sarladais, route de Souillac   ☎ 05 53 29 82 20
                      Motocross, endurance, trial biking and road trips.

Vézac   Plage de Vézac, Pont de Fayrac   ☎ 05 53 30 37 61
                      Open all year round. Booking necessary.

Potholing

Lalinde   Base de Loisirs de la Guillou   ☎ 05 53 61 02 91
                   ✉ *laguillou@wanadoo.fr*
                   (on the river Dordogne, east of Bergerac)

Périgueux   Spéléo Club de Périgueux,
                   91 rue Lagrange Chancel   ☎ 05 53 24 24 20

Roller Skating

Bergerac   Patineurs Bergeracois,
                   Patinage de Vitesse   ☎ 05 53 57 74 37
                   11 rue Théophile Gauthier. Minimum age six.

Fougueyrolles   Pro Glisse, Le Vieux Château   ☎ 05 53 74 60 33
                   (directly south of Montpon on the D708)
                   Roller skating practice Wednesdays and Saturdays 2 to 7pm
                   and Tuesday evenings from 8.30pm.

Périgueux   Le Torpilles de Périgueux, Maison des
                   Sportifs, 10bis rue Louis Blanc   ☎ 05 53 53 06 72
                   🖥 *www.torpilles.free.fr*
                   This roller skating club organises roller hockey, stunt and trick
                   sessions, roller discos and competitions.

                   'Roller Boulevard'
                   On the last Fridays in June, July and August the boulevards
                   in Périgueux are closed to traffic in the evenings and free
                   access is given to roller skaters of all ages, with ramps and
                   impromptu events being enjoyed by more and more skaters
                   each year.

Sarlat-la-Canéda   There's a skate park at Madrazès, by the stadium in the
                   north-east of the town.

Sailing

Mauzac   Club Nautique Mauzacois   ☎ 05 53 22 52 14
                   Open every day in July and August, weekends only in May,
                   June, September and the first two weeks of October.

Scuba Diving

Périgueux   Périgueux Plongée Sous Marine, Maison
                   des Sportifs, 10bis rue Louis Blanc   ☎ 05 53 53 06 72

Sarlat-la-Canéda   Club Subaquatique du Périgord Noir   ☎ 05 53 59 15 36
                   Contact Mr Courroy.

Shooting

Bergerac	USB Stade Gaston Simounet, 30 rue Anatole France	☎ 05 53 63 55 95
	Association Bergeracoise de Tir	☎ 05 53 58 87 81
Nontron	Association Nontronnaise de Tireurs Amateurs Contact Mr Desborde.	☎ 05 53 56 25 52
Sarlat-la-Canéda	Association des Tireurs Sarladais, Camping les Perrières Lessons, training and courses.	☎ 05 53 59 21 41

Snooker, Pool & Billiards

Some bars listed under **Bars & Nightlife** on page 92 also have billiards, pool or snooker tables.

Bergerac	Pool Marine, 46 avenue Pasteur Snooker club for over 18s.	☎ 05 53 61 89 44
Périgueux	Billard Club de la Rive – le Rive Gauche, 109 avenue du Maréchal Juin Open Tuesdays to Sundays for French billiards, pool and snooker.	☎ 05 53 07 49 62

Swimming

Bergerac	Piscine de Picquecailloux, Picquecailloux, allée Lucien Videau (on the east side of the town in the park) Indoor pool open all year round.	☎ 05 53 57 10 23
	Piscine Neptuna, allée Beau Rivage Outdoor pool open July and August.	☎ 05 53 57 97 37
Le Bugue	Piscine Municipale, Le Port Outdoor pool open only in the summer.	☎ 05 53 07 23 57
Montpon	Piscine Municipale, rue du Général Leclerc Three outdoor pools, open July and August.	☎ 05 53 80 30 84
Nontron	Piscine Municipale, Mas Viconteaux Outdoor pool open only in the summer.	☎ 05 53 60 72 93

| Périgueux | Piscine Municipale, Parc Aristide Briand, boulevard Lakanal | ☎ 05 53 53 30 36 |

Indoor pool.

Piscine d'Eté de Périgueux,
151 rue Alphée Maziéras   ☎ 05 53 03 49 58
Outdoor pool open only in the summer.

Ribérac   Piscine Municipale, avenue de Royan   ☎ 05 53 90 03 40
Three outdoor pools open June to September.

Sarlat-la-Canéda Stade Municipal de Madrazès,
route de Souillac   ☎ 05 53 31 12 08
Outdoor pool open July and August.

Tennis

Bergerac   Tennis Bergerac Millet Barrage,
chemin de la Fondaurade   ☎ 05 53 57 10 10

Le Bugue   Tennis Club Buguois   ☎ 05 53 07 27 87
July & August ☎ 05 53 07 28 15

Montpon   Tennis Club de Montpon   ☎ 05 53 80 31 90
There are courts at rue de Velines and at Ancien Gymnase, rue
Foix de Candalle. The club meets on Mondays at 5pm and
Wednesdays 10am to noon. Courts can also be hired by
the hour.

Nontron   Tennis Club de Nontron,
7 route de la Manganèse   ☎ 05 53 56 01 22
(on the south side of town on the road to Ribérac)
This is an active club with one indoor and five outdoor courts,
which can be booked by the hour at the shop Côté Court on
rue Carnot (☎ 05 53 56 00 32).

Périgueux   Club Olympique Périgueux Ouest,
Stade Maurice-Lacoin   ☎ 05 53 08 60 62
This is an active tennis club with a clubhouse and a variety of
court surfaces.

Stade Roger Dantou,
rue Alphée Maziéras   ☎ 05 53 53 35 92

Ribérac   rue du Stade   ☎ 05 53 90 03 10
July & August ☎ 05 53 90 27 62
Five courts available for hire by the hour.

Sarlat-la-Canéda	Tennis Club Sarladais, Madrazès, rue du Stade	☎ 05 53 59 44 23

Four outdoor and three indoor courts.

Waterskiing

Trémolat	Base de Loisirs	☎ 05 53 22 83 75

(on the Dordogne, south-west of Le Bugue)

Windsurfing

Mauzac	Club Nautique Mauzacois	☎ 05 53 22 52 14

(on the Dordogne, south-west of Le Bugue)
Every day in July and August, weekends only in May, June,
September and the first two weeks of October.

Tourist Offices

General   Comité Régional du Tourisme
d'Aquitaine, 23 Parvis des Chartrons,
33074 Bordeaux   ☎ 05 56 01 70 00
💻 *www.tourisme-aquitaine.info*

Comité Départemental du Tourisme de
la Dordogne, 25 rue Wilson, Périgueux   ☎ 05 53 35 50 24
💻 *www.perigord.tm.fr/tourisme*
💻 *www.perigorddecouverte.com*
💻 *www.dordogneguide.com*
💻 *www.dordogne-perigord.net*

Bergerac   97 rue Neuve d'Argenson   ☎ 05 53 57 03 11
💻 *www.bergerac-tourisme.com*
Mid-September to mid-June, Mondays to Saturdays 9.30am to
1pm and 2 to 7pm; mid-June to mid-September, Mondays to
Saturdays 9am to 7.30pm.

Le Bugue   Porte de la Vézère, rue Jardin Public   ☎ 05 53 07 20 48
💻 *www.perigord.com/bugue*
November to March, Tuesdays to Saturdays 9.30am to
12.30pm and 2.30 to 6.30pm; April to October, Mondays to
Saturdays 9.30am to 12.30pm and 2.30 to 6.30pm, Sundays
and bank holidays 10am to 1pm; July and August, every day
9am to 1pm and 3 to 7pm. There's a *bureau de change* in this
office, open the same hours as the tourist office.

Montpon   place Clémenceau   ☎ 05 53 82 23 77
✉ *ot.montpon@perigord.tm.fr*
October to April, Tuesdays to Fridays 9am to noon and 2 to

5.30pm, Mondays and Saturdays 2 to 5.30pm; May to September, Mondays to Saturdays 9am to 12.30pm and 2 to 6pm; July and August also Sundays 10am to noon.

Nontron   avenue du Général Leclerc   ☎ 05 53 56 25 50
⊠ *ot.nontron@wanadoo.fr*
September to June, Mondays to Saturdays 9am to 5pm; July and August, Mondays to Saturdays 9am to 7pm.

Périgueux   26 place Francheville   ☎ 05 53 53 10 63
🖥 *www.ville-perigueux.fr*
(from the town centre this office is down towards the river, to the left of Monoprix)
Open all year Mondays to Saturdays 9am to 7pm (July and August also Sundays 10am to 6pm).

Ribérac   place du Général de Gaulle   ☎ 05 53 90 03 10
🖥 *www.riberac.fr*
July and August, Mondays to Fridays 9am to 7pm, Saturdays 10am to 1pm and 2 to 7pm, Sundays 10am to 1pm; rest of the year, Mondays to Fridays 9am to noon and 2 to 5pm.

Sarlat-la-Canéda rue Tourny   ☎ 05 53 31 45 45
🖥 *www.ot-sarlat-perigord.fr*
🖥 *www.ville-sarlat.fr*
November to March, Mondays to Saturdays 9am to noon and 2 to 7pm; April to October, Mondays to Saturdays 9am to 7pm, Sundays and bank holidays 10am to noon and 2 to 6pm.

Tradesmen

Architects & Project Managers

General   Adams Gautier
☎ 05 49 64 42 96
🖥 *www.adamsgautier.com*
This is a British/French team of experienced architects, who also organise surveys and building permits and carry out project management for new builds, renovation, landscaping and pools.

Builders

General   Hautefort Renovation, Cherveix Cubas   ☎ 05 53 50 12 39
⊠ *lesflamands@tiscali.fr*
(north-east Dordogne)
English-speaking builder specialising in renovation.

Rema Services, St Pardoux   ☎ 05 53 60 76 20
⊠ *remaservices@voila.fr*

English-speaking company that undertakes building, roofing, electrics, plumbing and heating across the department.

Bergerac	Christophe Garrigue, 4bis rue Rosa Luxembourg	☎ 05 53 57 37 04
	New and renovation work.	
	Latour et Fils, 52 rue St Martin	☎ 05 53 57 18 26
	New and renovation work.	
Le Bugue	Rigaudie, ZA La Plaine	☎ 05 53 07 24 89
Montpon	EPM, La Jourdaire	☎ 05 53 80 37 01
	(south of the town, over the railway)	
Nontron	Lhomme et Dauriac, 6 rue Le Roy	☎ 05 53 56 13 70
	General builder.	
Périgueux	Becam 2, 18 rue Mobiles Coulmiers	☎ 05 53 09 01 23
	🖳 www.becam-24.com	
	General work on all types of building; renovation a speciality. Design service.	
	Bâtiment Restauration Maçonnerie (BRM), 31 avenue Jeanne d'Arc	☎ 05 53 35 20 77
Ribérac	JCM, Faye	☎ 05 53 90 54 75
	(north-east of Ribérac, towards Aubeterre) New and renovation, general building work, roofing and masonry.	
Sarlat-la-Canéda	Société Sarlandaise de Construction, La Gare Nord	☎ 05 53 59 18 35

Carpenters

Many carpentry firms that make wooden windows and doors also work in aluminium.

Bergerac	Tryba ABH, 141 avenue Pasteur	☎ 05 53 22 26 10
	🖳 www.tryba.com Windows, doors and shutters.	
Le Bugue	Peyridieu Serge, ZI La Plaine	☎ 05 53 07 40 04
	Staircases, balustrades and mezzanines made and installed.	
Montpon	Robert Rousseille, 27 rue Moulineaux	☎ 05 53 80 31 48
	General carpenter and cabinet maker.	
Nontron	JF Devaux, 34 rue Antonin Debidour	☎ 05 53 56 03 02
	General carpentry and roofing.	

Périgueux	AMEP, 120 rue Pierre Sémard Production and installation of stairs, parquet, etc.	☎ 05 53 09 26 01
	Jean-Luc Raynal, 11 rue Sainte Claire Kitchens, windows, parquet, shutters etc.	☎ 05 53 04 20 75
Ribérac	Sco.Me.Bat, route Périgueux General carpentry, including kitchens and stairs.	☎ 05 53 90 18 50
Sarlat-la-Canéda	Mercier Vaunac, Naudissou	☎ 05 53 59 41 46

Chimney Sweeps

Bergerac	Metifet et Fils, 3 rue Alfred de Musset	☎ 05 53 57 06 87
Le Bugue	Jean-Jacques Cabrillac, Sauveboeuf	☎ 05 53 61 15 08
Mussidan	Gombault, 12 rue Jean Jaurès (east of Montpon)	☎ 05 53 80 20 73
Périgueux	S Salleroi, 9 rue Denfert Rochereau	☎ 05 53 53 20 99
Ribérac	Sarl Rouby & Fils, 103 rue du 26 Mars	☎ 05 53 91 67 07
Sarlat-la-Canéda	Fournial Jean-Jacques, 24bis rue Xavier Vial	☎ 05 53 31 26 44

Electricians

General	Solec, La Chassagnole, Cressensac ✉ *solecfrance@yahoo.co.uk* General household electrics and electrical central heating systems. This company is run by an Englishman, who covers the eastern Dordogne.	☎ 05 65 37 79 26
Bergerac	André Tur, Le Petit Chai-Touterive General electrician, heating and plumbing.	☎ 05 53 57 75 58
Le Bugue	Lalot Etablissements, Le Bourg, Journiac Electricity and air-conditioning, new and renovation.	☎ 05 53 03 24 84
Montpon	Champeville et Fils, 92 avenue Georges Pompidou Electrics, heating and bathrooms.	☎ 05 53 80 73 89
Nontron	H. Masfrand, 18 rue Carnot General electrics and repair of household appliances.	☎ 05 53 56 04 83

Périgueux   Jacques Marty, 65 rue Pierre Sémard   ☎ 05 53 08 95 27
                 Electrics and heating, new installations and repair work.

Ribérac   Sarl Rouby et Fils, 103 rue du 26 Mars   ☎ 05 53 91 67 07
                 Electrics, heating and plumbing.

Sarlat-la-Canéda Mondial Chauffage – Muller Energie,
                 Centre Commercial, route de Brive   ☎ 05 53 31 20 89

Plumbers

Bergerac   Lambert Charles et Fils, 3 rue Fontaines ☎ 05 53 57 17 37
                 Plumbing, heating, bathrooms and water softeners.

Le Bugue   T Barthélémy, 59 route Campagne   ☎ 05 53 03 93 88

Montpon   Magie Serge, 41 rue Prés Wilson   ☎ 05 53 80 35 69
                 Central heating, plumbing, roofing and bathrooms.

Nontron   Sarl Lagarde, 78 rue de Périgueux   ☎ 05 53 56 02 63
                 General plumbing and installation and maintenance of central
                 heating systems.

Périgueux   S Salleroi, 9 rue Denfert Rochereau   ☎ 05 53 53 20 99
                 Heating and plumbing.

Ribérac   Sarl Rouby et Fils, 103 rue du 26 Mars   ☎ 05 53 91 67 07
                 Heating, plumbing and bathrooms.

Sarlat-la-Canéda Jouclas Quercy Périgord,
                 54 rue Fontaine de l'Amour   ☎ 05 53 31 05 59
                 General plumbing, heating, electrics and air-conditioning.

Stained Glass Windows

Nontron   LG Martin, 32 rue Picaud   ☎ 05 53 56 98
                 Designs, makes and restores stained glass windows.

Translators & Teachers

French Teachers & Courses

Aubeterre-sur-   Association Approches   ☎ 05 45 98 13 78
Dronne   ✉ *approches@infonie.fr*
                 (just north of Ribérac)
                 Individual and group French lessons.

Bergerac   Perf'Etudes, 58 rue Petit Sol   ☎ 05 53 58 33 43

	Université du Temps Libre French courses for English-speakers.	☎ 05 53 57 11 59

| Le Bugue | Espace Linguistique
Contact Marie-Christine, who runs courses in Le Bugue and
St Alvère. | ☎ 05 53 58 48 11 |

| Montpon | Greta Dordogne,
26bis avenue Georges Pompidou
🖥 *www.greta-dordogne.com*
Government-run organisation. | ☎ 05 53 82 46 79 |

| Nontron | Centre de Formation,
1 place des Droits de l'Homme | ☎ 05 53 60 31 93 |

| Périgueux | Europa Etudes, rue Charles Mangold
Individual and group lessons. | ☎ 05 53 53 26 22 |

| | Greta Dordogne, 80 rue Victor Hugo
🖥 *www.greta-dordogne.com*
Government-run organisation. | ☎ 05 53 03 29 48 |

| Sarlat-la-Canéda | Greta Dordogne, 4 avenue Dordogne
🖥 *www.greta-dordogne.com*
Government-run organisation. | ☎ 05 53 31 70 66 |

Translators

Mérignac	Christiane Gallagher, 503 avenue de Verdun A court-approved translator in neighbouring Gironde (33).	☎ 05 56 97 93 25

| Vanzains | James Anderson, Laygonie
🖥 *www.anderson.fr*
(south-west of Ribérac)
Translation and interpreting, including liaison
with tradesmen. | ☎ 05 53 91 38 60 |

Utilities

Electricity & Gas

Électricité de France/Gaz de France (EDF/GDF) is one company for the whole of France but operates its gas and electricity divisions separately. The numbers below are for general information; emergency numbers can be found on page 59.

| General | EDF/GDF Services Périgord, 5 rue Maurice Barat, Bergerac | ☎ 08 10 57 78 23 |
| | 🖳 *www.gazdefrance.com* | |

EDF/GDF local offices are listed below (there are no direct telephone numbers for these offices; you must dial the above number).

| Périgueux | 46 rue Nouvelle du Port |

| Ribérac | boulevard François Mitterrand |

| Sarlat-la-Canéda | 21 avenue Thiers |

Heating Oil

Bergerac	Total France, rue Docteur Vizerie	☎ 05 53 57 67 97
Chancelade	Alvéa, 6 ZI Les Gabares	☎ 05 53 08 62 04
Périgueux	Auchan Fioul	☎ 05 53 06 66 57
Ribérac	Alvéa, route Périgueux,	☎ 05 53 91 62 75

Water

The main water supply companies are listed below. If you aren't covered by one of these, your *mairie* will have details of your water supplier.

General	Compagnie des Eaux, place de la Petite Rigaudie, Sarlat-la-Canéda	☎ 08 01 14 70 17
	Générale des Eaux, 60 rue Anatole France, Bergerac	☎ 08 11 90 29 03
	Lyonnaise des Eaux	☎ 08 10 00 20 40
	emergencies	☎ 08 10 13 01 20
	SAUR, Terremale, Colombier	☎ 05 53 58 28 08
	SAUR, La Port, Razac-sur-L'Isle	☎ 05 53 54 60 38
	Service des Eaux, avenue Jean Moulin, Lalinde	☎ 05 53 24 95 19
	SIAEP, La Mairie, Le Bourg, Montazeau	☎ 05 53 63 42 02
	SIAEP, route Périgueux, Lalinde	☎ 05 53 61 22 40

SOGEDO, Plaines, Belvès   ☎ 05 53 29 01 39

SOGEDO, 10 avenue Pierre de
Bourdeilles, Brantôme   ☎ 05 53 05 72 53

SOGEDO, 11 avenue Docteur Tocheport,
Excideuil   ☎ 05 53 62 41 33

SOGEDO, rue Notre Dame, Monpazier   ☎ 05 53 22 62 42

SOGEDO, 88 rue 26 Mars 1944, Ribérac   ☎ 05 53 90 07 35

Wood

Eyliac	Grellier Forêt Exploitation, Saverdenne (east of Périgueux)	☎ 05 53 08 19 15
Gardonne	Jean-Luc Sylvestre, Mouthes (west of Bergerac)	☎ 05 53 27 89 69
St Michel-de- Villadeix	Dupont et Fils, route Lalinde (south of Périgueux)	☎ 05 53 54 91 62

Cahors

3

Lot

This chapter provides details of facilities and services in the department of Lot (46). General information about each subject can be found in **Chapter 1**. All entries are arranged alphabetically by town, except where a service applies over a wide area, in which case it's listed at the beginning of the relevant section under 'General'. A map of Lot is shown below.

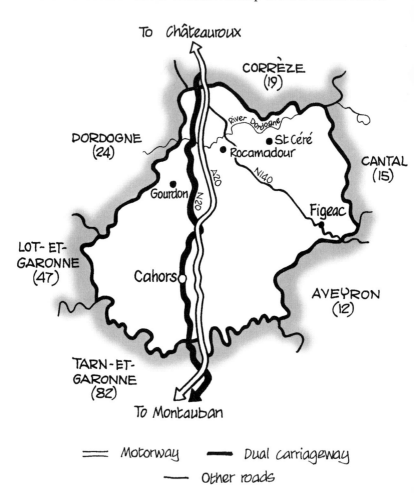

Accommodation

Camping

Cahors	Camping Rivière de Cabessut 🖳 *www.cabessut.com*	☎ 05 65 30 06 30

Beside the river Lot.
Open April to September inclusive.

Figeac | Les Rives du Célé | ☎ 05 65 34 59 00
Situated within a leisure complex, this campsite has a
swimming pool with wave machine and water slides. Open April
to September inclusive.

Gourdon | Camping Municipal Ecoute s'il Pleut | ☎ 05 65 41 06 19
Situated in a forest with leisure facilities all around. Open from
June to September inclusive.

St Céré | Camping Municipal, Soulhol | ☎ 05 65 38 12 37
(500m from the town centre)
Mobile homes and caravans for rent. Open April
to September.

Châteaux

Mercuès | Le Château de Mercuès | ☎ 05 65 20 00 01
🖥 *www.relaischateaux.fr/mercues*
This château was the summer residence of the bishop of
Cahors and has magnificent views over the surrounding
countryside. There's a gourmet restaurant and the wine cellars
can be visited. Rooms from €160 to €400 per night. Closed
from 1st November to Easter.

Meyronne | La Terrasse, le Bourg | ☎ 05 65 32 21 60
🖥 *www.hotel-la-terrace.com*
With double rooms up to €290 per night this is a very
comfortable three-star hotel within a feudal château alongside
the Dordogne. There's a pool, garden and restaurant with
panoramic view.

Gîtes And Bed & Breakfast

General | Maison du Tourisme,
place François Mitterrand, Cahors | ☎ 05 65 53 20 90
🖥 *www.gîtes-de-france-lot.com*
Bookings can be made by phone or internet.

Hotels

General | 🖥 *www.otedis.com*
This website has a comprehensive list of hotels, including
prices and booking information.

🖥 *www.tourisme-lot.com*
The tourist office website has details of hotel accommodation.

Bars & Nightlife

Alvignac   Casino d'Alvignac, route Padirac   ☎ 05 65 33 77 70
                   A casino and restaurant.

Cahors   Le Bowling, la Beyne   ☎ 05 65 35 71 46
                   (south of the river)
                   Video games, ten bowling alleys and a disco. Open Tuesdays
                   to Saturdays 7pm to 2am, Sundays 4pm to 2am.

                   Cahors Danse   ☎ 05 65 35 74 45
                   Organises evening dances with live bands or orchestras.
                   Leaflets available from the tourist office with forthcoming dates.
                   Bookings must be made between 7 and 8pm.

                   Club Oxygène, la Beyne   ☎ 06 77 13 15 36
                   (south of the town and the river)
                   Disco/nightclub.

                   Le Déclic, 39 rue Joffre   ☎ 05 65 35 95 32
                   Music bar with themed evenings and various events.

                   L'Irish Pub, place des Consuls   ☎ 05 65 53 15 15
                   Bar with concerts and shows.

                   Le Latino, quai Lagrive   ☎ 05 65 35 54 68
                   (alongside the river on the east side of the eastern loop)
                   Disco/nightclub.

There are a several bars and bistros in the old quarter of Figeac that are
open late into the evening, as well as the following:

Figeac   La Plage Verte, 2 allées Victor Hugo   ☎ 05 65 14 11 67
                   Music bar and restaurant open from 6pm to midnight Mondays
                   to Saturdays.

                   Le Palais, 4 boulevard de Juskiewenski ☎ 05 65 34 03 72
                   Karaoke evenings.

                   Le Pont d'Or, 2 avenue Emile Bouyssou ☎ 05 65 50 95 00
                   This cocktail bar within the Best Western hotel hosts a variety
                   of events during the year.

Gourdon   L'Hôtel Bissonnier,
                   51 boulevard des Martyrs   ☎ 05 65 41 02 48
                   🖳 www.hotelbissonnier.com
                   Themed evenings held all year round including jazz, Thai
                   and Latino.

| | Le Pub Med, 19 avenue Cavaignac | ☎ 05 65 41 09 65 |

Le Pub Med, 19 avenue Cavaignac   ☎ 05 65 41 09 65
Music bar with karaoke and cocktails.

Puybrun   La Guinguette & Le Club   ☎ 05 65 38 52 44
                (north-west of St Céré)
                La Guinguette offers 'apéritifs dansants' – tea dances without
                the tea but with the traditional music of tango, waltz, etc. Le
                Club is a nightclub at the same venue open on Fridays,
                Saturdays and bank holidays.

St Céré   Au Passé Simple,
                52 rue de la République   ☎ 05 65 38 39 61
                A piano bar in the centre of the town, open until around
                midnight, later at weekends.

                Thé Dansant, Le Casino,
                avenue Jean Mouliérat   ☎ 05 65 38 19 60
                Tea dances from 3 to 8pm every Sunday from late September
                to mid-May.

Souillac   Le Black Bar,
                62 boulevard Louis-Jean Malvy   ☎ 05 65 37 81 06
                Piano bar open until around 1am.

Business Services

Computer Services

General   Euro Laptops, Le Castelat, Gourdon ☎ 05 65 37 63 45
                💻 *www.gourdonnet.com*
                Software, hardware, upgrades, new computers and help with
                all aspects of setting up and using your computer by a British
                qualified IT trainer, who works across this whole region.

                PJS Informatique, Le Pereyrous,
                Musclat   ☎ 05 65 37 06 24
                💻 *www.pgsinformatique.com*
                Computer repairs, upgrades, web design and training
                sessions, run by Peter Smith and covering Cahors, Gourdon,
                Sarlat-la-Canéda and Souillac.

Cahors   INIT Informatique, 100 rue Jean Vidal ☎ 05 65 22 00 81
                💻 *www.init.fr*
                Computer sales and repairs.

Figeac   Informatique Avenir,
                53 Faubourg du Pin   ☎ 05 65 50 31 72
                Computer sales and accessories.

Gourdon	CB System, 15bis avenue Gambetta	☎ 05 65 41 11 3:
	🖥 *www.cbsystem.fr*	
	Repairs, accessories and sales, both new and second-hand.	

Employment Agencies

The main offices of ANPE, the state employment service, in Lot are listed below. There are also smaller offices throughout the department (see 🖥 *www.anpe.fr*).

Cahors	chemin Rural Mont St Cyr	☎ 05 65 20 46 5C
Figeac	8 avenue Carmes	☎ 05 65 50 35 8C
Souillac	avenue Martin Malvy	☎ 05 65 27 07 3C

Communications

Fixed Telephones

General	France Télécom: Dial 1014 or go to
	🖥 *www.francetelecom.fr*
	Local shops are listed below.

Cahors	101 boulevard Gambetta
	Mondays 1.30 to 6.30pm, Tuesdays 9.30am to 12.30pm and 1.30 to 6.30pm.

Figeac	1 place Carnot
	Mondays 1.30 to 6.30pm, Tuesdays 9am to noon and 1.30 to 6.30pm, Saturdays 9am to 5pm.

Internet Access

Cahors	Cyber Café, Les Docks,	
	430 allées des Soupirs	☎ 05 65 22 36 38
	(in the south-west corner of the town inside the loop of the river)	
	Tuesdays to Saturdays 2 to 6pm and Tuesdays, Thursdays and Fridays 8 to 10pm.	
	Bureau Information Jeunesse,	
	20 rue Frédéric Suisse	☎ 05 65 23 95 90
	Mondays to Fridays 9am to noon and 1 to 6pm, Saturdays 9am to noon and 1 to 5pm. Free on Wednesdays and Saturdays.	

Figeac	La Poste, avenue Fernand Pezet	☎ 05 65 34 87 02
	Mondays to Fridays 8.30am to 5.30pm, Saturdays 8.30am to 12.30pm.	

Cyber-K, 5 rue Balène   ☎ 05 65 34 58 03
🖳 *www.cyberk.fr.st*
Mondays to Saturdays 11am to 7pm.

Gourdon   Informatique Internet 46,
16 rue du Majou   ☎ 05 65 41 34 26
Mondays to Saturdays 10am to noon and 3 to 7pm.

St Céré   TiBox Informatique, 15 rue Faidherbe   ☎ 05 65 10 89 08
Tuesdays to Fridays 10am to 12.30pm and 3 to 7pm,
Saturdays 10am to 5pm.

Grand Café, 9 place de la République   ☎ 05 65 38 11 60
(opposite the tourist office)
There's a France Telecom machine inside the cafe that you can
use to access the internet; all you need is a telephone card.

Mobile Telephones

All France Télécom shops (see above) sell mobile phones, as do the following:

Cahors   Espace SFR, 15 place Galdemar   ☎ 05 65 22 21 11
Mondays 2 to 7pm, Tuesdays to Saturdays 9.30am to noon
and 2 to 7pm.

Figeac   Folie Phonie, 3 place Vival   ☎ 05 65 34 02 85
Tuesdays to Saturdays 9.30am to 12.30pm and 2.30 to 6pm.

Gourdon   Euro Protections, 37 avenue Cavaignac   ☎ 05 65 41 43 09
This shop also sells and installs security systems.

Domestic Services

Crèches & Nurseries

Figeac   Halte-Garderie, Place Vival   ☎ 05 65 50 91 76
Pre-school nursery for two- and three-year-olds.

Gourdon   Crèche Parentale & Halte-Garderie,
'Ecoute s'il Joue', 26 avenue Gambetta   ☎ 05 65 41 35 55

Point Information Jeunesse,
place Noël Poujade   ☎ 05 65 41 11 65
Babysitting available for residents of Gourdon and the
surrounding area. Open Mondays, Wednesdays and Fridays
3.30pm to 6.30pm and Thursdays noon to 2pm.

Equipment/Tool Hire

Cahors	Loca-Hydro, Rivière de Regourd	☎ 05 65 22 34 77
Le Vigan	Laho Equipement, ZA Millepoises 🖳 *www.laho.fr* (just east of Gourdon)	☎ 05 65 41 19 47
St Michel- Loubéjou	Locavente, la Croix Blanche (just north of St Céré)	☎ 05 65 38 76 71

Garden Services

General	Julian Urrutia, Bergerac	☎ 05 53 57 98 69

All aspects of tree surgery handled and a mobile sawmill to turn trunks into beams and planks. Fluent English spoken and, although based in Bergerac, covers all of this department.

Cahors	Vert Jardin, 28 rue Feydel	☎ 05 65 20 26 48

Design and maintenance, terraces and watering systems.

Cras	Agri Jardi Lot, Le Mas de Fiaule (central Lot, north of Cahors)	☎ 05 65 36 80 45

Design and garden maintenance.

Launderettes

Cahors	GTI Laverie Pressing, 208 rue Clémenceau Open every day from 7am to 9pm.	☎ 05 65 22 21 98
Figeac	Allô Laverie, rue Ortabadial (opposite the tourist office entrance) Open every day from 6am to 10pm.	☎ 05 65 50 17 12
Gourdon	Laverie du Majou, 27 rue du Majou (below the tourist office) Open every day from 7am to 10pm.	☎ 05 65 41 11 80
St Céré	EcoWash, Rond-Point de l'Europe (set back from the road by Leader Price) Open every day from 7am to 9pm.	☎ 06 07 48 03 37

Septic Tank Services

Cahors	Sanicentre, Combe des Carmes	☎ 05 65 35 05 71
Gourdon	Sanitra Fourrier, 4 boulevard Galiot de Genouillac	☎ 05 65 41 35 52

| St Michel-
Loubéjou | Containers Services Barnabé,
La Croix Blanche | ☎ 05 65 38 55 98 |

Entertainment

This section isn't intended to be a definitive guide but gives a wide range of ideas for the department. Prices and opening hours were correct at the time of publication, but it's best to check before travelling long distances.

Cinemas

| Cahors | Cinéma le Quercy, 871 rue Emile Zola | ☎ 05 65 22 20 05 |

Cinéma ABC, 24 rue des Augustins   ☎ 05 65 35 03 11
This cinema is mainly for art and cultural films.

| Figeac | Cinéma Charles Boyer,
2 boulevard Pasteur
🖳 *www.cculturel.figeac.free.fr* | ☎ 05 65 34 24 78 |

| Gourdon | Le Bourian, boulevard des Martyrs | |

programme info ☎ 08 92 68 06 14

| St Céré | MJC, 170 quai A. Salesse | ☎ 05 65 10 83 33 |

English Books

Cahors   France-Grande Bretagne, Bureau no. 22,
Espace Clement Marot, place Bessières   ☎ 05 65 22 68 44
This group has an English library available for members, open
Wednesday and Saturday mornings 11am to 1pm.

Meyrals   Association Culturelle Internationale de
Périgord, Carmensac Haut   ☎ 05 53 30 30 23
✉ *emboiling@wanadoo.fr*
(west of Sarlat-la-Canéda in Dordogne, signposted from the
D48 between St Cyprien and Les Eyzies)
This is an English library open Monday afternoons from 2 to
4pm and Wednesday mornings from 10am to noon (hours may
be extended in the future). You need to be a member of the
Association Culturelle Internationale de Périgord to use the
library. Membership costs €20 per year for a family or €15 per
person. There's an additional library membership fee of €15
per family or €10 per person.

Montcuq   Chimera, 13 rue Faubourg St Privat   ☎ 05 65 22 97 01
(south-west of Cahors)

This shop, run by a British lady, deals in second-hand English and French books.

Souillac   O'Leary's, 2 avenue Jean Jaurès   ☎ 05 65 37 09 42
(north-east of Gourdon)
This library operates an English book exchange system.

There are English-language books at all the following public libraries:

	Mon	Tue	Wed	Thu	Fri	Sat
Cahors 185 avenue Jean-Jaurès ☎ 05 65 20 38 50	closed	1.30–6.00	10.00–6.00	1.30–6.00	1.30–6.00	10.00–6.00
Figeac 2 boulevard Pasteur ☎ 05 53 07 59 08	2.30–6.30	4.30–6.30	10.00–12.00 2.30–6.30	2.30–6.30	2.30–6.30	10.00–12.00 2.30–5.30*
Gourdon Place Noël Poujade ☎ 05 65 41 30 92	closed	10.00–12.00 2.00–5.00	10.00–12.00 2.00–5.00	closed	3.00–6.00	10.00–4.00
St Céré Quai Jules Ferry ☎ 05 65 38 18 14	1.30–6.30	1.30–6.30	9.30–12.00 1.30–6.30	closed	4.30–6.30	9.30–1.00 2.00–4.00

* closed on Saturday afternoons in the summer

Festivals

There are many festivals in this department, and just a small selection is detailed here. Festivals are annual unless otherwise stated.

March/April   Figeac
Le Chainon Manquant   ☎ 05 63 04 92 97
Held over five days at the end of March and beginning of April and comprising over 60 shows in various venues.

May/June   Rocamadour
Fête des Fromages Fermiers   ☎ 05 65 33 22 00
A huge cheese fair.

July   Cahors
Cahors Blues Festival   ☎ 05 65 35 99 99
The last two weeks of July.

July/August   Figeac
Festival de Théâtre   ☎ 05 65 34 24 78

Prayssac
Festival Mondial de Folklore ☎ 05 65 22 40 57

Rocamadour
Les Mercredis de Rocamadour ☎ 05 65 33 22 00
Open-air concerts and films every Wednesday.

August Bélaye
Rencontres de Violoncelle de Bélaye ☎ 05 65 29 18 75
Concerts and seminars featuring the cello in the churches
in and around Bélaye for seven days at the beginning
of August.

Gindou
Recontres Cinématographiques de
Gindou ☎ 05 65 22 89 99
An outdoor film festival, held around the third week of August.

Gourdon
Grande Fête Médiévale ☎ 05 65 27 52 50
The first weekend in August.

Puy-l'Evêque ☎ 05 65 23 22 21
An independent wine-makers' fair.

Theatres

Cahors Théâtre de Cahors,
place François Mitterrand ☎ 05 65 20 88 60
(in the centre of town by the tourist office)

Video/DVD Hire

Cahors Vidéo Star 46, 48 avenue Anatole de
Monzie, St Georges ☎ 05 65 30 21 94
(south of the river, on the main road south towards Toulouse)
Mondays 3.30pm to 8pm, Tuesdays 10.30am to 12.30pm and
3.30 to 9pm, Wednesdays and Saturdays 10.30am to 12.30pm
and 3 to 8.30pm, Thursdays and Fridays 10.30am to 12.30pm
and 3.30 to 8.30pm, Sundays 4 to 8.30pm.

Figeac Accès Vidéo,
boulevard de Juskiewenski ☎ 06 16 12 75 55
DVD and video dispenser outside the shop, which is only open
for enquiries 6 to 7pm on Fridays.

Gourdon Vidéo Club,
avenue Gustave Larroumet ☎ 05 65 41 33 25

St Céré	Antoine Musique, 15 rue Pasteur	☎ 05 65 38 14 39

Open Tuesdays to Saturdays 9.30am to12.30pm and
2.30 to 8pm.
There's also an external dispenser for DVDs and videos.

Leisure Activities

This section isn't intended to be a definitive guide but gives a wide range
of ideas for the department. Prices and opening hours were correct at the
time of publication, but it's best to check before travelling long distances.

Art Classes

Cahors	Stage Peinture au Couteau	☎ 06 14 07 60 70

Courses in oils and acrylics.

Dessin Aquarelle Mandalas,
71 rue des Mirepoises   ☎ 05 65 35 96 05
Lessons and courses in watercolours.

| Gourdon | Centre de Loisirs, MJC,
place Noël Poujade | ☎ 05 65 41 11 65 |
|---|---|---|

✉ mjc.gourdon@wanadoo.fr
Drawing and painting classes, including watercolours
and oils.

St Céré	Quai A. Salesse	☎ 05 65 10 83 33

Sewing classes on Monday afternoons. Patchwork and
embroidery classes Tuesdays and Wednesdays. Painting on
silk, two Fridays a month. Pottery classes Tuesday evenings
and Thursday afternoons.

Bike Hire

| Figeac | Larroque et Fils,
1 avenue Georges Pompidou | ☎ 05 65 34 10 28 |
|---|---|---|

Open Mondays to Saturdays 8am to noon and 2 to 6pm.

Gourdon	Nature Evasion, 73 avenue Cavaignac	☎ 05 65 37 45 12

Hire, sale and repair of bicycles.

Puy-l'Evêque	Loca-Lot, Le Bourg	☎ 05 65 36 59 22

🖥 www.loca-lot.fr.st
(west of Cahors in the direction of Fumel)
Open every day from April to the end of September.

St Céré	St Chamant, rue Faidherbe	☎ 05 65 38 03 23

Hire of both traditional and mountain bikes.

Boat, Train & Wagon Rides

Boat Trips

Bouzies
Lot-Navigation   ☎ 05 65 24 32 20
Holiday boats for hire by the week. Open 8am to noon and
2 to 7pm.

Cahors
Babou Marine, Port St Mary   ☎ 05 65 30 08 99
🖳 *www.baboulene-jean.fr*
Hire of holiday cruisers for 2 to 12 people with access to 65km
(45mi) of navigable waterways.

Les Croisières Fénelon   ☎ 05 65 30 16 55
✉ *bateaufenelon@wanadoo.fr*
Various cruises available, including a full-day trip starting at
9.30am and consisting of a short tour of the town followed by a
cruise departing from Port Bullier, lunch and a visit to a
vineyard with a tasting at Parnac. Open all year.

Cajarc
Le Schmilblic, Mas de Gratufie   ☎ 06 03 03 08 04
Sightseeing trips aboard 'Le Schmilblic'. One trip every
afternoon during the last week of June and first week of
September, two or more trips every afternoon in July
and August.

Douelle
Crown Blue Line, Le Moulinat   ☎ 05 65 20 08 79
🖳 *www.crownblueline.com*
Week-long hire of holiday cruisers for two to ten people from
Easter to 1st November. Open Monday to Saturday 8.30am to
6pm. Departures are on Fridays and Saturdays.

Train Rides

Cahors
Le Petit Train de Cahors,
allée des Soupirs   ☎ 05 65 30 16 55
This 'train' drives through the town giving a commentary as
you pass places of interest. Operates from 1st April to
30th September.

Quercy Rail, place de la Gare   ☎ 05 65 23 94 72
✉ rb.murat@wanadoo.fr
Journeys along the picturesque Lot valley by rail.
Booking recommended.

Figeac
Petit Train Touristique de Figeac   ☎ 05 65 34 06 25
This 'train' travels around the streets of the town in July and
August with a 45-minute commentary.

Martel
Chemin de Fer Touristique du
Haut Quercy, la Gare   ☎ 05 65 37 35 81

A journey that follows the Dordogne valley on the old railway line hewn out of the cliff face, 80m above the river. Each trip is from Martel to Saint Denis and lasts a maximum of one and half hours. Trips are dependent on the weather and may have to be modified for technical reasons.

Wagon Rides

Castel-Aynac	Château d'Aynac	☎ 05 65 11 08 02

🖳 *www.castel-aynac.fr*
Horse-drawn wagons/caravans for hire by the week from March to November. Wagons are fully equipped wagons and travel at around four miles per hour – relaxation compulsory.

Bonsai

Cahors	Bonsaï Lotois, Bureau No.17,	
	Espace Clément Marot, place Bessières	☎ 05 65 22 27 07

Meetings on the second Sunday of the month. Contact Mr Montagne.

Boules & Pétanque

Cahors	Cahors Sport Boules, Boulodrome Couvert, Chemin de Peyrolis	☎ 05 65 35 54 73
Figeac	Pétanque Figeacoise, Boulodrome Jean Pramil	☎ 05 65 34 32 16

At the Londieu complex, practice Fridays 5.30 to 7pm.

Gourdon	Boule Gourdonnaise	☎ 05 65 41 03 97
St Céré	Gymnase, quai A. Salesses	☎ 05 65 38 31 12

Contact Mr St Chamand.

Bridge

Cahors	Bridge Club de Cahors, Bureau No.29, Espace Clément Marot, place Bessières	☎ 05 65 22 08 82

Mondays, Wednesdays and Fridays 2.15 to 6.15pm, Tuesdays and Saturdays 3 to 6pm and Thursdays 2 to 6pm.

Figeac	Club de Figeac, Ceint d'Eau	☎ 05 65 80 81 15

(a small village west of Figeac)
Regular tournaments held in the village school.

Gourdon	Club de Bridge de Gourdon	☎ 05 65 41 12 73
St Céré	Bridge Club de St Céré, Quai A. Salesse	☎ 05 65 10 83 33

Mondays and Thursdays 2.30 to 6pm.

Children's Activity Clubs

Figeac   Centre de Loisirs, Place Vival   ☎ 05 65 50 91 76
               Activities in the school holidays for children from 4 to 13.

Gourdon   Centre de Loisirs, MJC,
               place Noël Poujade   ☎ 05 65 41 11 65
               ✉ *mjc.gourdon@wanadoo.fr*
               Activities and trips for children from 4 to 17 on Wednesdays,
               Saturdays and school holidays.

St Céré   Centre de Loisirs, Ecole Soulhol,
               quai A. Salesses   ☎ 05 65 38 00 26
               Activities for schoolchildren Wednesdays and school holidays
               (excluding summer).

               Club des Petits Musclés, Gymnase,
               quai A. Salesses   ☎ 06 72 76 45 53
               Physical activity for young children, 10am to 10.45am for three
               to four-year-olds, 11am to noon for five to six-year-olds.

Circus Skills

Flaugnac   Ecole de Cirque, Carré Brune,
               Daudusson   ☎ 05 65 21 84 02

Dancing

Cahors   Cahors Danse Jazz, 9 impasse Séguier   ☎ 05 65 53 14 79
               Contact Mme Agasse.

               Association Rockercie, La Maison du
               Citoyen, avenue Maryse Bastié   ☎ 06 87 09 82 37
               Introductory sessions and courses in country dancing.

Figeac   Association Modern'Jazz, Espace F.
               Mitterrand, rue de Grial   ☎ 05 65 34 39 11
               Lessons Tuesday evenings and Saturdays. Minimum age five.

               Centre des Ateliers de Danse, Centre
               Culturel, boulevard Pasteur   ☎ 05 65 34 15 11
               Ballet, jazz and contemporary dance.

Gourdon   Centre de Loisirs, MJC,
               place Noël Poujade   ☎ 05 65 41 11 65
               ✉ *mjc.gourdon@wanadoo.fr*
               Contemporary, traditional and jazz classes for all ages.

St Céré   Danse Modern Jazz, MJC,
               quai A. Salesse   ☎ 05 65 10 83 33

Classes for children and adults, including tap dancing and
ballet, on various days.

Danse Contemporaine,
Gymnase de St Céré   ☎ 05 65 38 26 20
Lessons for children and adults.

Drama

Gourdon   Centre de Loisirs, MJC,
                 place Noël Poujade   ☎ 05 65 41 11 65
                 ✉ mjc.gourdon@wanadoo.fr
                 Theatrical workshops held throughout the week for different
                 age groups, from six-year-olds to adults.

St Céré   MJC, quai A. Salesse.   ☎ 05 65 10 83 33
                 Drama classes for children and adults: children on
                 Wednesdays from 2pm; adults on Thursdays at 9pm. €12 per
                 month or €30 per term.

Gyms & Health Clubs

Cahors   Mega Gym, 291 rue Anatole France   ☎ 05 65 35 17 13
                 Gym, cardio training, weights and fitness classes. Mondays,
                 Tuesdays, Thursdays and Fridays 10am to 1.30pm and 5 to
                 8.45pm, Wednesdays noon to 1.30pm and 5 to 8.45pm,
                 Saturdays 10am to 12.30pm.

Figeac   Haltéro Club Figeacois, Salle Occitane,
                 Espace François Mitterrand,
                 place Renaud   ☎ 05 65 34 68 80
                 Weights, sauna and cardio training. Open Mondays 11.30am to
                 8pm, Tuesdays, Fridays and Saturdays 9am to 8pm,
                 Wednesdays 9am to 7pm, Thursdays 10am to 2pm and
                 3 to 8pm.

                 Figeac Forme, Espace François
                 Mitterrand, place Renaud   ☎ 05 65 34 47 41
                 A series of fitness classes, including gym and step, held
                 throughout the week.

St Céré   Weight-Lifting, MJC, quai A. Salesse   ☎ 05 65 10 83 33
                 Thursday and Saturday evenings.

Karting & Quad Bikes

Castenau   Montratier Rando Quads 46,
                 Les Etangs du Quercy   ☎ 05 65 21 94 91
                 (directly south of Cahors)

Practice area and over 20km (14mi) of track. Guides available, and courses for children and adults. Booking necessary. Picnic area on site.

Model Clubs

Cahors   Cahors Model Club, bar 'Le Paris',
            107 boulevard Léon Gambetta   ☎ 05 65 35 59 82
            Model aeroplane club. Contact Mr Dutrieux.

Music

Figeac   Fa Si La, 12 avenue Fernand Pezet   ☎ 06 86 00 12 10
            Music school offering lessons for all ages from five years,
            including piano, organ, synthesizer and music theory.

Gourdon   Centre de Loisirs, MJC,
            place Noël Poujade   ☎ 05 65 41 11 65
            ✉ mjc.gourdon@wanadoo.fr
            Various instruments, including guitar and piano.

            Ecole de Musique,
            85 boulevard Galiot de Genouilhac   ☎ 05 65 41 42 77
            Organ, piano and synthesizer.

Off-Roading

Puy l'Evêque   Loca-Lot, Le Bourg   ☎ 05 65 36 59 22
            🖳 www.loca-lot.fr.st
            (west of Cahors in the direction of Fumel)
            Outings in 4x4s, from three hours to all day. Open every day
            from the beginning of April to the end of the September.

Paint Ball

Vézac   New Century Games,
            Combe-de-la-Serre   ☎ 06 76 47 75 39
            Open all year: June to September every day; rest of the year
            by appointment. Minimum age 12.

Photography

Cahors   Donner à Voir, Espace Clement Marot,
            Place Bessières   ☎ 05 65 22 20 07
            Contact Mr Spinosa.

Gourdon   Centre de Loisirs, MJC,
            place Noël Poujade   ☎ 05 65 41 11 65
            ✉ mjc.gourdon@wanadoo.fr
            Classes in digital photography and developing.

Pottery

Gourdon	Centre de Loisirs, MJC,	
	place Noël Poujade	☎ 05 65 41 11 65

✉ *mjc.gourdon@wanadoo.fr*
Pottery classes for adults Mondays 7.15 to 9.15pm and for children Wednesdays 2 to 3.15pm.

Roller Skating

Gourdon	Club de Roller, place Noël Poujade	☎ 05 65 41 11 65

✉ *mjc.gourdon@wanadoo.fr*

Valroufie	Club 'Skate Roller'	☎ 06 81 47 07 24

(north-east of Cahors)
Contact Mr Monells for venues and meetings.

Social Groups

Cahors	Cahors Accueil AVF, Bureau No.5,	
	Espace Clément Marot, place Bessières	☎ 05 65 22 28 73

A support group that organises a variety of activities and events for newcomers to Cahors and the surrounding area. Open Mondays 4 to 6pm and Thursdays 2.30 to 5pm.

France-Grande Bretagne, Bureau No.22,
Espace Clément Marot, place Bessières   ☎ 05 65 22 68 44
This group, which has both French and English members, aims to help English-speaking newcomers integrate into the French way of life. There's an English library available to members and French language workshops. Contact Mrs Smith for more information.

Gourdon	Rotary Club de Gourdon	☎ 05 65 41 16 88

Stamp Collecting

Cahors	Union Philatélique du Quercy, Bureau No.27,	
	Espace Clément Marot, Place Bessières	☎ 05 65 22 54 56

Sundays 10am to noon.

St Céré	Quai A. Salesse.	☎ 05 65 10 83 33

Meetings on the third Sunday of each month 10 to 11am.

Tree Climbing

Pradines	Cap Nature	☎ 05 65 22 25 12

🖳 *www.capnature46.com*
(just north-west of Cahors)

Explore the tree canopy on monkey bridges, rope ladders and aerial runways. Full safety equipment provided. Separate course for children. Booking recommended.

Walking & Rambling

Figeac | Randopattes de Figeac | ☎ 05 65 34 44 20
Weekly walks organised both mid-week and weekends. Contact Mr Cournac

St Céré | Around the area of St Céré are 480km (300mi) of paths open to walkers. Circuits range from 3 to 26km (2 to 16mi) and are divided into four categories. Details from the tourist office.

Randonnée Pédestre | ☎ 05 65 10 83 33
Organised walks on the first and third Thursdays and Sundays of the month.

Yoga

Gourdon | Centre de Loisirs, MJC,
place Noël Poujade | ☎ 05 65 41 11 65
✉ *mjc.gourdon@wanadoo.fr*
Both Hata and Nidra yoga.

St Céré | l'Usine, rue du Docteur Roux | ☎ 05 65 38 37 46
Beginners Mondays 6.30pm, gentle class Tuesdays 10am and advanced class Tuesdays 7.30pm. Contact Mr Gruyer.

Medical Facilities & Services

Ambulances

In the event of a medical emergency dial 15.

Cahors | ☎ 05 65 22 25 35
Figeac | ☎ 05 65 34 10 10
Gourdon | ☎ 05 65 41 02 68
St Céré | ☎ 05 65 10 80 80

Chiropractors

Eymet | Simon Pullen, 18 boulevard National | ☎ 05 53 23 32 21
(Eymet is on the southern border of Dordogne, close to Lot)
This is an English-speaking chiropractor.

Doctors

English-speakers may like to contact the following doctors:

Bretenoux	Dr Heredia, avenue Libération, Bretenoux (just north of St Céré)	☎ 05 65 38 43 55
Cahors	Dr Solignac, 94 rue Georges Clémenceau	☎ 05 65 22 15 34
Figeac	Dr Roudié, 4 place Edmond Michelet	☎ 05 65 34 11 41
Gourdon	Dr Tirand, La Clède (behind the hospital)	☎ 05 65 41 30 37

Dentists

English-speakers may like to contact the following dentists:

Cahors	Cabinet Dentaire, 22 boulevard Gambetta	☎ 05 65 22 32 87
Figeac	Dr Clarac, 14 chemin Miattes	☎ 05 65 34 13 47
St Céré	Cabinet Dentaire, 8 boulevard Léon Gambetta	☎ 05 65 38 13 34

Gendarmeries

Cahors	rue Hortes	☎ 05 65 35 17 17
Figeac	route de Cadrieu	☎ 05 65 40 65 17
Gourdon	boulevard de la Madeleine	☎ 05 65 41 73 50
St Céré	rue Faidherbe	☎ 05 65 38 00 17

Health Authority

General	CRAM Midi-Pyrénées, rue Georges Vivent, Toulouse ☎ 05 62 14 28 28 💻 *www.cram-midipyrenees.fr* This is the regional office for the Midi-Pyrénées and is open Mondays to Fridays 8am to 5pm.
Cahors	190 quai Eugène Cavaignac ☎ 05 65 22 20 63 This is the departmental office. Open Wednesdays 8.30am to 9.30am (no appointment necessary), Wednesdays 9.30am to noon and the second Tuesday and third Thursday morning of each month (by appointment).

| Figeac | CRAM, 22 rue Gaumont – place de l'Estang | ☎ 05 65 34 57 95 |

This office is open every Thursday 9 to 10am (no appointment necessary) and 10am to noon (by appointment).

| Gourdon | Centre Médico-Social, place Jacques Chapou | ☎ 05 65 22 20 63 |

There's a CRAM representative here the first Tuesday of each month (no appointment necessary) and in the morning of the third Thursday of each month (by appointment).

| St Céré | Centre Médico-Social, place Mercadial | ☎ 05 65 34 57 95 |

There's a CRAM representative here the fourth Wednesday morning of each month (by appointment).

Hospitals

All these hospitals have an emergency department:

Cahors	Centre Hospitalier, 335 rue Prés Wilson	☎ 05 65 20 50 50
Figeac	Centre Hospitalier, rue des Maquisards	☎ 05 65 50 65 50
Gourdon	Hospital de Gourdon, avenue Pasteur	☎ 05 65 27 65 27
St Céré	Avenue Docteur Roux, Saint Céré	☎ 05 65 10 40 00

Motoring

Breakers' Yards

| Laburgade | Jean-Marie Faurie Sarl, D10 (south of Cahors) | ☎ 05 65 31 62 62 |
| Montdoumerc | Récupération Services Auto Rochis, RN20 (south of Cahors) | ☎ 05 65 24 31 70 |

Car Dealers

Cahors	Audi/VW, CAP Sud Autos, route de Toulouse	☎ 05 65 22 54 00
	Citroën, Citroën Cahors, route de Toulouse	☎ 05 65 35 27 61
	Ford, Garage Ford, route de Toulouse	☎ 05 65 20 48 48

	Mazda, Polygone Auto, route de Toulouse	☎ 05 65 23 93 00
	Mercedes, Socadia, route de Toulouse	☎ 05 65 35 77 00
	Nissan, Laudis Autos, 1012 avenue Anatole de Monzie	☎ 05 65 53 23 23
	Peugeot, GGB Concess, route de Toulouse	☎ 05 65 35 02 02
	Renault, D Didier Autos, route de Toulouse	☎ 05 65 35 15 95
	Rover, Oustric, rue de Villefranche	☎ 05 65 22 50 06
	Toyota, Laville, 853 avenue Anatole de Monzie	☎ 05 65 22 11 15
Figeac	Audi, Réveillac, avenue de Cahors	☎ 05 65 34 18 78
	Citroën, P Bresson, avenue de Cahors	☎ 05 65 50 30 30
	Fiat, Forza Auto, avenue Rodez	☎ 05 65 34 77 99
	Peugeot, Garage Peugeot, 12 avenue Aurillac	☎ 05 65 34 01 56
	Renault, Rudelle et Fabre, route de Cahors, Saint Georges	☎ 05 65 34 00 23
	Vauxhall/Opel, Sadal Concess, 26 avenue Joseph Loubet	☎ 05 65 14 02 14
	VW, Réveillac, avenue de Cahors	☎ 05 65 34 18 78
Gourdon	Citroën, Espace Autos, route de Fumel	☎ 05 65 41 12 03
	Ford, Garage Poly Bernard, Grimardet	☎ 05 65 41 15 65
	Peugeot, Robert Navarre Auto, route de Fumel	☎ 05 65 41 17 62
	Renault, D Didier, route du Vigan	☎ 05 65 27 06 06
St Céré	Audi, Garage Payrot, 401 avenue Anatole de Monzie	☎ 05 65 38 01 07

	Citroën, Garage Delpech, la Croix Blanche, St Michel-Loubéjou	☎ 05 65 38 11 88
	Mercedes, Garage Payrot, 401 avenue Anatole de Monzie	☎ 05 65 38 01 07
	Peugeot, Bretenoux Autos, route St Céré, Bretenoux	☎ 05 65 38 45 60
	Renault, Garage Renault, avenue Anatole de Monzie	☎ 05 65 38 20 10
	VW, Garage Payrot, 401 avenue Anatole de Monzie	☎ 05 65 38 01 07

Tyre/Exhaust Centres

Cahors	Speedy, 407 avenue Beyne	☎ 05 65 21 06 23
Figeac	Figeac Pneus, 41 Faubourg du Pin	☎ 05 65 34 64 64
Gourdon	Garrigue, route de Salviac	☎ 05 65 41 00 71
St Céré	Formule 1, avenue Anatole de Monzie	☎ 05 65 10 88 80

Pets

Dog Training

Lacapelle-Marival	Laisse et Collier, Pech Rouge (north-west of Figeac)	☎ 05 65 40 42 03

Farriers

General	Didier Rouillon, le Bourg, Theminettes (north-west of Figeac)	☎ 05 65 40 89 00
	Marc Soulié, la Gravette, Cahors	☎ 05 65 31 62 11
	Stéphane Marty, Foncène, Cénac et St Julien (south-east Dordogne, near Lot border)	☎ 05 53 28 95 25

Horse Dentists

Vets don't deal with teeth rasping and there are specialist equine dentists. You need to telephone in advance to be booked onto the next circuit.

General	Christian Frémy, 19 boulevard Horizon, Penne d'Agenais ☎ 05 53 41 73 78
	(east of Villeneuve-sur-Lot in Dordogne)

Kennels & Catteries

Creysse	Pension et Toilettage La Roque, 21 La Roque ☎ 05 53 23 46 14
	(east of Bergerac in Dordogne) Kennels and cattery.

Lacapelle-Marival	Laisse et Collier, Pech Rouge ☎ 05 65 40 42 03
	(north-west of Figeac) Kennels only.

Pet Parlours

Cahors	Salon de Toilettage, 4 place Champollion ☎ 05 65 35 96 84
	Open all day during the week.

Figeac	La Belle & Le Clochard, 26 boulevard de Juskiewenski ☎ 05 65 14 02 20

Gourdon	Gourdon C'Ouaf, 14 avenue Léon Gambetta ☎ 05 65 41 66 36
	Open Tuesdays to Saturdays.

St Céré	Toilettage A Tout Poil, 12 rue Pasteur ☎ 05 65 38 08 86

Riding Equipment

Cahors	Siramon Sellerie, 2 rue St James ☎ 05 65 35 16 32
	(near the covered market in the centre of town)

St Céré	Siramon Sellerie, rue Jean de la Barrière ☎ 05 65 38 47 06
	(in the old bus depot 'Delbos')

SPA

Figeac	Association de Sauvegarde des Animaux, Nayrac ☎ 05 65 34 19 07

Veterinary Clinics

Cahors	Clinique Vétérinaire, avenue Beyne ☎ 05 65 35 04 78
	(south of the river – a continuation of avenue Anatole de Monzie)

Figeac	Clinique Vétérinaire, 9bis avenue Pierre Curie ☎ 05 65 34 24 86

Gourdon	Clinique Vétérinaire, route de Salviac	☎ 05 65 41 01 12
St Céré	Dr Patrick Garapin, avenue Europe	☎ 05 65 38 39 22

Places To Visit

This section isn't intended to be a definitive guide but gives a wide range of ideas for the department. Prices and opening hours were correct at the time of publication, but it's best to check before travelling long distances.

Animal Parks & Aquariums

Gramat   Parc Animalier, route de Cajarc   ☎ 05 65 38 81 22
            🖥 *www.gramat-parc-animalier.com*
            Over 150 species and 1,000 animals in this 40ha (100-acre)
            park, including a variety of wild, beautiful and rare animals.
            Drinks and snacks are available and there's a picnic area.
            Open April to the end of September 9.30am to 7pm; rest of the
            year 2 to 6pm. Adults €7.50, children €4.50.

Martel   Reptiland, RN140   ☎ 05 65 37 41 00
            🖥 *www.reptiland.fr*
            Nearly 100 species, including lizards, snakes, tortoise,
            crocodiles, scorpions and spiders. Open February to the end of
            June and September to the end of December 10am to noon
            and 2 to 6pm, closed Mondays; July and August 10am to 6pm
            every day. Adults €6.50, children €4.

Rocamadour La Forêt des Singes, l'Hospitalet   ☎ 05 65 33 62 72
            🖥 *www.la-foret-des-singes.com*
            Home to over 130 monkeys, which roam freely in a
            natural park. You can walk through this park and guides
            provide information about the monkeys. There's a
            restaurant/cafe and picnic area. Open 1st April to 30th
            June and the whole of September 10am to noon and 1 to 6pm
            every day; July and August 10am to 6pm every day; October
            to mid-November 10am to noon and 1 to 5pm on
            Sundays, bank holidays and school holidays.
            Adults €6.50, children €4.

            Le Rocher des Aigles   ☎ 05 65 33 65 45
            This eagle centre displays rare species in enclosures
            making it possible for visitors to discover the birds of prey
            in a reconstructed but 'natural' environment. Demonstrations
            include vultures flying up to 1,000m and returning in nose-dives
            at the command of their trainers. Open daily April to June
            and September 2 to 6pm; July and August noon to 6pm;
            October 2 to 4pm. Adults €6.50, children €4.50.

Beaches & Water Parks

Many towns and villages have a *plan d'eau*, which can be a lake or riverside location. It may be just for fishing and picnics or there may be facilities such as a beach, playground and crazy golf.

Bétaille-en-Quercy	Parc Aquatique – la Saule ☎ 05 65 32 55 75 This water park has a playground, lifeguards, pools for toddlers and inflatables. Cafe and pizza bar open lunchtimes and evenings. Open every day mid-June to mid-September 11am to 8pm. Adults €4.80, under 12s €4.10.	
Cahors	l'Archipel, quai Ludo Rollès ☎ 05 65 35 05 86 Outdoor pool with toboggan, water cannons and various games. Open every day from mid-June to mid-October 11am to 8pm.	
Figeac	Domaine du Surgié ☎ 05 65 34 59 00 This lake has fishing, open spaces and a playground. There's a swimming pool with toboggan and paddling pool and in July and August there's crazy golf, boat hire, trampolines and bouncy castles. Open April to June and September 2 to 7pm; July and August 11am to 10pm.	
Padirac	Loisirs - Espace Aquatique ☎ 05 65 33 45 15 A thousand square metres of swimming pool and a 150m of water chutes plus playground, volleyball court, trampolines, pétanque, pizza and snack bar and picnic area. Open July and August every day from 11am to 8pm. Under three-year-olds free, others €4.	
Sénaillac-Latronquière	Le Lac du Tolerme ☎ 05 65 40 31 26 A 38ha (95-acre) lake with windsurfing, fishing, beach, playground, paths around the lake, picnic areas, barbecues, pedalos, rowing boats, canoes and sailing boats. There's a small admission fee.	
Souillac	Quercyland Copeyre ☎ 05 65 32 72 61 Six pools for babies to adults plus trampolines, water chutes, crazy golf, bouncy castles, climbing wall, volleyball court and electronic games. Open every day from May to September 11am to 8pm. €5 entrance fee.	

Caves

Cabrerets	Grottes de Pech-Merle ☎ 05 65 31 27 05 🖳 *www.pechmerle.com* These caves contain many prehistoric drawings, and at the museum you can see a film about the cave art of the region. Open from the beginning of June to the beginning of November.	

Lacave   **Grottes de Lacave**   ☎ 05 65 37 87 03
💻 *www.grottes-de-lacave.com*
There are 12 chambers to visit once you've entered by electric train, one chamber being 60m (200ft) high. There are also lakes and remarkable visual effects. The visit takes around 75 minutes. Open March and October 10am to noon and 2 to 5pm; April to June 9.30am to noon and 2 to 6pm; July 9.30am to 12.30pm and 1.30 to 6pm; 1st to 25th August 9.30am to 6.30pm; 26th August to 30th September 9.30am to noon and 2 to 5.30pm. Adults €7, children from 5 to 14 €4.80.

Padirac   **Gouffre de Padirac**   ☎ 05 65 33 64 56
💻 *www.gouffre-de-padirac.com*
There's an underground river leading to a huge cavern with a lake and another cave with a 94m (300ft) high arched ceiling. The visit lasts around 90 minutes. Outside is a picnic area, playground and restaurant. Open April to the first week in July and all of September 9am to noon and 2 to 6pm; the remainder of July 9am to 6pm; August 8.30am to 6.30pm; beginning to second Sunday of October 9am to noon and 2 to 5pm. Adults €8, 6 to 12-year-olds €5.20.

Rocamadour   **Grotte Préhistorique des Merveilles**   ☎ 05 65 33 67 92
💻 *www.grotte-des-merveilles.com*
Only 100m from the tourist office are these rock formations and works of art painted nearly 20,000 years ago. The visit lasts around 35 minutes. April to June 10am to noon and 2 to 6pm; July and August 9am to 7pm; September to the end of the November holidays, 10am to noon and 2 to 6pm.

St Céré   **Les Grottes de Presque,**
route de Padirac   ☎ 05 65 38 07 44
💻 *www.grottesdepresque.com*
The visit to these caves last around 40 minutes through the well lit cave network containing many fragile and impressive rock formations, some 10m high. Open mid-February to the end of June and all of September 9.30am to noon and 2 to 6pm; July and August 9.30am to 6.30pm; October to mid-November 10am to noon and 2 to 5pm. Adults €6, 7 to 11-year-olds €3.

Châteaux

Assier   **Château d'Assier**   ☎ 05 65 40 40 99
Built around 1530, the buildings originally formed an enormous quadrangle richly decorated with carvings. Only the west wing remains, the decoration of which includes emblems, military scenes and scenes from the life of Hercules. Open all year except Tuesdays and bank holidays: January to April 10am to 12.30pm and 2 to 5.30pm; May to the first weekend in September 10am to 12.30pm and 2 to 6.45pm; the second week in September to December 10am to 12.30pm and 2 to 5.30pm. Adults €5, under 18s free.

Cenevières   Château de Cenevières   ☎ 05 65 31 27 33
A château dating from the 13th to the 16th century with a keep, gallery, furniture, tapestries and paintings from the end of the 16th century. Open from Easter to 1st November every day 10am to noon and 2 to 6pm (October only 2 to 5pm).

Cieurac   Château de Cieurac   ☎ 05 65 31 64 28
A 15th century château with a remarkable staircase, furnished rooms, tapestries, a French garden and a windmill. Open all of June and mid-September to 1st November weekends 2 to 6.30pm; July to mid-September every day 2 to 6.30pm.

Lacapelle-   Château de Lacapelle-Marival   ☎ 05 65 40 80 24
Marival   A medieval castle that was a fortress in the 13th century with a sentry walk and four corner watch towers. An enormous square keep was added in the 15th century and there are frescoes on the wall of the Great Hall.

Larroque-   Château de Larroque-Toirac   ☎ 06 12 37 48 39
Toirac   Taken several times by the English in the 14th century, this castle overlooks the Lot valley and has retained its entire medieval defensive system, as well as fine 15th century fireplaces and 16th century frescoes. There are also the remains of a troglodyte cave dwelling in the cliffs behind the castle and exotic plants in the terraced gardens. Open from the second week in July to mid-September every day from 10am to noon and 2 to 6pm; mid-June to mid-October every day for groups only by appointment.

Prudhomat   Château de Castelnau-Bretenoux   ☎ 05 65 10 98 00
Construction of the château was started in the 12th century with a dungeon and living quarters. In the late 19th century it was refurbished and now houses major collections of furniture and works of art from the Middle Ages to the 18th century. There's a guided tour, exhibitions and educational activities. Open January to April and September to December 10am to 12.30pm and 2 to 5.30pm (closed Tuesdays and bank holidays); May and June 9.30am to 12.30pm and 2 to 6.30pm (closed Tuesdays); July and August 9.30am to 7pm every day. Adults €6.10, under 18s free.

St Jean-   Château de Montal   ☎ 05 65 38 13 72
Lespinasse   A Renaissance château with architecture and sculptures of superb quality as well as a monumental staircase, tapestries and furniture from the 16th and 17th centuries. Open from the end of March to 1st November every day (except Saturdays) 9.30am to noon and 2.30 to 6pm. Adults €5, under 15s €2.50.

Mills

Lunan   Moulin de Seyrignac   ☎ 05 65 34 48 32
A 15th century windmill in full working order.

Open June to September every day from 10am to noon and
3 to 7pm; rest of the year by appointment. Adults €2.30,
children €1.70.

Martel   Moulin du Lac de Diane,
                route de Bretenoux   ☎ 05 65 37 40 69
                A walnut oil mill that uses a hydraulic press to crush the nuts.
                Open from Easter to mid-September Tuesdays to Sundays 2 to
                5.30pm. Demonstrations on Thursday and Saturday afternoons
                in July and August; the rest of the year by appointment.

Mayrinhac-   Moulin de Vergnoulet   ☎ 05 65 38 77 05
Lentour   This watermill is situated on the Alzou. Three pairs of
                grindstones crush wheat, maize and buckwheat. Open every
                Tuesday all year round by appointment.

Miscellaneous

Cahors   Cloître Chapelle St Gausbert,
                Cathédrale St Etienne   ☎ 05 65 53 20 65
                This cathedral was built between the 11th and 17th centuries
                and visits are available to both the cathedral and the St
                Gausbert chapel, which has 15th century murals. Open June to
                September Mondays to Saturdays 10am to 12.30pm and 3 to
                6pm. Closed bank holidays. €2.50 entrance.

Lacave   Parc Préhistorique   ☎ 05 65 32 28 28
                🖳 www.prehistologia.com
                Within a large wood the Parc Préhistorique recounts the history
                of man over the last 4.5 million years. It's one of the most
                extensive reconstructions in Europe, including life-size
                dinosaurs, flying reptiles and giant mammals. There's also a
                reconstruction of a Neolithic village.

Marcilhac-sur- Abbaye de Marcilhac-sur-Célé   ☎ 05 65 40 68 44
Célé   A Roman abbey that is now a partial ruin, with a gothic church
                constructed in the 16th century containing some
                remarkable frescoes.

Rocamadour   ☎ 05 65 33 23 23
                A distinctive village and one of the most visited in France, its
                medieval houses clinging to the cliffs. The Sanctuaires de
                Rocamadour are a place of pilgrimage, some pilgrims mounting
                the 140 steps to the shrines on their knees. The shrines are
                open every day: January to March 9am to 5.30pm; April to
                October 8.30am to 6pm; November to December 9am to
                6.30pm. Guided tours available: adults €5.30, 8 to
                13-year-olds €3.

                La Féerie   ☎ 05 65 33 71 06
                🖳 www.la-feerie.com

A 45-minute show using sound and light effects and over 200 computer-generated animations that took over 15 years to design and produce. Shows throughout the day from April to November. Adults €7, 4 to 12-year-olds €4.50. Adventure playground and picnic area.

Rempart de Rocamadour
These ramparts are the remains of the 14th century fortress designed to protect the shrines (see above). The ramparts overlook the Alzou canyon with views over the valley and of Rocamadour itself. Open January to March, November and December every day from 9am to 6.30pm; April to October every day from 9am to 6.30pm. Guided tours available. Adults €2.60, 8 to 13-year-olds €2.10.

Museums & Galleries

Cahors
Musée de la Résistance, Espace Bessères ☎ 05 65 22 14 25
There are six rooms retracing the Resistance movement in Lot, covering the armed resistance, repression, deportation and liberation. Open all year from 2 to 6pm (closed 1st January, 1st May and 25th December).

Cajarc
Galerie l'Acadie, 4 place de l'Eglise   ☎ 05 65 40 76 37
A gallery of contemporary art open April to September from Wednesday to Sunday 11am to 7pm, Monday and Tuesday by appointment.

Musée du Rail, cours de la Gare   ☎ 06 81 74 16 47
Free entry to this railway museum. Open every day from July to September.

Capdenac-le-Haut
Musée de Capdenac-le-Haut   ☎ 05 65 50 01 45
A medieval village, keep, museum and fountain. Open mid-June to mid-September every day from 10am to 12.30pm and 2 to 7pm; out of season Tuesdays to Saturdays 2 to 6pm. Adults €2.30, 12 to 18-year-olds €1.50.

Cardaillac
Musée Eclate, place de la Tour   ☎ 05 65 40 10 63
Guided tour around part of the village, including a barrel maker's house, clog maker's workshop, chestnut-drying oven, prune oven, walnut oil mill and press, and an early 20th century classroom. Tours at 3pm July to mid-September with a second tour at 4.30pm from mid-July to the third week in August. Fee €1.60.

Figeac
Musée Champollion,
4 rue Frères Champollion   ☎ 05 65 50 31 08
This museum, which is also the house in which Jean François Champollion was born, commemorates the life and work of the man who deciphered hieroglyphics and contains a collection of Egyptian art and temporary exhibitions and events. November

to February Tuesdays to Sundays 2 to 6pm; March to October Tuesdays to Sundays 10am to noon and 2.30 to 6.30pm (July and August also Mondays). Closed 1st January, 1st May and 25th December. Adults €3.10. Guided tours at 10am on Tuesdays in July and August: €4.95.

Galerie le Rire Bleu, 4 rue d'Ajouu   ☎ 05 65 50 05 39
💻 *www.le-rire-bleu.org*
A contemporary art gallery open April to the end of December, Tuesdays to Sundays 10am to 12.30pm and 3 to 7.30pm.

Padirac   Historial du Gouffre   ☎ 05 65 33 75 75
💻 *www.historial-de-padirac.com*
Museum with prehistoric objects, fossils and minerals, scenes relating to the discovery of the Padirac Chasm and a dinosaur park in a bamboo plantation. Open April to October every day from 9am to 7pm. Adults €5, 4 to 12-year-olds €4. Commentary available in English.

Rocamadour   Musée du Jouet Ancien Automobile,
place Ventadour   ☎ 05 65 33 60 75
Collection of Dinky toys and 100 pedal cars dating from 1910 to 1960. Open April to September every day 10am to noon and 2 to 6pm. Adults €3.80, under 14s €1.

Musée d'Art Sacré, place du Sanctuaire ☎ 05 65 33 23 23
17th century sculptures, paintings, gold and silver work. Open all year every day 9.30am to noon and 2 to 6pm (July and August 9am to 7pm).

St Céré   Galerie d'Art Exposition Jean Lurçat,
Casino, Avenue Jean Mouliérat   ☎ 05 65 38 19 60
A permanent exhibition of the works of Jean Lurçat and other artists. Temporary exhibitions at various times throughout the year.

St Pierre-Toirac Musée Rural Quercynois,
route de la Gare   ☎ 05 65 34 26 07
Fifty life-size models in traditional costumes with the tools of their trade. Collections of rare and unusual items, costumes, etc. A witchcraft room with ritual objects, six exhibitions and two gardens. Open July and August Sunday to Friday 2.30 to 6.30pm. By request the rest of the year.

Sauliac-sur-Célé Musée de Plein Air du Quercy,
Domaine de Cuzals   ☎ 05 65 22 58 63
Two reconstructed farms – one pre-Revolution, one 19th century – with their crops and animals, and 30 themed exhibitions on every aspect of traditional rural life, including water, fire, domestic life and machinery. Open April to October.

Parks, Gardens & Forests

Gramat
Les Jardins du Grand Couvent de
Gramat, 33 avenue Louis Mazet   ☎ 05 65 38 73 60
(50m from the station at Gramat)
A kilometre of paths through woods and colourful gardens.
Open May and June from 2 to 6pm; July and August 10am to
7pm; September to October 2 to 6pm. Adults €4, 5 to
12-year-olds €2.

Regional Produce

Caillac
Château Lagrezette   ☎ 05 65 20 07 42
💻 *www.chateau-lagrezette.tm.fr*
Wine has been made at this vineyard since 1503 and Mr Perrin
opens his doors every day from 10am to 7pm for visits to his
cellars and tastings.

Lamothe-
Fénelon
La Ferme de Foie Gras Jacquin, Emboly ☎ 05 65 37 65 67
Farm visits and tastings Monday to Saturday at 6pm. See the
birds, how the various products are prepared and a
demonstration of the techniques used.

Puy l'Evêque
Château Gautoul   ☎ 05 65 30 84 17
💻 *www.gautoul.com*
Visit the wine cellars and enjoy a free tasting. Booking required
for groups, but general visitors welcome at all times.

St Sozy
Coopérative Quercy Périgord Fermier   ☎ 05 65 32 22 88
This *foie gras* producer can be visited in July and August from
Wednesdays to Fridays to see how the birds are raised and
their products prepared. Free tastings of *foie gras* and
other pâtés.

Professional Services

The following offices have an English-speaking professional.

Accountants

Cahors   Mr Caussanel, résidence Verrerie   ☎ 05 65 22 65 26

Solicitors & Notaires

Cahors   Buytet, Mellac et Ferriz,
215 rue Victor Hugo   ☎ 05 65 35 31 41

Religion

Anglican Services In English

Cahors   Chapel, Centre Paroissial, Terre Rouge ☎ 05 65 21 20 07
               ✉ *rebill@wanadoo.fr*
               (on the Rodez road just under two miles out of Cahors centre)
               Services on Sundays at 10am. Evening Prayer and Holy
               Communion usually once a month. Organised by the
               Chaplaincy of Toulouse. Contact Susan Bill to confirm current
               services.

Protestant Churches

Selected churches are listed below.

Figeac   Assemblée Chrétienne de Figeac,
               4 rue Aujou   ☎ 05 65 34 65 03

St Céré   Culte Protestant Evangelique,
               168 avenue Victor Hugo   ☎ 05 65 38 25 02

Restaurants

Cahors   L'Auberge du Vieux Cahors,
               144 rue St Urcisse   ☎ 05 65 35 06 05
               Seafood is a speciality and there are set menus from €17 to
               €32. Open every day July to mid-September; rest of the year
               closed Tuesdays and Wednesdays.

               Au Fil de Douceurs,
               90 quai de la Verrerie   ☎ 05 65 22 13 04
               (a floating restaurant moored on the east bank of the eastern
               loop of the river Lot)
               This restaurant boat offers traditional, regional cuisine. Set
               menus from €13 to €43. Closed Sundays and Mondays.

               Le Chantilly,
               67 boulevard Léon Gambetta   ☎ 05 65 35 22 35
               (in the centre of town)
               This brasserie has a modern interior and corner position. Set
               menus from €9.40 to €20.

               La Chartreuse, St Georges   ☎ 05 65 35 17 37
               🖥 *www.hotel-la-chartreuse.com*
               (on the south bank of the river, south of the town)
               Set menus from €14 to €37 plus *à la carte* menu.
               Closed January.

Les Fondues de la Daurade,
27 place Chapou   ☎ 05 65 35 27 27
(by the Cathédrale St Etienne)
Fondues and *raclettes* a speciality. Closed Wednesday
lunchtimes and all day Tuesdays.

Le Gambetta, 19 allées Fénelon   ☎ 05 65 22 07 03
(in the centre of town beside the large fountain)
No set menus; dishes up to €17 each.

McDonald's, Regourd   ☎ 05 65 20 20 20
(north side of the town on the N20)

Le Méphisto, 10 avenue Jean Jaurès   ☎ 05 65 53 00 77
Set menu of the day €12; *raclettes* available if booked. Other
set menus €15 to €18. Closed Sundays.

L'ô à la Bouche, 134 rue St Urcisse   ☎ 05 65 35 65 69
Creative cuisine with set menus from €12.50 to €26 and *à la
carte* menu.

Le Palais, 12 boulevard Gambetta   ☎ 05 65 35 31 23
Open every day until midnight. Set menus from €8.40 to €25.

Le St Urcisse, place St Urcisse   ☎ 05 65 35 06 06
(close to the river on the eastern side of Cahors)
Traditional and innovative cuisine. Monday to Friday
lunchtimes, set menu €11.80. Other set menus up to €39 plus
à la carte menu. Closed Sundays and Mondays.

There are many restaurants tucked away in the small side streets of the old
quarter of Figeac, including some of the following:

Figeac   La Chandeleur, 3 rue Boutaric   ☎ 05 65 34 02 70
(in a tiny road leading off place Champollion)
This crêperie has set menus from €11 to €16.50. Closed
Tuesday evenings and all day Wednesdays. Closed Sundays
during January and February.

La Dinée du Viguier, 4 rue Boutaric   ☎ 05 65 50 08 08
(in a tiny road leading off place Champollion)
This is a formal restaurant with set menus from €25 to €65.
Closed Saturday lunchtimes, Sunday evenings and all day
Mondays.

Le Four à Bois, 26 rue Caviale   ☎ 05 65 34 72 12
Restaurant, grill and pizzeria with set menus from €18.50 and
an extensive *à la carte* menu. Closed all day Sundays, Monday
lunchtimes and the last two weeks of both June and November.

Le Marrakech, 7 rue Maquisards   ☎ 05 65 34 69 25
Moroccan cuisine with a €10 set menu. Open Tuesday to
Sunday lunchtimes.

McDonald's, chemin Moulin de Laporte ☎ 05 65 40 37 88
(on the south-east side of the town)

La Puce à l'Oreille, 5 rue St Thomas   ☎ 05 65 34 33 08
(tucked away up a tiny alley off rue Seguier)
A formal restaurant with set menus from €13.50 to €35. Closed
Sunday evenings and all day Mondays out of season and for
ten days in June and three weeks in October.

La Tourmaline, 8 rue Maquisards   ☎ 05 65 34 26 09
Indian and Chinese cuisine. Set menus from €14.50 to €20, set
lunch menu €10. Closed all day Tuesdays and Sunday and
Monday evenings.

To Chau, 8 place 12 Mai 1944   ☎ 05 65 34 28 57
Vietnamese and Chinese food, including take-away. €10 mid-
week lunch menu. Closed Mondays.

Gourdon   Au P'tit Bouchon,
31 boulevard Cabanes   ☎ 05 65 41 13 25
Lunchtime set menus Mondays to Saturdays €9 and €11.20,
other menus €18 to €24 and *à la carte* menu.

Le Central, 45 boulevard Mainiol   ☎ 05 65 41 07 38
Pizzeria with a large selection of bottled beers. No set menus.

Le Croque Note, 12 rue Jean Jaurès   ☎ 05 65 41 15 43
Traditional and modern cuisine. Set menus from €18 to €23.80.

L'Hôtel Bissonnier,
51 boulevard des Martyrs   ☎ 05 65 41 02 48
💻 *www.hotelbissonnier.com*
Restaurant open all year with concert dinners from around €30.

Le Palais, 91 boulevard Aristide Briand ☎ 05 65 41 14 89
Outside seating and a dining room at the rear. Set lunchtime
menu €13, other set menus €16 to €19. Open every day,
lunchtimes and evenings, in summer; closed all day Sundays
and Monday evenings the rest of the year.

La Promenade,
48 boulevard Galiot de Grenouilhac   ☎ 05 6541 41 44
💻 *www.lapromenadegourdon.fr*
Set menus from €9.60. Open all year.

Gramat	Château de Roumégouse, route de Rocamadour, Rignac ☎ 05 65 33 63 81

Gramat   Château de Roumégouse,
            route de Rocamadour, Rignac   ☎ 05 65 33 63 81
            A high-quality hotel and restaurant in a grand château. Menus
            from €35 plus *à la carte* menu. Closed from November to just
            before Easter.

Mercues   Le Château de Mercues   ☎ 05 65 20 00 01
            🖳 *www.relaischateaux.com/mercues.fr*
            (north-west of Cahors towards Villeneuve-sur-Lot)
            A formal restaurant with set menus from €50 to €88. Closed all
            day Mondays, lunchtimes Tuesdays to Thursdays and from
            November to mid-April.

St Céré   Côté Jardin, Tauriac   ☎ 05 65 38 49 51
            (a few kilometres north-west of St Céré, near the river)
            Regional cuisine concentrating on healthy eating and local
            products. Set menus €18 to €25. Open all day Fridays,
            Saturday evenings and Sunday lunchtimes

            Domaine de Granval,
            Saint Michel-Loubéjou   ☎ 05 65 38 63 99
            🖳 *www.domainedegranval.com*
            (set back on the main road between Bretenoux and St Céré)
            Set menus from €14 to €28, closed Sundays.

            Pizzeria Caprice, 2 rue Pasteur   ☎ 05 65 38 34 22
            Shaded terrace at the back and a good selection of salads and
            pasta as well as pizzas. Closed weekend lunchtimes and all
            day Mondays. No set menus.

            La Puymule, 1 place de l'Eglise   ☎ 05 65 10 59 10
            Set menus from €10 to €20. Open noon to 2pm and 7 to
            9.30pm evenings, 10pm at weekends. Closed Saturday
            lunchtimes and all day Mondays.

Rubbish & Recycling

Metal Collection

Bagnac-sur-Célé Aymard Sarl, 5 avenue Castors   ☎ 05 65 34 90 26
            (north-east of Figeac)

Lamagdelaine Prévost Environnement, Pech de Clary,
              415 route Mels   ☎ 05 65 35 30 60

Shopping

When available, opening hours have been included, but these are liable to
change and it's wise to check before travelling to any specific shop.

Alcohol

Cahors	Lafon Frères, 21 rue Blanqui	☎ 05 65 53 01 94

Wine by the litre and open Tuesdays to Saturdays.

Figeac	R. Malaret et Fils, place de la Halle	☎ 05 65 34 02 14

(in the centre of the town)
Wine sold by the litre.

Gourdon	Les Vins du Soleil,	
	boulevard de Martyrs	☎ 05 65 41 21 65

Wine sold by the litre.

St Céré	Le Cave Biarnaise, 74 avenue de la	
	République, Biars-sur-Cère	☎ 05 65 10 96 44

(on the left as you travel north through Biars)
Wine sold by the litre. Open Tuesdays to Saturdays.

Architectural Antiques

Cahors	Occitanie Pierres, RN20, St Henri	☎ 05 65 35 54 92

Garden statues, chimneys and stonework for construction and
pavements.

Building Materials

Cahors	Chausson Matériaux, Regourd	☎ 05 65 35 28 92

🖳 *www.chausson-materiaux.fr*
(north of Cahors on the D911)

Figeac	Point P, 33 avenue Président Georges	
	Pompidou	☎ 05 65 34 40 33

🖳 *www.pointp.fr*

Gourdon	De Nardi, 9 avenue Madeleine	☎ 05 65 41 18 73

🖳 *www.de-nardi.fr*

Caravans & Camper Vans

Gourdon	Oliver Vergne, route Salviac Fumel	☎ 05 65 41 04 33

Sales, repairs and second-hand caravans.

DIY

Cahors	Obi, route de Toulouse	☎ 05 65 22 59 00

🖳 *www.obi.fr*

Figeac	Weldom, 7 avenue Président Georges	
	Pompidou	☎ 05 65 34 26 42

| Gourdon | Bricomarché, La Peyrugue | ☎ 05 65 41 13 06 |

| St Céré | Bricorama, 211 rue Actipole les Tours, St Laurent-les-Tours | ☎ 05 65 38 06 41 |

(on the northern outskirts of St Céré)
Mondays to Saturdays 9am to noon and 2 to 7pm.

Fabrics

| Cahors | B. Jacques Tissus, place Jean Jacques Chapou | ☎ 05 65 35 03 52 |

Furnishing fabrics.

| Figeac | Dallara Mieulet, 24 boulevard de Juskiewenski | ☎ 05 65 34 12 59 |

| St Céré | Galerie du Mercadial, 5 place Mercadial | ☎ 05 65 38 13 76 |

Frozen Food

| Cahors | Thiriet, avenue de Toulouse | ☎ 05 65 35 72 31 |

Sundays 9.30am to 12.30pm, Mondays 2.30 to 7pm, Tuesdays to Saturdays 9.30am to 12.30pm and 2.30 to 7pm.

Garden Centres

| Cahors | Gamm Vert, Plaine du Pal | ☎ 05 65 20 46 80 |

Mondays to Saturdays 9am to noon and 2 to 7pm.

| | Jardinerie du Quercy, avenue Maryse Bastié | ☎ 05 65 30 10 97 |

Open Sundays.

| Figeac | Gamm Vert, place du Foirail | ☎ 05 65 34 22 77 |

Summer: Mondays 9am to noon and 2 to 6pm, Tuesdays to Fridays 8.30am to noon and 2 to 6.30pm, Saturdays 8.30am to noon and 2 to 6pm. Winter: Tuesdays to Saturdays 8.30am to noon and 2 to 6pm.

| | Les Jardins de Figeac, route de Toulouse | ☎ 05 65 14 15 04 |

| Gourdon | Gamm Vert, La Peyrugues, route de Salviac | ☎ 05 65 41 01 05 |

Mondays to Fridays 9am to noon and 2 to 7pm, Saturdays 6pm.

| St Céré | Gamm Vert, avenue Europe | ☎ 05 65 10 83 00 |

Tuesdays to Saturdays 8.30am to noon and 2 to 6.30pm (Saturdays till 6pm).

Hypermarkets

Cahors	Carrefour, route de Toulouse	☎ 05 65 35 27 19

Mondays to Saturdays 9am to 8.30pm (Fridays until 9pm).

	Leclerc, route de Luzech	☎ 05 65 20 34 51

(south-west the Lot river on the road to Toulouse)
Mondays to Saturdays 9am to 8pm (Fridays until 8.30pm).

Kitchens & Bathrooms

Specialist stores for kitchens and bathrooms can often be found on the large retail parks (see page 213).

Cahors	Jean Gilet Cuisines, 305 avenue du 7ème RI 🖵 *www.cuisinespegelec.com*	☎ 05 65 22 01 33

Figeac	Espalux, quai Albert Bessières 🖵 *www.espalux.fr* Closed Monday mornings.	☎ 05 65 14 06 60

Markets

Bretenoux   Tuesday and Saturday mornings.

Cahors   Regular markets Wednesday and Saturday mornings with fairs the first and third Saturdays of each month.

Figeac   All-day market every Saturday and a fair the second and last Saturday of each month.

Gourdon   Tuesday and Saturday mornings all year round with a fair the first and third Tuesdays of each month.

A local farmers' market Thursday mornings in July and August.

Gramat   Tuesday and Friday mornings all year round and Sunday mornings from May to September.

The big fair is on the second and fourth Thursdays of each month, replaced by the 31st of the month in October and December.

Limogne-en-Quercy   Sunday mornings.

Truffle markets Friday mornings from December to March and a summer truffle market on Sunday mornings June to August.

Martel	Wednesday and Saturday mornings.
	A truffle market joins the regular market in December and January.
Prayssac	Friday mornings.
	A local farmers' market on Sunday mornings in July and August.
	The big fair is the 16th of each month, brought forward to 15th if 16th is a Sunday and usually in July and August.
Rocamadour	A large cheese fair towards the end of May each year.
St Céré	Saturday mornings and a fair the first and third Wednesdays of each month. If the Wednesday is a bank holiday, the fair is the day before.
Souillac	Friday mornings, with fairs on the first and third Fridays of each month.
	A local farmers' market from 5 to 8pm on Wednesdays in July and August.
Vayrac	Thursday and Saturday mornings, with fairs on the first and third Thursdays of each month.

Music

Cahors	Alain Pugret, 105 rue du Château du Roi	☎ 05 65 22 09 11
Figeac	Au Joyeux Fa Dièse, 1bis place Vival All types of instruments sold new and second-hand, and instrument hire.	☎ 05 65 34 15 66

Organic Food

Cahors	La Vie Claire, 26 place St Maurice Tuesdays to Saturdays 9am to 12.30pm and 3 to 7pm.	☎ 05 65 35 59 13
Figeac	Figeac Nature, 23 rue Caviale Open Tuesdays to Saturdays.	☎ 05 65 34 54 68
Gourdon	Brin de Nature, 4 avenue Léon Gambetta Open Tuesdays to Saturdays.	☎ 05 65 37 15 83

St Céré	Coloquinte, 1 boulevard Léon Gambetta Open Tuesdays to Saturdays.	☎ 05 65 38 33 53

Retail Parks

Cahors   South of the town along the RN20 is a retail park including:

- ● BUT – general furniture and household accessories;

- ● Carrefour – hypermarket;

- ● Intersport – sports goods.

Second-Hand Goods

Cahors	Capelle, 45 boulevard Gambetta	☎ 05 65 22 08 65
Figeac	Antiquité Rye Patrice, 17 rue Clermont	☎ 05 65 34 34 98
	Le Grenier, rue des Maquisards	☎ 05 65 50 05 67
Gourdon	Antiquités Brocantes, avenue Cavaignac A small shop on a busy road leading out of town.	☎ 05 65 41 04 41

Sports Goods

Cahors	Sport 2000, 759 chemin Belle Croix	☎ 05 65 22 12 40
Figeac	Sport 2000, 31bis avenue Jean Jaurès	☎ 05 65 34 18 18
Gourdon	Intersport, 23 boulevard Cabanes	☎ 05 65 41 31 09
St Céré	Flo'Sports, 41 rue Faidherbe Open Tuesdays to Saturdays.	☎ 05 65 38 11 29

Swimming Pool Equipment

General	Pool Serve, Domipech, Prayssas This company is run by a UK qualified pool engineer and builds, refurbishes and maintains pools from its base in Lot-et-Garonne.	☎ 05 53 95 98 62
Cahors	Piscine Services 46, La Beyne (directly south of the town off the main road) Maintenance, repair and renovation of pools, plus consumables, liners and covers.	☎ 05 65 53 04 46

St Céré	JPB Piscines, 8 avenue du Docteur Roux ☎ 05 65 38 27 22
	Construction, renovation, maintenance, and products and accessories for swimming pools, spas and saunas.

Sports

The following is just a selection of the activities available, the large towns having a wide range of sports facilities. Full details are available from the tourist office or the mairie.

Aerial Sports

Flying

Cieurac	Aéro Club du Quercy Aérodrome	☎ 05 65 21 05 96

Figeac	Aéro Club Figeac-Livernon, Aérodrome de Figeac	☎ 06 85 21 31 33
	Aeroplanes and microlights.	

Parachuting

Cieurac	Centre Ecole de Parachutisme de Cahors, Aérodrome Cieurac	☎ 05 65 21 00 54
	(south of Cahors)	

Archery

Cahors	1ère Compagne d'Arc de Cahors	☎ 05 65 22 32 67
	Contact Mr Sarrazin.	

Figeac	Les Archers de Figeac, Salle Jean Pramil, Londieu	☎ 05 65 40 77 90
	Training Tuesdays from 4pm and Thursdays from 6pm. Contact Mr Pendaries. Minimum age ten.	

Gourdon	Tir à l'Arc, place Noël Poujade	☎ 05 65 41 11 65

Badminton

Figeac	Association Figeacoise de Badminton, COSEC, Gymnase Collège Marcel Masbou, 1 avenue Flandres Dunkerque 1940	☎ 05 65 45 61 66
	Monday, Wednesday and Thursday evenings. Adults only.	

Gourdon	Club de Badminton, place Noël Poujade ☎ 05 65 41 11 65
	✉ *mjc.gourdon@wanadoo.fr*
	Mondays 6.30 to 8.30pm and Wednesdays 7 to 10pm.

St Céré   Gymnase de St Céré   ☎ 05 65 38 55 13
                 Mondays and Wednesdays 8.30 to 11pm for adults, Tuesdays
                 6.30 to 8pm for youngsters.

Canoeing & Kayaking

Cahors   Club Canoë Kayak Cahors,
                 impasse de la Charité   ☎ 05 65 22 62 62

Cajarc   Maison des Guides, le Plan d'Eau   ☎ 05 65 14 10 69
                 🖳 *www.maisondesguides.com*
                 (between Cahors and Figeac)
                 Open every day in July and August from 10.30am to 7.30pm;
                 June and September 2 to 6pm; rest of the year by appointment.

Figeac   Figeac Eaux Vives, Centre Social,
                 Place Vival   ☎ 05 65 50 05 48
                 Open 15th July to the end of August. Lessons, courses and
                 accompanied trips. Single day or several day hire.

St Céré   Plan d'Eau, Base de Loisirs, Tauriac   ☎ 05 65 32 20 82
                 🖳 *www.portloisirs.com*
                 (a few kilometres north-west of St Céré)
                 Canoe and kayak hire at various locations along the river,
                 including St Sozy, Creysse and Gluges as well as Tauriac.
                 English spoken.

Vayrac   Antinéa Loisirs   ☎ 05 65 37 44 87
                 🖳 *www.canoe-safaraid-dordogne.com*
                 (west of St Céré)

Canyoning

Cajarc   Maison des Guides, le Plan d'Eau   ☎ 05 65 14 10 69
                 🖳 *www.maisondesguides.com*
                 (between Cahors and Figeac)
                 Open every day in July and August from 10.30am to 7.30pm;
                 June and September 2 to 6pm; rest of the year by appointment.

Padirac   ☎ 06 84 90 03 69
                 Contact Mr Virgoulay

St Cirq-Lapopie Bureau des Sports Nature, Conduche   ☎ 05 65 24 21 01
                 🖳 *www.perso.wanadoo.fr/bureau-sports-nature*
                 (south of Figeac)
                 Potholing, canyoning and climbing.

Clay Pigeon Shooting

Figeac   Cible Figeacoise, Stand Nayrac,
                 avenue de Nayrac   ☎ 05 65 34 01 56

(west of the town near the equestrian centre)
Every Sunday 9.30am to 1pm at Stand Nayrac. Contact
Mr Calmejane.

Climbing

Autoire Les Falaises
(directly east of St Céré)
Offering 120 different climbs from 10 to 20m, Scales 5 to 7+, on
a variety of rock faces. A user guide (charte d'utilisation) is
provided, including a plan of the area and advice on
preserving the site.

Cajarc Maison des Guides, le Plan d'Eau ☎ 05 65 14 10 69
🖳 www.maisondesguides.com
(between Cahors and Figeac)
Open every day in July and August from 10.30am to 7.30pm;
June and September 2 to 6pm; rest of the year by appointment.

Creysse Port Loisirs, Camping du Port ☎ 05 65 32 20 82
🖳 www.portloisirs.com
This organisation arranges potholing, climbing and
other activities.

Figeac Association Spéléo de Figeac ☎ 05 65 11 40 66
Climbing in Lot and neighbouring departments. Open to all.
Contact Mr Jacquet.

Gourdon Escalade le Pied Noir ☎ 05 65 41 33 10

St Cirq-Lapopie Bureau des Sports Nature, Conduche ☎ 05 65 24 21 01
🖳 www.perso.wanadoo.fr/bureau-sports-nature
(south of Figeac)
Potholing, canyoning and climbing.

Cycling

Cahors Cahors Cyclisme, Espace Associatif
Marot, Place Bessières ☎ 05 65 35 13 72
Contact Mr Danglot.

Figeac Association des Cyclotouristes
Figeacois ☎ 05 65 34 37 36
Road cycling and mountain biking, with rides every week.
Contact Mr Maruejouls.

Gourdon Club Cyclotourisme Gourdonnais ☎ 05 65 31 02 18

Around the area of St Céré are 480km (300mi) of paths open to mountain
bikers. Circuits range from 3 to 26km (2 to 16mi) and are divided into four
categories. Details are available from the tourist office.

St Céré   Mr Auguie   ☎ 05 65 34 63 97
                        Rides Wednesdays and Saturdays at 2pm.

Fishing

If there's a lake locally, permits will be on sale at a nearby tabac or at the mairie; some tourist offices also sell permits.

Maps are available from fishing shops and tourist offices showing the fishing waters in the department. There's also information on the species found in the area, the prices of fishing permits and the fishing season.

Further information can be obtained from:

General   Fédération du Lot, 182 quai Cavaignac,
                        Cahors   ☎ 05 65 35 50 22
                        🖥 *www.pechelot.com*
                        This comprehensive website gives details of where and when
                        you may fish, plus details of fishing permits – from €6 a day.

Golf

St Céré   Golf de Montal, St Jean-Lespinasse   ☎ 05 65 10 83 09
                        Two 9-hole courses totalling 5,028m. Open to the general public.
                        Dominated by cliffs to the south and overlooking the valley of St
                        Céré to the north, this course offers an exceptional setting.
                        Terraced greens, many bunkers and sloping fairways. The
                        clubhouse has a fast food restaurant, practice range and pro shop
                        renting out clubs and golf carts. Green fees €18 to €26.

Souillac   Souillac Country Club   ☎ 05 65 27 56 00
                        9 holes, par 33, 2,002m. Pro shop, restaurant and bar, putting
                        green, covered and open driving ranges, golf carts to hire. Also on
                        site: pool, tennis court and chalets. Green fees from €25 to €30.

Horse Riding

Cahors   Club Hippique de Quercy,
                        117 chemin du Club Hippique   ☎ 05 65 35 20 61
                        Open all year round. Lessons for all from three years old,
                        beginners and improvers; hacks from one hour to all day.

Figeac   Club Figeacois du Cheval et du Poney,
                        avenue de Nayrac   ☎ 05 65 34 70 57
                        Closed the first two weeks of September. Beginners and
                        improvers; hacks and week-long camps for children.

Milhac   Le Haras des Ausiers, Les Ausiers   ☎ 05 65 41 53 78
                        (directly north of Gourdon)
                        Hacks from one hour to all day.

St Céré — Around the area of St Céré are 480km (300mi) of paths open to riders. Circuits range from 3 to 26km (2 to 16mi) and are divided into four categories. Details from the tourist office.

Ecole d'Equitation de Siramon ☎ 05 65 38 19 32
Lessons, competitions, hacks and day trips.

Judo

Cahors — Judo Club Cadurcien, Gymnase de Cabessut, chemin Ludo Rollès ☎ 05 65 22 37 13

Figeac — Association Fenêtre Ouverte, Ancien CES, rue Victor Delbos ☎ 05 65 40 05 92
Classes for children and adults.

Gourdon — Club de Judo ☎ 06 07 02 52 95

St Céré — Salle de Combat, Gymnase, quai A. Salesses ☎ 06 83 24 02 13
Classes for all ages throughout the week. Contact Mr Lafage.

Motorcycle Riding

Cahors — Moto Club Cadurcien, café 'Le Bordeaux', boulevard Gambetta ☎ 05 65 35 27 83
Several motorbike clubs are based at this cafe. Contact Mr Rolland.

Gourdon — Moto-Club de Gourdon ☎ 05 65 41 12 60
Telephone for venues and meeting dates.

Potholing

Cahors — Groupe Spéléologique du Quercy, 413 rue Fonrodenque ☎ 05 65 35 11 85
Contact Mr Milhas.

Cajarc — Maison des Guides, le Plan d'Eau ☎ 05 65 14 10 69
🖥 www.maisondesguides.com
(between Cahors and Figeac)
Open every day June to September: July and August 10.30am to 7.30pm; June and September 2 to 6pm. Rest of the year by appointment only.

Creysse — Port Loisirs, Camping du Port ☎ 05 65 32 27 59
🖥 www.portloisirs.com
This organisation arranges potholing trips, rock climbing and other activities.

Figeac	Association Spéléo de Figeac	☎ 05 65 11 40 66

Expeditions in Lot and other neighbouring departments. Open to all. Contact Mr Jacquet.

Spéléo Club de Figeac, Salle de l'OIS,
2 avenue du Général de Gaulle   ☎ 05 65 31 14 23
Meetings on the second Monday of the month at 8.30pm.
Contact Mme Bizot. Minimum age 18.

Roller Skating

Gourdon   Club de Roller, place Noël Poujade   ☎ 05 65 41 11 65
✉ *mjc.gourdon@wanadoo.fr*

Valroufie   Skate Roller   ☎ 06 81 47 07 24
Contact Mr Monells for details of venues and dates.

Rowing

Cahors   Aviron Cadurcien, quai Regourd   ☎ 05 65 35 44 95
Contact M. Balmary

Shooting

Cahors   AST La Cible Cadurcienne,
125 rue des Thermes   ☎ 05 65 35 28 00

Gourdon   Association Sportive de Tir   ☎ 05 65 37 00 28

Snooker, Pool & Billiards

Cahors   Cahors Billard Club, Room 307,
Espace Associatif Clément Marot,
place Bessières   ☎ 05 65 23 99 79
French billiards.

Swimming

Cahors   l'Archipel, quai Ludo Rollès   ☎ 05 65 35 05 86
Outdoor pool with toboggan, water cannons and various games. Open mid-June to mid-October every day from 11am to 8pm.

Piscine Couverte, avenue Maréchal Juin ☎ 05 65 35 16 68
Indoor pool open September to June.

Figeac   Piscine Municipale, Espace de Loisirs,
Domaine du Surgié   ☎ 05 65 34 18 76
(on eastern edge of the town, by the river)

St Céré   Piscine Municipale, quai A. Salesses   ☎ 05 65 38 00 91
Outdoor pool complex open only July and August.

Tennis

Cahors   Cahors Tennis Club,
175 rue des Pensées   ☎ 05 65 30 11 92

Figeac   Tennis Club de Figeac   ☎ 05 65 34 53 31
Outdoor courts on rue Prairie des Pratges, indoor courts at
Espace F. Mitterrand, place Renaud. Outdoor courts open
Tuesdays to Saturdays 10am to noon and 2 to 7pm at Prairie
des Pratges; indoor courts by appointment.

Gourdon   Tennis Club Gourdonnais   ☎ 05 65 41 00 45

St Céré   quai A. Salesses   ☎ 05 65 38 25 30
Five courts, two with floodlights. Training on various days of the
week (in the gymnase if raining). For lessons, contact Mr
Lafont, Ecole de Tennis (☎ 06 80 60 91 32).

Waterskiing

Cajarc   Plan d'Eau   ☎ 05 65 40 66 81
Regular skiing 1st May to 15th October from 11am; rest of the
year by appointment. July to September contact the club at
the above number; rest of the year contact Mme de Villefort
(☎ 06 79 86 32 40).

Tourist Offices

General   Comité Régional du Tourisme,
54 boulevard de l'Emouchure,
31022 Toulouse   ☎ 05 61 13 55 48
🖳 www.tourisme-midi-pyrenees.com

Comité Départemental du Tourisme du
Lot, 107 quai Cavaignac, Cahors   ☎ 05 65 35 07 09
🖳 www.tourisme-lot.com

Cahors   place François Mitterrand   ☎ 05 65 53 20 65
🖳 www.mairie-cahors.fr
November to March Mondays to Saturdays 9am to 12.30pm
and 1.30 to 6pm; April to June Mondays to Saturdays 9am to
12.30pm and 1.30 to 6.30pm; July and August Mondays to
Fridays 9am to 6.30pm, Saturdays 9am to 6pm, Sundays and
bank holidays 10am to 12.30pm; September and October
Mondays to Saturdays 9am to 12.30pm and 1.30 to 6.30pm.

Figeac	Hôtel de la Monnaie, place Vival	☎ 05 65 34 06 25

💻 *www.ville-figeac.fr*
💻 *www.quercy.net/figeac*
Mid-September to May Mondays to Saturdays 10am to noon
and 2 to 6pm; June Mondays to Saturdays 10am to noon and 2
to 6pm and Sundays 10am to 1pm; July to mid-September
Mondays to Sundays 10am to 7.30pm.

Gourdon	24 rue du Majou	☎ 05 65 27 52 50

💻 *www.quercy.net/quercy/gourdon*
(in a narrow pedestrian road leading up to the church)
Open Mondays to Saturdays all year: November to February
10am to noon and 2 to 5pm; March to June, September and
October 10am to noon and 2 to 6pm; July and August 10am to
7pm. Open Sundays 10am to noon June to September only.

Rocamadour	Maison du Tourisme	☎ 05 65 33 22 00

Mid-November to March, Mondays to Fridays 10am to noon
and 2 to 5.30pm; April and mid-September to mid-November
Mondays to Fridays and Sundays 10am to noon and 2 to 6pm;
May to mid-July and end of August to mid-September every
day 10am to 12.30pm and 2 to 6.30pm; mid-July to last week
of August every day 10am to 7.30pm.

St Céré	place de la République	☎ 05 65 38 11 85

💻 *www.tourisme-saint-cere.com*
October to May Mondays to Saturdays 10am to noon and 2 to
6pm; June and September Mondays to Saturdays 9.30am to
12.30pm and 2 to 6pm; July and August Mondays to Saturdays
9.30am to 12.30pm and 2 to 7pm, Sundays 10am to 12.30pm.

Souillac	boulevard Louis Jean Malvy	☎ 05 65 37 81 56

September to June Mondays to Saturdays 10am to noon and 2
to 6pm; July and August Mondays to Sundays 9.30am to
12.30pm and 2 to 7pm.

Tradesmen

Architects & Project Managers

General	Adams Gautier	☎ 05 49 64 42 96

💻 *www.adamsgautier.com*
This is a British/French team of experienced architects, who also
organise surveys and building permits and carry out project
management for new builds, renovation, landscaping and pools.

Builders

Cahors	Custodio Frères,	
	208 rue Georges Clémenceau	☎ 05 65 22 34 16

| Figeac | MCM Constructions, 17 rue des Maquisards | ☎ 05 65 50 00 97 |

| Gourdon | Entreprise de Nardi, avenue de Grimardet | ☎ 05 65 41 03 73 |
General masonry and restoration work.

| St Céré | Les Constructions du Haut-Quercy, Latronquière | ☎ 05 65 40 24 09 |
General building, restoration and tiling.

Carpenters

| Cahors | Menuiseries Faugère, 512 avenue Jean Jaurès | ☎ 05 65 35 51 01 |

| Figeac | Quercymo, 18 avenue Général de Gaulle | ☎ 05 65 34 66 64 |
Carpentry and general building work.

| Gourdon | Les Vérandas du Quercy, route de Cahors | ☎ 05 65 41 67 67 |
General carpentry, including conservatories and shutters.

| St Céré | Menuiserie Alain Plas, 80 Pré de Viguié | ☎ 05 65 38 11 98 |

Electricians

| General | Solec, La Chassagnole, Cressensac | ☎ 05 65 37 79 26 |
✉ *solecfrance@yahoo.co.uk*
General household electrics and electric central heating systems. This company is run by an Englishman.

| Cahors | Confort Elec 46, 283 avenue Pierre Semard | ☎ 05 65 20 65 65 |
Electrical and heating engineers.

| Figeac | Technic'Service, chemin Crêtes | ☎ 05 65 34 42 30 |

| Gourdon | Beggiato Philippe, 28 rue Marché Vieux | ☎ 05 65 41 71 81 |

| St Céré | Montal Jean-Marie, 4 boulevard Jean Lurçat | ☎ 05 65 38 14 64 |

Plumbers

| Cahors | Calderon François, Rivière de Fontanet | ☎ 05 65 35 36 29 |
Plumbing and heating, installation and repair work.

| Figeac | Didier Counor, Puy de Corn | ☎ 05 65 34 46 01 |
Plumbing, heating and air-conditioning.

| Gourdon | Brico-Services, 19 boulevard Cabanès | ☎ 05 65 41 30 58 |

A general tradesman, who undertakes plumbing, building work, emergency repairs, and tiling.

| St Céré | ASTB, Pauliac, Prudhomat | ☎ 05 65 38 47 00 |

Heating, sanitary and plumbing services.

Robert Bladou, route Hortes, Bretenoux ☎ 05 65 38 43 21
Heating, sanitary and plumbing services.

Chimney Sweeps

Cahors	Au Service du Temps, 264 rue Nationale	☎ 05 65 20 45 79
Figeac	Marc Lionnet, avenue Cahors	☎ 05 65 34 24 68
Gourdon	D Treneuille, rue Calmon	☎ 05 65 41 16 90
St Céré	Robert Bladou, rue Hortes, Bretenoux	☎ 05 65 38 43 21

Translators & Teachers

French Teachers & Courses

| Cahors | Greta du Lot, 273 avenue Henri Martin | ☎ 05 65 35 43 91 |

💻 *www.greta-lot.ac-toulouse.fr*
A government-run organisation.

France-Grande Bretagne, Bureau no. 22,
Espace Clément Marot, place Bessières ☎ 05 65 24 51 89
This bilingual group holds French language workshops for all abilities. Contact Mr Eugster for more information.

| Figeac | Greta, Maison de la Formation, 6 avenue Bernard Fontanges | ☎ 05 65 34 66 43 |

A government-run organisation.

| Gourdon | Alison Downing, Loupiac | ☎ 05 65 41 92 28 |

(north of Gourdon towards Souillac)
Individual and group lessons for children and adults.

Mr Dalet, St Germain ☎ 05 65 31 02 59
(15 minutes south-east of Gourdon)
Individual and group lessons. First lesson free. Depending on location, lessons can be held at your home.

| St Céré | ABC, 3 quai A. Salesses | ☎ 05 65 38 37 70 |

Translators

Francoulès	Trans Europe Express Translations, Chemin du Mas de Sert ✉ *teet@teet.fr* (north of Cahors)	☎ 05 65 36 05 46
St Géry	Susan Baxter, chemin du Mas ✉ *susan.guide.lot @wanadoo.fr*	☎ 06 22 56 35 25

Utilities

Electricity & Gas

Électricité de France/Gaz de France (EDF/GDF) is one company for the whole of France but operates its gas and electricity divisions separately. The numbers below are for general information; emergency numbers can be found on page 59.

General	EDF/GDF Services Lot, rue Pomme, Souillac 💻 *www.edf.fr*	☎ 08 10 04 60 46

EDF/GDF local offices are listed below (there are no direct telephone numbers for these offices; you must dial the above number).

Cahors	283 avenue Pierre Sémard	
Figeac	place Vival	
Gourdon	42 boulevard Galliot de Genouillac	
St Céré	343 rue Henri Rouzet	
	Energie Sud Ouest, Pasturat, Arcambal	☎ 05 65 31 40 30
	Energie Sud Ouest, Le Bourg, Montbrun	☎ 05 65 40 72 77
	Energie Sud Ouest, Meymes, Prayssac	☎ 05 65 22 46 9L

Heating Oil

Cahors	Alvéa, 66 rue Portail Alban	☎ 05 65 35 04 45
	Milhau SD	☎ 05 65 35 59 34

| Castelfranc | Cassan Produits,
route Prayssac, Les Plantades | ☎ 05 65 36 20 15 |
| | Milhau SD, Le Bourg | ☎ 05 65 36 20 98 |

Water

The main water supply companies are listed below. If you aren't covered by one of these, your mairie will have details of your water supplier.

General	Lyonnaise des Eaux France, Iffernet, Flaujac-Poujols	☎ 08 10 82 58 10
	emergencies	☎ 08 10 82 48 24
	SAUR, 1 chemin l'Oustalet, Montcuq	☎ 05 65 33 23 00
	SAUR, 6 rue Sainte Marthe, Figeac	☎ 05 65 50 15 74
	SAUR, avenue Léon Gambetta, Gramat	☎ 05 65 33 23 00
	SAUR, Meymes, Prayssac	☎ 05 65 22 42 69
	Sicom Eaux de Bournac, Le Bourg, Varaire	☎ 05 65 31 50 75
	Sicom Eaux Ségala, Lavitarelle, Montet-et-Bouxal	☎ 05 65 40 20 58

Wood

| Cremps | Castelnau Ets. Beuzac
(south-east of Cahors) | ☎ 05 65 31 61 79 |
| Monteils | Scierie Carles | ☎ 05 65 29 63 58 |

Church of St Nicolas, Nérac

4

Lot-et-Garonne

This chapter provides details of facilities and services in the department of Lot-et-Garonne (47). General information about each subject can be found in **Chapter 1**. All entries are arranged alphabetically by town, except where a service applies over a wide area, in which case it's listed at the beginning of the relevant section under 'General'. A map of Lot-et-Garonne is shown below.

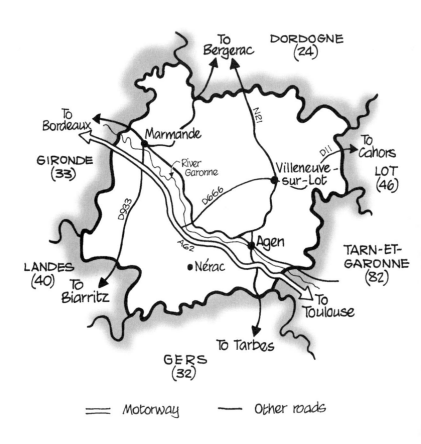

Accommodation

Camping

Agen   Moulin de Mellet,
              St Hilaire de Lusignan   ☎ 05 53 87 50 89
              💻 *www.perso.wanadoo.fr/moulin.mellet*
              Pool, fishing and chalets for hire.

Barbaste	Les Martinets, Le Bourg (on the D408 north-east of Nérac)	☎ 05 53 65 55 32
Marmande	Camping Municipal de la Filhole, RN113	☎ 05 53 64 63 05
Villeneuve-sur-Lot	Camping Municipal du Rooy, le Rooy, RN21	☎ 05 53 70 24 18

Châteaux

Casteljaloux   Château de Hautelande-Ruffiac, Ruffiac ☎ 05 53 93 18 63
This château overlooking the mountains and valleys
was originally a 14th century clergyman's residence.
This three-star hotel offers a shaded terrace, park and
billiards room. Double rooms from €58 to €88 per night.
There's no restaurant at the château.

Gîtes And Bed & Breakfast

Tourist offices have details of bed and breakfast facilities in their area and
may display a list in their window. Some communes also have gîtes
available for renting via the mairie.

Hotels

Agen, Marmande and Villeneuve-sur-Lot all have a wide selection of
hotels, including national chains such as those listed on page 46, and
therefore aren't included here.

General   💻 *www.lot-et-garonne.fr/vivre*
The departmental tourist office website, which includes an
online hotel booking service.

Nérac   Henri IV, 4 place Général Leclerc   ☎ 05 54 65 00 63
A small, comfortable hotel in the centre of town with rooms from
€35 to €42 per night.

Hôtel d'Albret, 40 allées d'Albret   ☎ 05 53 97 41 10
Rooms from €42 per night.

Hôtel du Château,
7 avenue Mondenard   ☎ 05 53 65 09 05
(to the left of the tourist office)
This hotel has a gourmet restaurant and rooms from
€45 to €69.

Bars & Nightlife

Agen	Cohiba Café, 75 Péristyle du Gravier Club and music bar.	☎ 05 53 48 13 33
	Le Dandy , 520 rue Gergovie Disco/nightclub.	☎ 05 53 66 54 82
	Eldorado, 7bis boulevard de la République	☎ 05 53 66 14 77

Disco/nightclub open Thursdays to Sundays and bank holidays.

Espace Billard, Centre Château de'Oct,
Le Passage   ☎ 05 53 96 97 19
(on the left just after the bridge on the road west out of
the town)
Pool, snooker and French billiards. Bar serving pizzas. Open
Tuesdays to Sundays in the summer 8pm to 2am;
Wednesdays, Saturdays and Sundays 3pm to 2am, Tuesdays,
Thursdays and Fridays 8pm to 2am in winter. Beginners'
sessions Tuesdays and Thursdays, pool competitions
Wednesdays at 8.30pm.

	Le Loft Club Privé, 32 rue Garonne Disco/nightclub.	☎ 05 53 66 76 91
Lavergne	Le Club, Le Bourg Bar/nightclub open Mondays to Saturdays from 5pm.	☎ 05 53 93 01 03
Marmande	La Galazie, place Lestang/ avenue Paul Gabarra Nightclub.	☎ 05 53 64 46 90

TNT, Espace de Nuit, Parc des
Expositions, route de Bordeaux   ☎ 05 53 20 66 10
There are two clubs at this venue: Le Carrousel for the 30 to 40
age group and Le Platinum for all ages. Both open from 11pm.
Occasional themed evenings.

Nérac	Le Gambetta, 100 rue Gambetta Music bar.	☎ 05 53 65 18 71
	Le Winger, 13 quai Lusignan Disco/nightclub.	☎ 05 53 65 92 92
Ste Bazeille	La Guinguette, RN13	☎ 05 5364 12 75

Retro, disco and rock. Open Thursdays from 7pm, Fridays and
Saturdays from 9.30pm and Sundays from 3pm.

In Villeneuve-sur-Lot there are many bars in the town centre open until around 1am all year. In the summer, there are concerts every Friday at Place Lafayette and every Wednesday at Cale de la Marine by the river (the stage is actually on the river Lot), and many bars hold their own concerts.

Villeneuve-sur-Lot	There are many bars in the town centre open until around 1am	
	La Luna, 2 place 4 septembre Disco/nightclub.	☎ 05 53 40 09 27
	Les Années Tubes, 18 avenue Agen Disco/nightclub.	☎ 05 53 70 30 17

Business Services

Computer Services

General	Euro Laptops, Le Castelat, Gourdon 💻 *www.gourdonnet.com* Software, hardware, upgrades, new computers and help with all aspects of setting up and using your computer by a British qualified IT trainer, who works across this whole region.	☎ 05 65 37 63 45
Agen	LP Composants, 142 boulevard de la République Sales, repairs and accessories.	☎ 05 53 66 69 20
Eymet	MCD Informatique, 3 place Gambetta ✉ *dean@mcd-informatique.com* (on the border of Dordogne and Lot-et-Garonne) Sales, service, repairs and websites and internet connections. Bilingual staff.	☎ 05 53 23 65 45
Nérac	LP Composants, 60 allées d'Albret Sales, repairs and accessories.	☎ 05 53 97 11 08
Villeneuve-sur-Lot	JLM Informatique, 12 rue Gambetta	☎ 05 53 70 76 97

Employment Agencies

The main offices of ANPE, the state employment service, in Lot-et-Garonne are listed below. There are also smaller offices throughout the department (see 💻 *www.anpe.fr*).

Agen	161 boulevard de la Liberté	☎ 05 53 69 14 50

Marmande	rue Stade	☎ 05 53 20 38 00
Villeneuve-sur-Lot	rue Fontanelles	☎ 05 53 41 52 00

Communications

Fixed Telephones

General	France Télécom: Dial 1014 or go to *www.francetelecom.fr* Local shops are listed below.
Agen	26 rue Molinier Mondays to Fridays 9.30am to 12.30pm and 1.30 to 6.30pm, Saturdays 9.15am to noon and 1.30 to 6.30pm.
Marmande	16 rue Charles de Gaulle Mondays 1.30 to 6.30pm, Tuesdays to Fridays 9.30am to noon and 1.30 to 6.30pm, Saturdays 9.30am to noon and 2 to 6.30pm.
Nérac	61 allées d'Albret Mondays 1.30 to 6pm, Tuesdays to Fridays 9.15am to noon and 1.30 to 6pm (Thursdays opens at 9.30am).
Villeneuve-sur-Lot	5 rue de Paris Mondays 1.30 to 6.30pm, Tuesdays to Fridays 9.30am to noon and 1.30 to 6.30pm, Saturdays 9.30am to 12.30pm and 2 to 6pm.

Internet Access

Agen	N@uteus, 83 cours Victor Hugo ☎ 05 53 87 91 60 Mondays to Saturdays 10am to 10pm, Sundays 2 to 8pm.
	Espace Public Multimédia, rue Henri Dunant ☎ 05 53 69 48 20 Mondays and Wednesdays 10am to 7pm, Tuesdays 1 to 6pm, Thursdays 1 to 8pm, Fridays 10am to 6pm, Saturdays 1 to 5pm.
Marmande	Espace Multimedia, 23 rue de la République ☎ 05 53 20 94 95 Tuesdays, Thursdays and Fridays 2 to 6pm, Wednesdays 9am to noon and 1.30 to 6pm, Saturdays 9am to noon and 2 to 6pm.

Nérac	Espace d'Albret, quai de la Baïse	☎ 05 53 97 40 55

(within the library, which is a modern building on the left, immediately over the bridge on the road to Agen)
Tuesdays, Thursdays and Fridays 2 to 6pm, Wednesdays 9am to noon and 2 to 6pm, Saturdays 9am to 12.30pm and 1.30 to 5.30pm.

Villeneuve-sur-Lot	La Poste, 1 rue Collège	☎ 05 53 40 45 50

Mondays to Fridays 8am to 6.30pm and Saturdays 8am to noon.

Mobile Telephones

All France Télécom shops (see above) sell mobile phones.

Agen	Espace SFR, 90 boulevard de la République	☎ 05 53 77 28 88

Mondays to Saturdays 10am to 7pm.

	Club Bouygues, 37 boulevard de la République	☎ 05 53 47 30 33
Marmande	Espace SFR, 14 boulevard de Maré	☎ 05 53 20 98 47

Mondays 2 to 7pm, Tuesdays to Fridays 9am to noon and 2 to 7pm, Saturdays 9am to 6pm.

	Phone Mobile, 35 rue Léopold Faye	☎ 05 53 93 57 95

Mondays to Saturdays 10am to 12.30pm and 2.30 to 7pm.

Villeneuve-sur-Lot	Télécom Boutique, 14bis place Lafayette	☎ 05 53 71 58 09

Mondays 2 to 7pm, Tuesdays to Saturdays 9am to noon and 2 to 7pm.

Domestic Services

Crèches & Nurseries

Agen	Crèche Halte-Garderie le Temps des Tout-Petits, 7 rue Roger Johan	☎ 05 53 66 00 81
	Halte-Garderie les Petits Coeurs, 41 rue Pallisy	☎ 05 53 66 47 25
Marmande	Halte-Garderie Municipale, rue Pierre Bérégovoy	☎ 05 53 64 75 02
	Maison Petite Enfance, rue Pierre Bérégovoy	☎ 05 53 64 64 14

| Nérac | Halte-Garderie Crèche Comptine, rue Remparts | ☎ 05 53 65 35 34 |

| Villeneuve-sur-Lot | Crèche Darfeuille, 8 rue Darfeuille | ☎ 05 53 70 09 07 |

Equipment & Tool Hire

| Castelculier | Cellerier Manutention, la Tuque, route Toulouse
🖥 *www.cellerier.com*
(on the eastern outskirts of Agen) | ☎ 05 53 68 30 67 |

| Marmande | Cellerier Ventes Locations, route Bordeaux | ☎ 05 53 89 64 00 |

| Nérac | Gascogne Location, route de Lavardac
🖥 *www.gascogneequipment.fr* | ☎ 05 53 97 19 68 |

Fancy Dress Hire

| Villeneuve-sur-Lot | Caverne d'Anni Baba, 17 rue Convention | ☎ 05 53 70 04 10 |

Garden Services

| General | Julian Urrutia, Bergerac   ☎ 05 53 57 98 69
All aspects of tree surgery handled and a mobile sawmill to turn trunks into beams and planks. Although based in Bergerac, covers all of this department. Fluent English spoken. |

| | Lorenti's, l'Ancienne Gare, Monbahus   ☎ 05 53 71 40 31
Landscaping, maintenance and garden design.
English spoken. |

| Jusix | Michel Guignan, Le Passage   ☎ 05 53 94 41 58
(on the north-west border of the department)
Design and maintenance, hedge cutting and garden clearance. |

| Laroque-Timbaut | Averous Espace Verts, ZAC Pourret   ☎ 05 53 68 86 40
(north-east of Agen)
Design and garden maintenance. |

Launderettes

| Agen | Lav'1 Max,
3 avenue du Général de Gaulle   ☎ 05 53 47 15 64
(at the end of the parade of shops on the east bank of the Garonne) |

| Marmande | Laverie de la Tomate,
28 boulevard Meyniel | ☎ 05 53 89 17 55 |

| Villeneuve-sur-Lot | Laverie, rue de la Fraternité
(in the town centre) | |

Septic Tank Services

| Boé | Rieux, 4 ZAC Rigoulet | ☎ 05 53 96 43 45 |

| Bon-Encontre | Méridionale d'Environnement,
ZI Jean Malèze, 33 rue Denis Papin | ☎ 05 53 66 78 82 |

| Sérignac-sur-Garonne | Roussille Thierry, Jouanisson | ☎ 05 53 68 71 55 |

Entertainment

This section isn't intended to be a definitive guide but gives a wide range of ideas for the department. Prices and opening hours were correct at the time of publication, but it's best to check before travelling long distances.

Cinemas

| Agen | CGR Carnot, 78 boulevard Carnot
programme information | ☎ 05 53 47 06 95
☎ 08 92 68 04 45 |

| | Montreurs d'Images, 6 rue Ledru Rollin ☎ 05 53 48 23 51
Art and cultural films. |

| Marmande | Comédia, 30 rue Léopold Faye
programme information | ☎ 05 53 64 21 32
☎ 08 92 68 01 74 |

| | Plaza, 32 boulevard de Maré
programme information | ☎ 05 53 20 95 12
☎ 08 92 68 01 74 |

| Nérac | Le Margot, place Général de Gaulle
🖳 *www.ville-nerac.fr* | ☎ 05 53 65 25 25 |

| Villeneuve-sur-Lot | Cinéma Cyrano,
9 boulevard de la Marine | ☎ 08 92 68 70 12 |

English Books

All the public libraries detailed below have English books and are closed on Mondays.

	Tue	Wed	Thu	Fri	Sat
Agen place Armand Fallières ☎ 05 53 66 50 52	1.30–6.00	10.00–12.00 1.30–6.00	1.30–6.00	1.30–6.00	10.00–12.00 1.30–6.00
Marmande 23 rue de la République ☎ 05 53 20 94 95	1.30–6.00	9.00–12.00 1.30–6.00	8.45–12.00 1.30–6.00	1.30–6.00	8.45–12.00 2.00–5.00
Nérac Espace d'Albret, Quai de la Baïse ☎ 05 53 97 40 55	2.00–6.00	9.00–12.00 2.00–6.00	2.00–6.00	2.00–6.00	9.00–12.30 1.30–5.30
Villeneuve-sur-Lot Centre Culturel, 23 rue Etienne Marcel ☎ 05 53 70 19 38	10.00–12.00 2.00–6.30	10.00–6.30	2.00–6.30	2.00–6.30	10.00–12.00 2.00–5.00

Festivals

There are many festivals in this department, and just a small selection is detailed here. Festivals are annual unless otherwise stated.

July	Agen

Agen
Les Nuits d'Eté   ☎ 05 53 69 41 74
Organised by the regional Conseil Général, this is a series of
classical and rock concerts, shows and short operas, held in
the grounds of the Conseil Général on the right bank of
the Garonne.

Villeneuve-sur-Lot
Festival du Rire   ☎ 05 53 40 04 53
A festival of humour and comedy at the beginning
of July.

Villeneuve-sur-Lot
Festival de Jazz en Villeneuvois   ☎ 05 53 36 17 30
A series of jazz concerts held at Cale de la Marine on the river
around the second week of July.

July/August   Sainte Livrade
A plum-stone spitting competition – not exactly a festival
but an event worthy of a mention due to its unusual
nature. Over 130 contestants from a
dozen countries.

August	Marmande	
	Music and Lyric Festival	☎ 05 53 64 44 44

This festival is internationally known and growing in popularity
and attendance each year.

Miramont-de-Guyenne
Festival des Arts de la Rue ☎ 05 53 93 20 52
During the first weekend of August the streets are full
of artists.

Monflanquin
Festival 'Grange de Piquemil' ☎ 05 53 36 55 76
Evening piano recitals over a period of five days towards the
end of the month.

Theatres

Agen   Espace Culturel François Mitterrand,
          avenue François Mitterrand, Boé   ☎ 05 53 48 10 82
          🖳 *www.ville-boe.fr*

          Théâtre Ducourneau,
          place Docteur Esquirol   ☎ 05 53 66 26 60

          Théâtre du Jour, 21 rue Paulin Régnier   ☎ 05 53 47 82 08

Nérac   Espace d'Albret, quai de la Baïse   ☎ 05 53 97 40 50
          (a modern building on the left immediately after the bridge
          on the road to Agen)

Villeneuve-sur- Théâtre Georges Leygues,
Lot   boulevard Georges Leygues   ☎ 05 53 70 37 24

          Théâtre du Terrain Vague,
          Château Bonrepos   ☎ 05 53 01 76 65

Video & DVD Hire

Agen   Vidéo Futur, 51 boulevard Pellatan   ☎ 05 53 47 89 70
          Open every day from 11am to 1pm and 3pm to 9pm.
          24-hour dispenser outside.

Marmande Canal Vidéo,
          34 boulevard Docteur Fourcade   ☎ 05 53 93 91 47
          Open 4 to 10pm.

Nérac   Evasion Vidéo, 75 allées d'Albret   ☎ 06 89 89 42 62
          Mondays to Fridays 6 to 7.30pm, Saturdays 6 to 8pm. There's
          a 24-hour video and DVD dispenser outside the shop.

Villeneuve-sur-Lot	Vidéo Futur, 16 avenue Général Leclerc	☎ 05 53 40 03 27

Mondays 3 to 8pm, Tuesdays to Sundays 10am to noon and 3 to 8pm.

Leisure Activities

This section isn't intended to be a definitive guide but gives a wide range of ideas for the department. Prices and opening hours were correct at the time of publication, but it's best to check before travelling long distances.

Amateur Radio

Villeneuve-sur-Lot — Radio Club Villeneuvois   ☎ 05 53 70 06 73
Training and promotion of amateur radio.
Contact Mr Lopez.

Aqua Gym

Agen — ASPTT Aqua Gym   ☎ 05 53 98 28 39
✉ *asptt47.agen@wanadoo.fr*
Contact Mme Albrespy.

Villeneuve-sur-Lot — Piscine de Malbentre, rue de Malbentre, Pujols   ☎ 05 53 70 97 26
(on the south-west side of the town)

Art Classes

Agen — l'Atelier Créatif, 18 rue Jacquard   ☎ 05 53 47 78 45
This art shop run courses for both adults and children. Open Tuesdays to Saturdays 10am to 7pm.

Détente et Loisirs sur le Plateau de St Ferréol, St Ferréol, Bon-Encontre   ☎ 05 53 96 59 22
(south-east out of Agen)
Various courses, including painting, sewing and painting on silk.

Villeneuve-sur-Lot — Art Vivant   ☎ 05 53 70 40 53
Contact Mr Leclerc.

StARTup   ☎ 06 19 99 67 77
Painting, music and theatre. Contact Mr Bohéra.

L'Atelier de Peinture   ☎ 06 70 17 10 34
Various painting courses. Contact Mme Paillaud for details.

Ballooning

St Jean-de-Duras	Montgolfière Domaine de Durand 💻 *www.domainededurand.com* Flights for individuals and families. Open all year; flights dependent on weather.	☎ 05 53 89 02 23
Serignac-sur-Garonne	Montgolfières de la Garonne	☎ 05 53 47 12 68

Bike Hire

Agen	Tourist Office, 107 boulevard Carnot	☎ 05 53 47 36 09
	Vélo & Oxygène, 18 avenue du Général de Gaulle	☎ 05 53 47 76 76
Feugarolles	'Maintenant', route de Thouars (north of Nérac) Bike hire from €6 for half a day, €50 for a week. Open all year.	☎ 05 53 67 46 67
Fumel	AJF Cycles, 8 place Postel (south-east of Agen)	☎ 05 53 71 14 57
Montayral	'Cadams' (east of Fumel) Mountain bikes for hire, repairs and courses; itineraries available. Open weekends April to October and weekdays from mid-June to mid-September, 8.30am to12.30pm and 1.30 to 6pm.	☎ 05 53 36 07 00
Prayssas	Néguenou Loisir, le Lac (north-east of Agen) 245km (155mi) of paths and 15 circuits, mountain bike hire and washing point for bikes.	☎ 05 53 95 00 67

Boat & Train Rides

Agen	Bateau l'Agenais, Quai de Dunkerque A variety of cruises available, including sightseeing and passion fruit-and Armagnac-tasting trips.	☎ 05 53 87 51 95
Fumel	Au Fil du Lot A gentle 15km (9mi) cruise along the Lot passing châteaux and mills. Sundays in June at 3pm; four departures a day in July and August; two departures each afternoon 1st to 15th September (closed Mondays). Adults €5.50, 5 to 13-year-olds €3. Minimum of eight passengers per trip.	☎ 05 53 71 13 70

| Nérac | Les Croisières du Prince Henri, quai de la Baïse ☎ 05 53 65 66 66 |

One-hour cruises with commentary on the river Baïse from Nérac. Tasting cruises available in the summer. April and October cruises on Sunday and bank holiday afternoons; May to September three to four cruises every day, the morning cruise includes a regional product tasting. Adult €7, under 13s €4.50.

Train Touristique de l'Albret, Gard de Nérac, 12ter avenue du 19 Mars 1962   ☎ 05 53 67 21 23
Trains run between Nérac and Mézin providing a two-hour return journey through the countryside. April, May and September weekends and bank holidays at 10am, 2.15pm and 4.45pm, Tuesdays to Fridays by appointment; June to August Tuesdays to Sundays. Adults €8.50, children €5.50.

Villeneuve-sur-Lot   Bâteaux Promenades Electriques, Berges du Lot, Ponton de l'Aviron   ☎ 05 53 36 17 30
Small electric boats for hire.

Boat Hire

Agen   Locaboat Plaisance, quai de Dunkerque   ☎ 05 53 66 00 74
Cruisers for hire for 2 to 20 people; no licence required.

Buzet-sur-Baïse   Aquitaine Navigation, Port de Buzet   ☎ 05 53 84 72 50
🖥 *www.aquitaine-navigation.com*
Boat hire without licence for 2 to 12 people, for the day or the week. Also based at Capitainerie du Port, Nérac.

Boules & Pétanque

Agen   Pétanque du Pont de la Garde   ☎ 05 53 96 89 42
Based at bar 'Chez Mario', 30 boulevard de la Liberté.

Marmande   Association Sportive des Cheminots – Pétanque, Garde de Marmande, place du 11 novembre   ☎ 05 53 20 45 63

Nérac   Pétanque du Petit Nérac   ☎ 05 53 65 10 41
Contact Mr Jouan.

Villeneuve-sur-Lot   Pétanque Villeneuvoise   ☎ 05 53 70 35 65
Contact Jacques Vesconi.

Bouncy Castle Hire

Montaigu-de-Quercy   J-M Asport, Teillefer   ☎ 05 63 94 30 44
Hire of bouncy castles, delivered and set up.

Bridge

Agen	Bridge Club Agenais, 139 avenue Jean Jaurès	☎ 05 53 66 55 74
Marmande	Bridge Cub de Marmande Contact Mr De Mirman.	☎ 05 53 64 09 46
Nérac	Club de Bridge Contact Mme Tomachot.	☎ 05 53 65 31 47
Villeneuve-sur-Lot	Bridge Club Villeneuvois An active club with regular competitions. Contact Mr Buy.	☎ 05 53 49 08 84
	Bridge Club, 8 boulevard de la Marine Beginners Wednesdays 2 to 5pm and matches Fridays at 2pm.	☎ 05 53 70 35 34

Circus Skills

Villeneuve-sur-Lot	Le Jongléreur Contact Mr Depaire.	☎ 05 53 70 22 67
	Lézard du Cirque Contact Simone Schaming for details of current courses.	☎ 05 53 49 29 17

Dancing

Agen	ABC Danse, avenue de Vérone Including rock and roll, cha cha, waltz and tango. Individual or group lessons. Contact Mme Bouquet.	☎ 05 53 66 97 55
	Association Danse la Vie Oriental and Egyptian dance; courses, workshops and individual lessons. Contact Mme d'Jouder.	☎ 05 53 95 76 72
	Les Chaussons Rouges, 15 rue d'Albret Ballet classes. Contact Mme Pauliard.	☎ 05 53 47 52 69
	Ecole de Danse, Prés Carnot Various classes, including ballet and jazz.	☎ 05 53 47 20 67
	Ecole Nationale de Musique et de Danse, 11 rue Lakanal Contact Mme Julié.	☎ 05 53 66 11 66
Marmande	InTi, Association de Tango	☎ 05 53 94 11 78
Nérac	Ecole de Danse, 12 rue du Lys	☎ 06 75 13 00 38

| Villeneuve-sur-Lot | Club Villeneuvois de Danse de Société
Contact Mr Santini. | ☎ 05 53 70 02 22 |

Danse et Expression
Contemporary dance. Contact Mme Frias. ☎ 05 53 70 85 43

Genération Claquettes
Tap dance. Contact Mr Bonizzoni. ☎ 05 53 70 00 79

Dog Clubs

Marmande
Club Canin
Contact Mr Ducan. ☎ 05 53 20 93 31

Drama

Agen
Compagnie de l'Escalier qui Monte,
Centre Culturel, 10 rue Ledru Rollin ☎ 05 53 87 48 59
Contact Mme Barthe.

Ecole Supérieure d'Art Dramatique,
21 rue Paulin Régnier ☎ 05 53 47 82 09
Contact Mme Bouillon.

Marmande
Amicale Laïque Théâtre,
Ecole Edouard Herriot ☎ 05 53 64 27 27
Contact Mr Dutel.

Atelier Jean-Pierre Plazas, Petit Théâtre,
allées des Tabacs ☎ 05 53 94 11 78
Theatrical and improvisation courses held throughout the
week for children and adults.

Nérac
Atelier Théâtre de l'Escalier,
Espace d'Albret ☎ 05 53 87 48 59
Theatre courses for six to ten-year-olds Tuesdays at 5.30pm
and Wednesdays 3.45pm, 11 to 14-year-olds Wednesdays
2pm and adults Tuesdays 8 to 10pm.

Villeneuve-sur-Lot
Les Apartés
Local theatre group. ☎ 05 53 41 96 48

Les Compagnons de l'Aurore
Medieval stage shows. ☎ 06 70 62 10 08

Gyms & Health Clubs

Agen
Olympie, 43 rue Camille Desmoulins ☎ 05 53 48 03 09
Weights, cardio equipment and beauty rooms.

Gym Carreras,
27 boulevard Edouard Lacour ☎ 05 53 96 67 18
Cardio equipment, weights and sauna.

Marmande   Aquaval, rue Portogruaro ☎ 05 53 20 40 53
This swimming complex has a gym with cardio equipment,
weights, sauna and solarium. Open every day: Mondays and
Thursdays 10am to 8pm, Tuesdays and Fridays 10am to 9pm,
Wednesdays and Saturdays 10am to 7pm, Sundays
8.30am to 12.30pm.

Villeneuve-sur- Eden Body, 40 rue Pujols ☎ 05 53 49 05 80
Lot   Cardio equipment and weights. Open Tuesdays and
Thursdays 9am to 9pm, Mondays, Wednesdays and
Fridays 9am to noon and 3 to 9pm, Saturdays 9am
to noon.

Karting & Quad Bikes

Agen   Karting Club d'Agen ☎ 05 53 87 84 52
Contact Mr Garcia.

Bonaguil   ATV Adventures ☎ 05 53 41 76 23
(in the extreme north-west of the department, on the border
with Lot)
Off-road excursions in maximum groups of four quad bikes.
No experience required, just a car or motorbike licence.
Passengers go free. From half an hour to half a day.

Caudecoste   Loisirs Karting 47, Base de Loisirs ☎ 05 53 87 31 42
🖥 www.karting47.fr
(15km/11mi south-east of Agen)
A new outdoor karting circuit with karts for all ages from
three-years-old. Trial circuits, lessons and courses. Open all
year from 10am to 12.30pm (except Tuesdays) and 2pm to
midnight (9pm in summer). Closed all day Tuesdays in winter.
Prices from €9.

Marmande   Karting Club Marmandais, ZI Nord,
route de Beaupuy ☎ 05 53 64 99 97
Contact Mr Di Palma.

St Sernin-de- Moto Sport Loisirs, Courtaou ☎ 05 53 94 18 68
Duras   (north of Marmande, near Duras and next to
lake Castelgaillard)
Both motorbikes and quad bikes can be taken round this
course. Introductory sessions and courses; motocross and
grass track. Open all year by appointment. From €35
per person.

| Ste Bazeille | Kart'Ind, route de Bordeaux, RN113   ☎ 05 53 76 04 3C |
| | A 400m indoor track, adult and junior karts (from seven-years-old) and mini motorbikes. Open Wednesdays to Sundays. |

| Villeneuve-sur-Lot | Karting du Villeneuvois   ☎ 05 53 70 64 28 |
| | Contact Mme Bouhet. Minimum age 16. |

Model Clubs

| Villeneuve-sur-Lot | Model Air Club Villeneuvois   ☎ 05 53 40 03 77 |
| | For nine-year-olds and upwards. Contact Mr Laparre. |

Music

| Agen | Ecole Nationale de Musique et de Danse, 11 rue Lakanal   ☎ 05 53 66 11 66 |
| | Contact Mme Julié. |

Fédération Musicale Aquitaine, Centre Culturel, rue Ledru Rollin   ☎ 05 53 96 16 83
Contact Mr Fondriest, who is involved in a variety of musical organisations across Agen.

Routes du Rock   ☎ 05 53 66 13 61
✉ routesdurock@aol.com
Contact Mr Desméroux.

| Marmande | Printemps Musical du Marmandais   ☎ 05 53 20 84 44 |
| | Contact Mr Cazassus. |

| Nérac | ☎ 05 53 67 11 55 |
| | Guitar lessons. Contact Mme Hélène Groussolles. |

L'Ecole de Musique, Espace Culturel, avenue de Lattre de Tassigny   ☎ 05 53 97 40 52

| Villeneuve-sur-Lot | Batterie Fanfare Jeunes Villeneuvois   ☎ 05 53 70 13 22 |
| | Drum lessons. |

Orchestre Municipal d'Harmonie   ☎ 05 53 70 28 63
Rehearsals and shows, musicals and performances at official ceremonies.

Off-Roading

| Agen | Club 4x4 47   ☎ 05 53 66 44 47 |
| | Contact Mr Rouquier. |

| Marmande | Club 4x4
Contact Mr Daousse. | ☎ 05 53 64 00 49 |

| Villeneuve-sur-Lot | Loisir 4x4
Minimum age 18. Contact Mr Clerc. | ☎ 05 53 98 37 84 |

Paint Ball

| Caudecoste | Loisirs Karting 47, Base de Loisirs
🖳 *www.karting47.fr*
(15km/11mi south-east of Agen)
Open all year from 10am to 12.30pm (except Tuesdays) and 2pm to midnight (9pm in summer). Closed all day Tuesdays in winter. Paintball from €11. | ☎ 05 53 87 31 42 |

| Villeneuve-sur-Lot | Logistique Paintball, RN21
(off the N21 at Villeneuve-sur-Lot, then marked to Pujols)
Day and evening sessions available. From €16 for adults, €14 for under 17s. | ☎ 05 53 71 83 23 |

Photography

| Agen | Photo Club de Agen
Contact Mr Moreno. | ☎ 05 53 67 05 25 |

| Marmande | ASPTT Photographie, Complexe Carpète, rue Jean Memoz
Contact Mr Duranteau. | ☎ 05 53 20 97 04 |

| Villeneuve-sur-Lot | Cercle Photo
Contact Mr Courtine. | ☎ 05 53 70 24 38 |

| | Objectif Image – Photo Club PTT
Contact Mr Seyler. | ☎ 05 53 70 77 05 |

Scouts & Guides

| Agen | Scouts de France
Contact Mr Volpato. | ☎ 05 53 66 93 80 |

| Marmande | Scouts de France
Contact Mme Darribehaude. | ☎ 05 53 94 25 90 |

| Nérac | Scouts Unitaires de France
Contact Mme de Lisleferme. | ☎ 05 53 65 80 25 |

Social Groups

| Agen | Agen Accueil
A group to help newcomers to Agen meet people and learn about the area. Contact Mme Lalot. | ☎ 05 53 47 22 94 |

Nérac	Nérac Accueil, contact Mme Josse	☎ 05 53 65 01 33

Welcome group for newcomers to Nérac and the
surrounding areas.

Villeneuve-sur-Lot	AVF Villeneuve/Lot	☎ 05 53 49 32 69

A group to welcome new arrivals to Villeneuve-sur-Lot and the
surrounding area. Contact Mr Gas.

Comité Jumelages Villeneuve & Troon   ☎ 06 70 37 78 81
This is the town twinning committee for Villeneuve-sur-Lot and
Troon in Scotland.

Boulevard Fifties   ☎ 05 53 41 72 01
Lovers of rock music, cars and motorbikes from the '50s.
Contact Patrick Vidal.

Groupe d'Animations Musicales
Villeneuvois   ☎ 05 53 70 71 10
Tea dances, variety evenings and shows.
Contact Mr Barde.

Rotary Clubs

Agen	Rotary Club d'Agen	☎ 05 53 66 78 20
	Contact Mr Dardaud	
Nérac	Rotary Club de Nérac	☎ 05 53 97 41 10
	Based at Hôtel d'Albret, allées d'Albret.	
Villeneuve-sur-Lot	Rotary Club Villeneuve	☎ 05 53 70 61 12
	Contact Mr Uhnanue.	

Spas

Casteljaloux	Le Thermes, la Bartère	☎ 05 53 20 59 00

🖳 *www.eurothermes.com*
A spa complex dedicated to health and relaxation,
including some treatments for specific health problems.
Three-star accommodation and packages from
two to six nights.

Stamp Collecting

Agen	Cercle Philatélique de l'Agenais,	
	Centre Culture, rue Ledrun Rollin	☎ 05 53 67 15 28

✉ *dominique.tallet@wanadoo.fr*

Marmande	Amicale Philatélique du Marmandais	☎ 05 53 64 03 33
	Contact Mr Biras.	

| Villeneuve-sur-Lot | Le Club Philatélique du Villeneuvois, 47 rue de Pujols | ☎ 05 53 41 91 81 |

Villeneuve-sur-Lot   Le Club Philatélique du Villeneuvois,
47 rue de Pujols   ☎ 05 53 41 91 81
An active club that organises exchanges. Meets the first Sunday in the month at 10am and the fourth Thursday at 8.30pm. Contact Mr Bertrand.

Tree Climbing

Lacapelle-Biron   Parc en Ciel, Moulin de Courrance   ☎ 05 53 71 84 58
🖳 *www.parc-en-ciel.com*
(north-east corner of Lot-et-Garonne)
Situated in a huge woodland this is an adventure up in the tree tops, including monkey bridges, rope ladders and aerial runways. There are five routes for different abilities. Full safety equipment provided. Minimum height 1.20m (4ft). There's also a small area with farm animals, crazy golf, a snack bar and a picnic area.

St Vincent-de-Cosse   Airparc Périgord, Port d'Enveaux   ☎ 05 53 29 18 43
(between the river and railway line)
Explore the tree tops whilst negotiating rope ladders, swing bridges and more. Trainers/sports shoes recommended. Full safety equipment provided.

Vintage Cars

Marmande   Vieilles Roues Marmandaises   ☎ 05 53 89 50 24
Contact Mr Joret.

Villeneuve-sur-Lot   Vieilles Voitures Villeneuvoises   ☎ 05 53 40 14 62
Contact Mr Hasse.

Walking & Rambling

Agen   Comité Départemental de la Randonnée
Pédestre, 4 rue André Chénier   ☎ 05 53 48 03 41
🖳 *www.cdrp47.asso.fr*
The organisation responsible for walking groups and routes in the department. Maps and details of walks available. Office open Mondays to Fridays 9am to 5.30pm.

Les Randonneurs de l'Agenais, Centre
Culturel, rue Ledru Rollin   ☎ 05 53 66 46 31
Contact Mlle Derruppe.

There's a footpath alongside the canal at Agen, some sections of which are lit at night.

Marmande   ASPTT de Marmande,
Randonnée Pédestre   ☎ 05 53 20 01 07
Contact Mr Dall'Agnese.

| Nérac | Nature Orientation Randnée Détente | ☎ 05 53 97 09 48 |
| | Contact Mme Coudert. | |

| Villeneuve-sur-Lot | Groupe des Randonneurs Villeneuvois | ☎ 05 53 01 33 71 |
| | Contact Mr Della'Corte. | |

Yoga

| Agen | Yoga d'Agen | ☎ 05 53 68 03 23 |
| | Contact Mme Accary. | |

| | Association Auma Yoga, | |
| | 14bis rue des Droits de l'Homme | ☎ 05 53 95 65 03 |

| Marmande | Ananda Beyssac Yoga | ☎ 05 53 64 34 29 |
| | Contact Mme Hombert. | |

| Nérac | Auma Yoga | ☎ 05 53 65 65 03 |
| | Contact Mme Arbizu. | |

| Villeneuve-sur-Lot | Cercle Diffusion de Yoga | ☎ 05 53 70 98 28 |
| | Contact J. Marchio. | |

| | Association Reliance, boulevard Danton | ☎ 05 53 40 09 14 |

Medical Facilities & Services

Ambulances

In the event of a medical emergency dial 15.

Agen	☎ 05 53 98 25 25
Marmande	☎ 05 53 20 66 66
Nérac	☎ 05 53 65 02 31
Villeneuve-sur-Lot	☎ 05 53 01 27 27

Chiropractors

Eymet	Simon Pullen, 18 boulevard National	☎ 05 53 23 32 21
	(Eymet is on the southern border of Dordogne, close to Lot-et-Garonne)	
	This is an English-speaking chiropractor.	

Doctors

English-speakers may like to contact the following doctors.

Agen	Dr Tapesar, 39 rue Alsace Lorraine	☎ 05 53 66 06 01
Marmande	Dr Monguillot, 37 avenue Maréchal Joffre	☎ 05 53 20 97 97
Nérac	Dr Macky, 13 allées d'Albret	☎ 05 53 65 00 16
Villeneuve-sur-Lot	Dr Mourgues, 37 rue Pujols	☎ 05 53 70 30 01

Dentists

English-speakers may like to contact the following dentists.

Agen	Dr Welsch-Beitz, 2 rue Pierre Courbet	☎ 05 53 87 53 53
Marmande	Dr Camps, 4 rue Lozes	☎ 05 53 64 34 28
Nérac	Dr Bonnet, 57 allées d'Albret	☎ 05 53 65 39 90
Villeneuve-sur-Lot	Groupe Dentaire, 11 cours Victor Hugo	☎ 05 53 40 32 32

Gendarmeries

Agen	15 rue Valence	☎ 05 53 69 30 00
Marmande	40 boulevard Meyniel	☎ 05 53 64 83 00
Nérac	43 avenue Maréchal Foch	☎ 05 53 97 44 30
Villeneuve-sur-Lot	11 boulevard Danton	☎ 05 53 49 75 00

Health Authority

General	CRAM Aquitaine, 80 avenue de la Jallère, Bordeaux 💻 *www.cram-aquitaine.fr* This is the regional office.	☎ 05 56 11 64 13
Agen	2 rue Diderot Open Mondays to Fridays 8am to 5pm (no appointment necessary).	☎ 05 53 66 45 57
Marmande	38 avenue Pierre Buffin Open Mondays to Fridays 8am to noon and 1 to 4.30pm (no appointment necessary).	☎ 05 53 76 01 20

Nérac	Centre Haussmann, Salle Lapeyrusse ☎ 05 53 66 45 57
	Every Wednesday 9 to 10.30am without appointment, 10.30am to noon by appointment.

Villeneuve-sur-Lot	Hôtel de Ville, boulevard de la République ☎ 05 53 66 45 57
	Mondays and Fridays 9am to noon and Thursdays 1.30 to 4.30pm (no appointment necessary); Mondays 1.30 to 4.30pm by appointment.

Hospitals

All these hospitals have an emergency department.

Agen	Centre Hospitalier d'Agen, St Esprit ☎ 05 53 69 70 71

Marmande	Centre Hospitalier Marmande Tonneins, 76 rue Docteur Courret ☎ 05 53 20 30 40

Nérac	Hôpital de Nérac, 14 rue Sainte Claire ☎ 05 53 97 61 00

Villeneuve-sur-Lot	Centre Hospitalier St Cyr, 2 boulevard St Cyr de Cocquard ☎ 05 53 40 53 40

Motoring

Breakers' Yards

Allez-et-Cazeneuve	Auto Carambolage 47, route de Bordeaux ☎ 05 53 01 43 33
	(west of Villeneuve-sur-Lot)

Lafox	Le Parc Automobile, Pont de Lafox Nord ☎ 05 53 68 53 19
	(on the N113 south-east of Agen)

Car Dealers

Agen	Audi, Auto Sun 47, Métairie de Beauregard, Le Passage ☎ 05 53 77 70 30
	BMW, Auto Ville et Campagne, RN 113, Boé ☎ 05 53 96 29 55
	Citroën, Bigot Autos, 70 avenue de Bigorre, Boé ☎ 05 53 77 55 55

Daewoo, Espace Découverte Auto II,
avenue d'Aquitaine, Boé   ☎ 05 53 96 04 42

Chrysler/Jeep, Dutheil Auto,
Foulayronnes   ☎ 05 53 95 85 85

Ford, Malbet Auto,
avenue Maréchal Leclerc   ☎ 05 53 77 15 40

Hyundai, Manfé, route de Bordeaux,
Colayrac St Cirq   ☎ 05 53 47 02 32

Kia, Espace Découverte Auto I,
2 boulevard Edouard Lacour   ☎ 05 53 96 44 75

Mazda, Agen Motors, route de Toulouse,
Castelculier   ☎ 05 53 77 74 74

Mercedes, Garage Legrand,
31 boulevard Edouard Lacour   ☎ 05 53 77 28 30

Peugeot, Macard Ets, rue André Boillot   ☎ 05 53 77 46 46

Renault, Garage ADREA, rue du Midi,
ZAC Agen Sud   ☎ 05 53 77 70 00

Saab, Espace Découverte Auto II,
avenue d'Aquitaine, Boé   ☎ 05 53 96 04 42

Seat, 1089 avenue Maréchal Leclerc   ☎ 05 53 68 69 99

Skoda, Beauregard Auto, Pont de
Beauregard, Le Passage   ☎ 05 53 77 70 95

Suzuki, Espace Découverte Auto II,
avenue d'Aquitaine, Boé   ☎ 05 53 96 04 42

Toyota, Dartus Autos, RN113,
Gimbrède, Colayrac St Cirq   ☎ 05 53 67 65 20

Vauxhall/Opel, Auto Aquitaine,
avenue Docteur Jean Bru   ☎ 05 53 77 88 88

VW, Auto Sun 47, Métairie de
Beauregard, Le Passage   ☎ 05 53 77 70 30

Marmande	Audi, Garage Fréchic, route de Bordeaux	☎ 05 53 76 05 50
	BMW, Garage Raymond, route de Bordeaux	☎ 05 53 64 07 59
	Daewoo, Center d'Auto de Lestang, avenue Paul Gabarra	☎ 05 53 64 14 39
	Fiat, Garage Auto Aquitaine, 130 avenue Jean Jaurès	☎ 05 53 64 75 71
	Peugeot, GGA, 95 avenue Jean Jaurès	☎ 05 53 64 34 47
	Renault, AMC, route de Bordeaux, Sainte Bazeille	☎ 05 53 20 80 80
	Rover, Centre d'Auto de Lestang, avenue Paul Gabarra	☎ 05 53 64 14 39
	Saab, Centre d'Auto de Lestang, avenue Paul Gabarra	☎ 05 53 64 14 39
	Suzuki, Centre d'Auto de Lestang, avenue Paul Gabarra	☎ 05 53 64 14 39
	Toyota, Garage Raymond, route de Bordeaux	☎ 05 53 64 07 59
	Vauxhall/Opel, Aquitaine Auto, route de Bordeaux, Sainte Bazeille	☎ 05 53 83 83 33
	VW, Garage Fréchic, route de Bordeaux	☎ 05 53 76 05 50
Nérac	Citroën, D Soubiran, route de Condom	☎ 05 53 65 69 42
	Peugeot, JJ Beaumont, route de Bordeaux	☎ 05 53 65 03 42
	Renault, Garage d'Albret, place du Foirail	☎ 05 53 65 38 73
	Vauxhall/Opel, D Bellandi, route de Bordeaux	☎ 05 53 65 08 19

Villeneuve-sur-Lot	Alfa Romeo, Franzin, route de Bordeaux, Bias	☎ 05 53 70 13 05
	Audi, Auto Sun 47, route de Bordeaux, Bias	☎ 05 53 40 31 22
	Citroën, Bigot Autos, ZA Parasol, route de Fumel	☎ 05 53 40 06 90
	Fiat, Franzin, route de Bordeaux, Bias	☎ 05 53 70 13 05
	Ford, Garage Malbet, Souilles, Bias	☎ 05 53 40 29 77
	Honda, Boudou, 1 avenue d'Agen	☎ 05 53 49 07 57
	Mitsubishi, Franzin, 33 avenue d'Agen	☎ 05 53 01 19 18
	Nissan, Laudis Autos, Souilles, Bias	☎ 05 53 40 08 79
	Peugeot, Macard 47, 111 route de Bordeaux, Bias	☎ 05 53 40 56 05
	Renault, Villeneuve Autos, route de Bordeaux, Bias	☎ 05 53 40 55 55
	Toyota, Best Auto, 438 route de Bordeaux, Bias	☎ 05 53 49 55 95
	Vauxhall/Opel, Garage Parise, 67 avenue Général Leclerc	☎ 05 53 70 89 32
	Volvo, Soverauto, route de Bordeaux, Bias	☎ 05 53 49 21 44
	VW, Auto Sun 47, route de Bordeaux, Bias	☎ 05 53 40 31 22

Tyre & Exhaust Centres

Agen	Midas, 182 avenue Jean Jaurès	☎ 05 53 47 04 44
Marmande	Point S, 123 avenue Jean Jaurès, route de Bordeaux	☎ 05 53 89 26 74
Nérac	Villeneuve-sur-Lot Pneus, Seguinot	☎ 05 53 65 81 07
Villeneuve-sur-Lot	FAP, ZAC de Parasol	☎ 05 53 49 58 60

Pets

Dog Training

Ste Colombe-de-Villeneuve	Chenil des Lauriers, Pech de Laborde (south-west of Villeneuve-sur-Lot)	☎ 05 53 70 51 78
Villeneuve-sur-Lot	Club Education Canine Contact Jacky Fabre.	☎ 05 53 70 04 95

Farriers

General	Christian Fremy, 19 boulevard Horizon, Penne d'Agenais (east of Villeneuve-sur-Lot)	☎ 05 53 41 73 78
	Alain Charlot, 444 rue Gaston Imbert, Miramont de Guyenne (in the north of the department)	☎ 05 53 93 37 56

Horse Dentists

Vets don't deal with teeth rasping and there are specialist equine dentists. You need to telephone in advance to be booked onto the next circuit.

General	Christian Frémy, 19 boulevard Horizon, Penne d'Agenais (east of Villeneuve-sur-Lot)	☎ 05 53 41 73 78

Kennels & Catteries

Agen	Centre Canin Moulié, RN21, Foulayronnes Kennels only.	☎ 05 53 47 33 60
Ste Colombe-de-Villeneuve	Chenil des Lauriers, Pech de Laborde (south-west of Villeneuve-sur-Lot) Kennels and cattery.	☎ 05 53 70 51 78

Pet Parlours

Agen	Au Chien Chic, boulevard Sylvain Dumon	☎ 05 53 66 17 20
Marmande	Toilettage de la Gravette, 13 rue Jean Goujon	☎ 05 53 20 79 88
Nérac	Toutou Flash, 31 rue Brèche (just below the tourist office going towards the river)	☎ 05 53 65 30 67

Villeneuve-sur-Lot   Au Salon du Chien, rue des Elus   ☎ 05 53 71 22 84

Riding Equipment

Agen   Booka Equitation,
4 boulevard de la République   ☎ 05 53 66 90 70

SPA

Agen   SPA du 47, 29 rue Baudin   ☎ 05 53 47 32 62

Refuge de Brax, 1 chemin Franchinet,
Brax
(directly east of Agen)   ☎ 05 53 96 77 97

Caubeyres   SPA du 47, Lasgraouettes
(north-east of Nérac)   ☎ 05 53 88 05 71

Veterinary Clinics

Agen   Clinique Vétérinaire Saint Jacques,
1497 avenue Maréchal Leclerc   ☎ 05 53 68 22 33
(south of the town centre, beside the Parc des Sports)

Marmande   Clinique Vétérinaire du Docteur Ziani,
21 rue Jean Mermoz   ☎ 05 53 20 88 43

Nérac   Cabinet Vétérinaire des Allées,
37 allées d'Albret   ☎ 05 53 65 02 80
English is spoken at the practice with open consultations
every day 2 to 4pm.

Villeneuve-sur-Lot   Cabinet, 4 rue du Docteur Pierre
Mourgues   ☎ 05 53 40 10 33
Dr Blineau at this practice speaks English.

Places To Visit

This section isn't intended to be a definitive guide but gives a wide range of ideas for the department. Prices and opening hours were correct at the time of publication, but it's best to check before travelling long distances.

Beaches & Water Parks

Many towns and villages have a *plan d'eau*, which can be a lake or riverside location. It may be just for fishing and picnics or there may be facilities such as a beach, playground and crazy golf.

Cancon	Centre Touristique du Lac	☎ 05 53 01 60 24

(north of Villeneuve-sur-Lot)
Leisure park with fishing, swimming pool, crazy golf, bar, restaurant and table tennis. Open 1st June to 30th September. Free admission.

Mézin-Réaup	Base de Loisirs de Lislebonne	☎ 05 53 65 65 28

(south-west of Nérac)
Lakeside bathing, restaurant, barbeques, canoes and kayaks, pony rides and mountain biking. Open 1st June to 30th September every day 8.30am to 10.30pm.

Châteaux

Duras	Château de Duras	☎ 05 53 83 77 32

🖳 *www.chateau-de-duras.com*
A 12th to 18th century château, also known as the Château des Ducs, with 32 rooms open to visitors, workshops and an audiovisual presentation. The armoury workshop traces the development of metalwork from prehistoric times to the end of the Middle Ages with demonstrations in the high season. Guided tours available. Open November to the beginning of the February weekends and school holidays only 2 to 6pm; March to May and October every day 10am to noon and 2 to 6pm; June and September every day 10am to 12.30pm and 2 to 7pm; July and August every day 10am to 7pm. Adults €4.30, children €2.30.

Grézet-Cavagnan	Château de Malvirade	☎ 05 53 20 61 31

This 16th century château has battlements, towers and a large park. Every Thursday in the summer there are medieval evenings with candlelight, period music and people in costume.

Fumel	Le Château de Bonaguil, St Front-sur-Lemance	☎ 05 53 71 13 70

🖳 *www.bonaguil.org*
Built at the end of the 15th century, this château was modelled on a fort. Open February, March and October every day 11am to 1pm and 2.30 to 5.30pm; April, May and September every day 10.30am to 1pm and 2.30 to 5.30pm; June to August every day 10am to 6pm; November and December Sundays and bank holidays only 2.30 to 5pm. Adults €4.50, 7 to 16-year-olds €3.

Madaillan	Château Féodal de Madaillan	☎ 05 53 87 56 23

Dating from the 13th to 15th centuries, this château's architecture exemplifies the influence of the French/English wars during the 14th and 15th centuries. Open all year round on Sunday afternoons at 3.30pm; April to July and September Friday to Monday afternoons; August every afternoon. Concerts are held in July and August. Adults €5, under 7s free.

| Nérac | Château Henri IV | ☎ 05 53 65 21 11 |

In the heart of the old town this magnificent Renaissance building is alongside the river Baïse and was home to the family Albret, including the future Henri IV. It currently houses an archaeological museum. Open June to September 10am to noon and 2 to 7pm; October to May 10am to noon and 2 to 6pm. Closed Mondays. Guided tours available in July and August. Adults €4, under 12s free.

| Poudenas | Château de Poudenas, Mézin | ☎ 05 53 65 78 86 |

(south-west of Nérac)
This château was first built in the 13th century and was added to until the 17th century. The interior is beautifully furnished and can be hired out for functions for 20 to 500 people. Guided tours mid-July to the end of August, Tuesdays to Sundays between 3 and 6pm.

| Villeneuve-sur-Lot | Château de la Sylvestrie | ☎ 05 53 40 08 09 |

A château built between the 12th and 16th centuries and enclosed by a medieval courtyard. Open 15th July to the end of August from 3 to 6pm.

Caves

| Castella | Grottes de Fontirou, RN 21 | ☎ 05 53 41 73 97 |

💻 *www.grottes-fontirou.com*
These many-coloured caves contain a wide range of formations. Guided tours take around 40 minutes. Open May to mid-June Sundays and bank holidays 2 to 5.30pm; the last two weeks of June and the first two weeks of September every day 2 to 5.30pm; July and August every day 10am to 12.30pm and 2 to 6pm. Outside there's a crazy golf area and sandwich bar.

| Ste Colombe-de-Villeneuve | Grottes de Lastournelles | ☎ 05 53 40 08 09 |

These caves are more than 25,000 years old with spectacular stalagmites and curtain formations. Open every day in July and August 10am to noon and 2 to 7pm.

Regional Produce

| Beaupuy | Cave de Beaupuy | ☎ 05 53 76 05 10 |

💻 *www.cavedebeaupuy.com*
(just north of Marmande)
Production, sale and distribution of red, rosé and white Côtes du Marmandais wines from 160 local wine-makers. Open all year from 8.30am to noon and 2 to 6.30pm (till 7pm June to September). Free visit and tastings.

Duras	Le Cabri, route de Savignac ☎ 05 53 83 81 03

This goat farm introduces you to their breeding and the production of goat's cheese. Products are on sale at the farm shop. Open from mid-March to the end of December.

Lannes	Château de Lagrangerie ☎ 05 53 65 70 97

Originally a monastery, in the 12th century, this château is now a winery, producing Floc de Gascogne, armagnac and Pruneaux d'Agen. Open every day 9am to noon and 1.30 to 7.30pm.

Le Temple-sur-Lot	Ferme Biologique de Roche, Roche ☎ 05 53 01 21 28

This organic farm grows fruit and vegetables as well as using its produce to make bread, pastries, desserts and fruit juices. Farm shop open Tuesdays and Fridays 5 to 7pm; farm visits by appointment.

Marmande	Foie Gras Farm, Mauveain-sur-Gupie ☎ 05 53 94 20 48

Messieurs Daniel and Thomas Regaud welcome you to their farm, where for the last four generations their family has produced *foie gras*. You can taste goose and duck pate and visit a museum of preserving techniques. Mondays 2 to 6pm, Tuesdays to Fridays 8am to noon and 2 to 6pm.

Mézin	Ferme de Gagnet ☎ 05 53 65 73 76

Producers for three generations, the family Tadieu-Lorenzon invite you to discover some of their products: *foie gras*, *confits des canards*, *eau de vie*, armagnac and Floc de Gascogne. Tasting, commentary and free visits. Open all year 8am to 12.30pm and 3 to 8pm.

Montesquieu	Ferme Roques ☎ 05 53 68 60 39

(on the D119 in the direction of Mont-de-Marsan, 15 minutes from Agen)
Fruit farm, growing applies, pears, kiwi fruit and peaches, as well as the plums that become the regional speciality – prunes. These prunes are available as jams, covered in chocolate, and as juice, liqueur or *eau de vie*. Open Mondays to Saturdays all year, 10am to noon and 2 to 7pm.

Nérac	Château du Frandat, le Frandat ☎ 05 53 65 23 83

Sale of home-made armagnac and wines of Buzet and visits to the *chai* (above-ground cellar for wine in casks). Open 10am to noon and 2 to 6pm. Visit and tasting free.

St Jean-de-Duras	Vins AOC Côtes de Duras, Domaine d Durand ☎ 05 53 89 02 23

🖳 *www.domainededurand.com*

Organic raisin juice and jam made from wild fruit in September and October. Open all year from 9am to noon and 2 to 7pm every day (Sundays by appointment out of season).
Free tastings.

Ste Maure-de-Peyriac — La Ferme d'Armagnac, Masin et Fils   ☎ 05 53 65 60 44
Organic armagnac produced and bottled on the farm. Open all year Mondays to Saturdays 10am to 7pm.

Soumensac — Château 'La Boissière'   ☎ 05 53 94 75 79
Red, rosé and white AOC wines are produced here and are available in bags or boxes. Free tasting. Open all year round from 9am to noon and 2 to 6pm.

Miscellaneous

Agen — Hippodrome d'Agen la Garenne   ☎ 05 53 96 51 06
Various race meetings held throughout the year, from trotting to flat racing.

Casteljaloux — Base de Loisirs de la Taillade   ☎ 05 53 93 00 93
An outdoor centre with a permanent orienteering course, archery, crazy golf, and mountain biking and walking trails. Meals available by appointment. Open all year from 9am to 8pm. €9.15 for the day.

Douzains — Asinerie de Pinseguerre   ☎ 05 53 36 92 35
Donkey rides and rambles.

Gontaud-de-Nogaret — Moulin de Gibra,
chemin du Gal de Cambes   ☎ 05 53 83 42 46
(south-east of Marmande)
An 18th century windmill restored in 1981 to full working order, milling grain if the weather is suitable. Open by appointment with the tourist office (telephone number above). Adults €2, children €0.50.

Lacapelle-Biron — P'Arc en Ciel, Moulin de Courrance   ☎ 05 53 71 84 58
💻 *www.parc-en-ciel.com*
Nature discovery park with 'walks' up into the tree canopy. Five routes of varying difficulty and for various ages. Minimum height 1.2m (4ft). Also picnic area, animals, gardens, fountains, waterfalls and crazy golf. July and August every day 9am to 8pm; April to June, September and October weekends and school holidays 10am to 6pm. Prices from €15 to €21.50.

Lafitte-sur-Lot — Dedal'Prune, Domaine du Gabach   ☎ 05 53 84 00 69
A maize maze covering 1.5 ha (3.75 acres) with a picnic area by the river Lot. Open 1st to 14th July and 25th to 15th September 9am to noon and 2 to 7pm; 15th July to 24th

| | August 9am to 7pm (till 9pm on Wednesdays). Sundays and bank holidays 3 to 7pm. Adults €3.80, children €3.20. | |

| Layrac | Sculpteur Ferronnier d'Art, route de Caudecoste (just south of Agen) | ☎ 05 53 67 00 48 |

Sculptures made to order in copper, bronze and other metals, using various techniques – both traditional and contemporary. Workshop open 9am to noon and 2 to 7pm.

| Nérac | Chocolaterie La Cigale, 2 rue Calvin | ☎ 05 53 65 15 73 |

This chocolate craftsman opens his workshop to the public Mondays to Fridays 9am to noon and 2 to 6.30pm, Saturdays 9.30am to 12.30pm and 2.30 to 6pm. Visits available all year by appointment except December.

Eglise St Nicolas, place St Nicolas
Contains stained glass windows and wall paintings from the end of the 19th century.

| Roquefort | Walibi Aquitaine, Château de Caudouin 🖳 *www.sixflagseurope.com* (south-west of Agen) | ☎ 05 53 96 58 32 |

A large theme park with rides and attractions, live entertainment and special events, set around an 18th century château. Open from April to October from 10am (closing times depend on time of year). Adults €21.50, 3 to 11-year-olds €16.

| Vianne | Joël Gallo, 'La Gare' | ☎ 05 53 97 50 49 |

Mr Gallo is a master glass blower and his showroom is open every day. Telephone in advance for times of glass-blowing demonstrations.

| Villeneuve-sur-Lot | Hippodrome, route de Fumel | ☎ 05 53 70 96 31 |

Race days throughout the year.

| | Haras National, rue des Haras | ☎ 05 53 36 17 30 |

This national stud farm was opened in Agen in 1804 and moved to Villeneuve-sur-Lot in 1811. Guided tours leave the tourist office Wednesday afternoons in July and August, or there's a signposted route you can follow unaccompanied on Monday to Friday afternoons all year.

Museums & Galleries

| Agen | Musée des Beaux-Arts, place du Docteur Esquirol | ☎ 05 53 69 47 23 |

This art gallery is in a building which was four private hotels in the 16th and 17th centuries, which provide a diverse and beautiful backdrop to the art collection. This is varied, with works from the 18th to 20th centuries, including works by the Impressionists as well as by local artists. Open every day except Tuesdays, 10am to 6pm. Adults €3, under 18s free.

Musée des Beaux Arts,
place du Docteur Esquirol   ☎ 05 53 69 47 23
An archaeological collection as well as paintings from the 16th to 20th century. Open every day 10am to 6pm, except Tuesdays and 1st January, 1st May, 1st November and 25th December. Adults €3.50, free for under 18s and for everyone the first Sunday of the month.

Musée de la Résistance et De La
Déportation, 40 rue Montesquieu   ☎ 05 53 66 04 26
A remarkable museum showing the involvement of the people of Lot-et-Garonne in the Resistance movement, including documents, photographs, press articles, paintings and medals. Open Tuesdays to Saturdays 2.30 to 6pm. Free admission.

Clairac

Musée du Train, Place de l'Eglise   ☎ 05 53 79 34 81
Over 100 years of railway history – from mechanical to electric trains – in this large museum with reproductions and genuine exhibits. Open September to December and January to June 10am to 6pm; July and August 10am to 7pm. Adults €4.

Duras

Musée du Château des Ducs,
Château de Duras   ☎ 05 53 83 77 32
This magnificent medieval fortress was the home of the Durfort family and their descendants and now houses a museum of ethnology and archaeology, portraying rural life, traditions and agriculture around the turn of the 19th and 20th centuries, in vaulted rooms. Open July and August 10am to 7pm; June and September 10am to 12.30pm and 2 to 7pm; March to May and October 10am to noon and 2 to 6pm; November to February weekends and school holidays 10am to noon and 2 to 6pm. Adults €4.60, under 14s €2.30.

Musée Conservatoire du Parchemin   ☎ 05 53 20 77 55
🖥 *www.museeduparchemin.com*
This is a working museum of parchment, where you can see each stage in the process of making a medieval manuscript: the parchment, the inks and the gold leaf. You can watch calligraphists and artists at work and have lessons in calligraphy (by appointment). The shop sells parchment,

ink, reeds and quills. Open April to September every day
from 11am to 1pm and 3 to 8pm.

Frespech	Musée du Foie Gras, Souleilles	☎ 05 53 41 23 24

🖥 *www.souleilles-foiegras.com*
Discover the history of *foie gras* from ancient Egyptian times to
the present day, with videos (available in English) explaining
current production techniques, visits to the breeding centre and
tastings. Open February to December 3 to 7pm (10am to 7pm
in the summer). Adults €4, under 14s free.

Marmande	Musée Albert Marzelles,	
	15 rue Abel Boyé	☎ 05 53 64 42 04

Situated in the heart of the town in a totally restored building,
this museum contains a Roman mosaic from the fourth
century in the entrance hall and a large collection of art and
sculptures – regional, national and international. Open
Tuesdays to Fridays 3 to 6pm, Saturdays 10am to noon
and 3 to 6pm and one Sunday a month from 3 to 6pm.
Free admission.

Mézin	Musée du Liège et du Bouchon	☎ 05 53 65 68 16

🖥 *www.lot-et-garonne.fr/htm/museeemezin*
Mézin was once a major centre for the cork industry, producing
literally millions of corks daily, and this museum deals with
cork and cork manufacture – from harvesting the bark in the
forests to shaping corks in family workshops. Open July to
September daily 10am to noon and 2 to 7pm; April to June
and October Tuesdays to Sundays 2 to 6pm. Closed
every bank holiday except 14th/15th July. €3.50 adults,
under 13s free.

Nérac	Musée du Château d'Albret,	
	impasse Henri IV	☎ 05 54 65 21 11

Château d'Albret was built between the 14th and 16th centuries
and is currently home to the municipal museum housing
numerous objects and papers relating to the Albret family and
court life at Nérac. The archaeology section is dedicated to the
territory and history of Albret. Open October to May 10am to
noon and 2 to 6pm; June to September 10am to noon and 2 to
7pm. Closed Mondays. Adults €4, under 12s free.

St Pierre-de-Buzet	Musée de l'Ecole d'Autrefois	☎ 05 53 84 74 14

Two classrooms have been reconstructed to recreate a bygone
rural school life. The first is typical of an 1830s classroom, the
other a classroom of the 1880s – with the school furniture,
maps and rare books of each period. Open every day July and
August 3 to 6.30pm. Adults €4, children €2.

Ste Bazeille	Musée Archéologique André Larroderi,	
	Place René Sanson	☎ 06 85 23 60 52

Visitors are taken on a journey through more than 2,000 years of Marmandais history – prehistoric, Gallo-Roman and medieval – with a video presentation on the discovery of the four mosaics of Sainte Bazeille. Open all year on Sundays 2.30 to 6pm, other days by appointment (open Wednesdays to Mondays 2.30 to 6.30pm in July and August). Adults €2, under 14s free.

Soumensac

Musée de l'Outil Ancien, Le Bourg   ☎ 05 53 93 85 46
This a museum houses over 1,500 tools and utensils. Open June to August inclusive 2 to 7pm. Free admission.

Poupées Folkloriques, rue du Musée   ☎ 05 53 93 85 46
An exhibition of over 250 dolls, with others for sale. Open June to August 2 to 8pm; rest of the year by appointment. Free admission.

Villeneuve-sur-Lot

Musée de Gajac, 2 rue des Jardins   ☎ 05 53 40 48 00
Housed in the old mill of Gajac, this is a permanent art exhibition, with Impressionist and religious paintings, copper engravings, sculptures and Gallo-Roman objects. Open October to mid-June Wednesdays to Mondays 2 to 6pm (except bank holidays); mid-June to September every day 10am to noon and 2 to 6pm. Adults €2, children €1.

Site Archéologique d'Eysses,
place St Sernin d'Eysses   ☎ 05 53 70 65 19
The Gallo-Roman town of Eysses was situated in the northern quarter of Villeneuve-sur-Lot at the crossroads of two major strategic routes: from Bourges to Spain and from Bordeaux to Lyons. The surviving ruins form an archaeology 'museum' that complements a visit to the town, presenting medieval objects such as craftsmen's tools, money and glassware. Open July and August every day 2 to 6pm; rest of the year by appointment. Adults €1.50, children €0.80.

Zaintrailles

Musée de l'Abeille   ☎ 05 53 65 90 26
At this working museum you will learn all about bees and honey production – both ancient and modern. Open every day July and August 3 to 7pm; the remainder of the year by appointment.

Parks & Gardens

Agen

Parc du Conseil Général de Lot-et-Garonne
(in the grounds of the Conseil Général on the south side of the town centre)
This elegant park comprises 23 areas with a variety of themes: there's an alley of cedars, cherry trees and Japanese flowers. Free access.

Casteljaloux	Jardin Public	☎ 05 53 93 00 00

Protected by walls, moats and marshland the château of Casteljaloux was constructed in a strong position between the Landes moors and the Garonne valley. The château's grounds, which became a public park in 1954, contains magnificent wooded and floral areas. Casteljaloux has been awarded a 'three flowers' classification, largely due to this site.

Colayrac-St Cirq
Végétales Visions Serres Exotiques, RN113   ☎ 05 53 67 07 77
💻 *www.vegetalesvisions.com*
A botanical garden with plants from all over the world, including more than 1,000 varieties of tropical, sub-tropical and carnivorous plants and bonsai. From May to October there's an exotic vegetable garden, with guided tours on Sundays at 3pm. Open Tuesdays to Saturdays 10am to noon and 2 to 6pm, Sundays 10am to noon (July and August Mondays to Saturdays 9am to noon and 2 to 7pm, Sundays 9am to noon). Closed 1st January, 25 December and from 15th to 31st January.

Fargues-sur-Ourbise
Forêt Domainale de Campet, Maison Forestière du Bourdineau   ☎ 05 53 93 04 52
This forest is open at all times and contains an '*écomusée*' on the subject of tree and forest conservation.

Marmande
Jardin du Cloître de l'Eglise Notre Dame   ☎ 05 53 64 44 44
Within these cloisters at Marmande is a classic garden of French topiary consisting of three gardens of different themes. Open all year with free access.

Pont-du-Casse
Jardin Botanique de Darel, route de Cassou   ☎ 05 53 77 83 37
Produced and designed by the Société des Sciences Naturelles Agricoles de l'Agenais, this garden covers around 2.5ha (6 acres) and contains wild plants, including orchids, medicinal plants and a collection of trees native to the region. Open 15th March to 15th October from 2 to 6pm. Free admission.

Ste Livrade-sur-Lot
La Roseraie Vicart, 'Cocar'   ☎ 05 53 41 04 99
A 2.5km (1.5mi) path coloured and perfumed by 7,500 roses in 300 varieties, from the English Tea Rose to miniature roses. Open every day May to September from 9.30am to noon and 2.30 to 7pm. Adults €2.50, under 12s free.

Professional Services

The following offices have an English-speaking professional.

Accountants

Agen   KPMG Entreprises, 21 avenue Michelet   ☎ 05 53 77 59 00

Solicitors & Notaires

Agen   Lauzin-Roy et Boudey,
                70 rue Lamouroux   ☎ 05 53 47 01 73

Religion

Anglican Services In English

Monteton   Eglise de Monteton
                (in the north-west corner of the department near Duras)
                Services held here at 10.30am on the first Sunday of the
                month and 3pm on the third Sunday of the month. Contact
                the Revd Michael Selman, 1 Lotissement de la Caussade,
                Floirac (☎ 05 56 40 05 12) for further information or a copy
                of the monthly Aquitaine Chaplaincy newsletter.

Protestant Churches

Selected churches are listed below.

Agen   Assemblée Chrétienne,
                657 avenue Gaillard   ☎ 05 53 95 67 02

                Eglise Evangélique Méthodiste,
                1874 avenue Maréchal Leclerc   ▤ 05 53 96 84 32

                Eglise Réformée, 21 rue Gabriel Griffon ☎ 05 53 66 14 20

Nérac   Eglise Réformée, 35 bis allées d'Albret ☎ 05 53 65 01 32

Ste Bazeille   Eglise Evangélique, 4 rue Joliot Curie ☎ 05 53 64 37 95
                (north-east of Marmande on the N113)

Synagogues

Agen   Acia, 52 rue Montesquieu   ☎ 05 53 48 29 17

Marmande   Mosquée, rue de Langeot   ☎ 05 53 20 78 03

Restaurants

Agen   Las Aucos, 33 rue Voltaire   ☎ 05 53 48 13 71
                A formal restaurant with set menus from €15 to €39.

Closed Monday evenings, all day Tuesdays and
Saturday lunchtimes.

La Boucherie,
boulevard Sylvain Dumon   ☎ 05 53 67 08 60
(on the corner opposite the railway station)
Steak house-style restaurant open every day. Set menus
from €10 to €22.10, express menu €8.40 Monday to
Friday lunchtime.

Brasserie de la Poste,
82 boulevard Carnot   ☎ 05 53 66 37 73
There are no set menus at this brasserie, with main courses
at around €12. Open every day.

Buffalo Grill, Artigueloube, Boé   ☎ 05 53 96 73 25
(on the retail park south of Agen)
Steak house-style restaurant open until 11pm every day.

China Town, 169 boulevard Carnot   ☎ 05 53 66 17 18
Chinese restaurant with set menus from €14.50 to €20.60.
Take-away service available. Closed all day Sundays.

La Cinquième Saison,
14 place du Maréchal Foch   ☎ 05 53 95 87 11
This *crêperie* is tucked away by the Cathédrale St Caprais.

Le Cyrano, boulevard Carnot   ☎ 05 53 66 30 56
Bar, brasserie and grill open every day with service until
midnight during the week and 1am at weekends.

La Fleur de Sel,
66 rue Camille Desmoulins   ☎ 05 53 66 63 70
Gastronomic cuisine with set menus from €20 to €36.
Closed Saturday lunchtimes, all day Sundays and
Monday lunchtimes.

La Lafayette, 67 rue Lafayette   ☎ 05 53 66 70 02
(in a small side street opposite the tourist office)
This intimate restaurant has set menus from €10.70
to €25.50.

La Malmaison, 36 cours Gambetta   ☎ 05 53 47 25 46
Facing the river, this restaurant has set menus from €16 to
€25 and is closed all day on Sundays.

Le Marrakech,
122 boulevard de la République   ☎ 05 53 47 74 65
Moroccan cuisine, with set menus from €12 to €23. Closed
Monday lunchtimes.

McDonald's, rue Prune☎ 05 53 47 35 82
(north-east of the town centre)

L'Oasis, 46 rue Molinier   ☎ 05 53 66 89 33
A small restaurant in the pedestrian area of the town. No set
menu but main courses average €13.

Osake, 38 boulevard Sylvain Dumon   ☎ 05 53 66 31 76
(near the railway station)
Japanese restaurant. Closed Sunday evenings and all
day Mondays.

Le Vietnam, 43 rue des Ambans   ☎ 05 53 47 36 62
Vietnamese cuisine with no set menus. Open Monday evenings
to Saturday evenings.

Marmande Le Chiang Mai, 28 rue de la République ☎ 05 53 64 39 88
Thai cuisine, with set lunchtime menus from €9 to €11.50.
Closed Monday lunchtimes and all day Sundays.
English spoken.

Crêperie l'Atlantide,
36 rue Léopold Faye   ☎ 05 53 20 29 77
An extensive *à la carte* menu, no set menus. Closed Sundays,
Mondays and bank holidays.

Ganesha, rue de la République   ☎ 05 53 79 94 12
Indian and Sri Lankan cuisine. Set menus from €18.20 to
€21.25 and lunchtime menus Mondays to Fridays from
€8.50 to €10.

Le Lion d'Or, 1 rue de La République ☎ 05 53 64 21 30
Within a two-star hotel, this restaurant has set menus from
€17 to €40.

Les Nenuphars, 46 rue Léopold Faye   ☎ 05 53 64 10 69
Indian restaurant with take-away service.

Le Trianon, route d'Agen   ☎ 05 53 64 16 14
Set menus from €18 to €28. Closed Saturday and Monday
lunchtimes and all day Sundays.

McDonald's,
avenue François Mitterrand   ☎ 05 53 64 05 88
(on the north-west outskirts of the town)

Viet-Nam, avenue du Maréchal Joffre ☎ 05 53 64 54 01
Vietnamese restaurant with no set menus and an average main
course price of €9.50. Take-aways available.

Nérac	**D'Albret, 40 Allées d'Albret** ☎ 05 53 97 41 10

D'Albret, 40 Allées d'Albret ☎ 05 53 97 41 10
Monday to Friday lunchtime set menu €10.50, other menus
from €15 to €25. Closed Sunday evenings.

La Cheminée, 28 allées du Centre ☎ 05 53 65 18 88
(in the town centre)
Set menus from €10.50 to €27 and *à la carte* menu.
Closed Tuesday and Sunday evenings and all
day Sundays.

La Crêperie du Roy,
24 avenue de Lattre de Tassigny ☎ 05 53 97 12 33
Pancakes, salads and grills. Open every lunchtimes and
evenings (until 11pm in summer).

L'Escadron, 7 rue Henri IV ☎ 05 53 97 19 04
(directly in front of the château)
Outside seating in summer. Set menus from €15.20 to €30
and *à la carte* menu. Closed Tuesday evenings and all
day Mondays.

Le Marcadieu, 73 allées d'Albret ☎ 05 53 65 00 59
Café/brasserie open for lunch Mondays to Fridays, with set
menus from €8 to €13.

Restaurant du Château,
7 avenue Mondenard ☎ 05 53 65 09 05
(left of the tourist office)
Menus from €17 to €38 plus *à la carte* menu. Closed
Friday to Sunday evenings and Saturday lunchtimes
out of season.

Le Riad, 69 rue Gambetta ☎ 05 53 97 04 34
Moroccan cuisine. No set menu. Closed Mondays.

La Sardaigne, 4 rue A. Fallières ☎ 05 53 65 33 91
(in the town centre near the church)
Italian restaurant.

Le Lys de Saigon,
16 avenue Maurice Rontin ☎ 05 53 65 90 65
Vietnamese cuisine. Open Tuesday to Friday lunchtimes. No
set menus; average main course €9.

Villeneuve-sur- Bombay Restaurant, 33 rue des Cieutat ☎ 05 53 70 43 60
Lot Indian restaurant open every day with a set menu at
lunchtime from €8 to €10 and other set menus from
€16 to €20.

La Brocherie, rue de la Convention   ☎ 05 53 71 64 40
An intimate restaurant in a small side street. Set menus from
€18 to €24. Closed Tuesday and Sunday evenings and
all day Mondays.

Buffalo Grill, ZAC Parasol   ☎ 05 53 01 07 44
(on the retail park on the eastern side of the town)
Steak house-style restaurant open until 11pm every day.

L'Intermezzo, 18 rue Parmentier   ☎ 05 53 70 18 51
Pizzas cooked in open ovens and set lunchtime menus
from €9.20 to €13. Closed Sunday and
Monday lunchtimes.

La Mine, 36 place Lafayette   ☎ 05 53 01 46 61
Outside seating under the archways around the enclosed
square. Set menus from €8 to €15.40.

McDonald's, avenue Bordeaux, Bias   ☎ 05 53 36 13 77
(on the north-west side of Villeneuve-sur-Lot)

L'Oustal, 24 rue de la Convention   ☎ 05 53 41 49 44
Specialities of seafood and Basque cuisine. €12 lunchtime
menu Mondays to Fridays, other set menus €17 to €26. Closed
Tuesday and Wednesday evenings and all day Sundays.
English spoken.

Le Parmentier, 13 rue Parmentier   ☎ 05 53 70 35 02
Lunchtime set menu €12.50, other menus from €17 to €26.
Closed Sunday evenings and all day Mondays out
of season.

Rubbish & Recycling

Metal Collection

Boé	Etablissements Jach, ZI Boé (south of Agen)	☎ 05 53 96 38 40
Villeneuve-sur-Lot	Brangé Sarl, Souliès, route de Bordeaux, Bias	☎ 05 53 70 99 19

Shopping

Alcohol

Agen	Paradis des 4 Saisons, 27 place Jean Baptiste Durand	☎ 05 53 48 26 67

Marmande	Saveur des Vins, RN 113	☎ 05 53 20 50 60

Mézin   Cave des Coteaux du Mézinais,
         1 boulevard Colomé   ☎ 05 53 65 53 55
         (south-west of Nérac)

Villeneuve-sur- La Dive Bouteille,
Lot   7 rue de la Convention   ☎ 05 53 41 41 99
                 Wine sold by the litre. Open Tuesdays to Saturdays 9.15am
                 to 12.15pm and 2.30 to 7pm.

Architectural Antiques

Bajamont   Hervé Soulie, Caussida, D656   ☎ 05 53 67 92 18
            🖳 www.materiaux-anciens-agen.com
            (on the eastern outskirts of Agen in the direction of Cahors)
            Timber beams, oak rafters, fireplaces, stone, tiles
            and paving.

British Groceries

Eymet   The English Shop, 22 rue du Temple   ☎ 05 53 23 79 39
         (south of Bergerac on the border of Dordogne and
         Lot-et-Garonne)
         Traditional British groceries, including bacon, sausages
         and cheese, and gifts and books. Open Tuesdays to
         Saturdays 9.30am to 6.30pm and Sundays 9.30am
         to 12.30pm

Building Materials

Agen   Point P, Riols, quai de la Garonne, Boé   ☎ 05 53 66 09 12
        🖳 www.pointp.fr
        Mondays to Fridays 7.30am to noon and 1.30 to 6.30pm,
        Saturdays am to noon.

Marmande   Bardusco, 3 route Périgueux   ☎ 05 53 64 25 45
            Shop and tool hire. Mondays to Saturdays.

Nérac   Sarreméjean, ZI Barre   ☎ 05 53 65 92 31

Villeneuve-sur- Chausson Matériaux,
Lot   ZI Glady-Cami de Pastourel   ☎ 05 53 70 04 50

Caravans & Camper Vans

Agen   Destinéa, route de Toulouse, RN113,
        Castelculier   ☎ 05 53 95 15 15
        🖳 www.destinea.com
        (south-east of Agen)

Agen Loisirs, route Toulouse, Boé ☎ 05 53 96 13 02
(on the retail park south of Agen)

Department Stores

Agen Nouvelles Galeries,
72 boulevard de la République ☎ 05 53 47 20 21
Mondays to Fridays 9.15am to 7pm, Saturdays
9.15am to 7.30pm.

Villeneuve-sur- Nouvelles Galeries,
Lot 8 cours Victor Hugo ☎ 05 53 36 16 11

DIY

Agen Castorama, ZAC Agen Sud ☎ 05 53 66 15 32
🖳 *www.castorama.fr*

Marmande Monsieur Bricolage, route Bordeaux ☎ 05 53 20 93 20
(on the retail park south-west of the town)

Nérac Weldom, ZA Larrousset,
route de Condom ☎ 05 53 65 36 35

Villeneuve-sur- Quincaillerie Lafon Christian,
Lot 2 avenue Jacques Bordeneuve ☎ 05 53 70 30 21

Fabrics

Agen Le Casaquin Doré, 32 rue Cornières ☎ 05 53 66 83 95
Dress-making fabrics.

Patrick de Vincenz,
6 boulevard de la République ☎ 05 53 47 49 65
Furnishing and household fabrics.

Marmande Billaud, 47 rue Charles de Gaulle ☎ 05 53 64 69 60

Villeneuve-sur- Côté Tissus, 16 rue Casseneuil ☎ 05 53 70 38 99
Lot

Frozen Food

Agen Picard, avenue M. Luxembourg ☎ 05 53 48 11 80
Mondays 3 to 7.30pm, Tuesdays to Fridays 9.30am to
12.30pm and 3 to 7.30pm, Saturdays 9.30am to 1pm
and 2.30 to 7.30pm.

Marmande	Thiriet, avenue Pierre Buffin	☎ 05 53 20 69 54

Sundays 9am to noon, Mondays 2.30 to 7pm, Tuesdays to Saturdays 9.30am to 12.30pm and 2.30 to 7pm.

Garden Centres

Agen   Jardiland, rue du Midi, ZAC Sud, Boé   ☎ 05 53 77 72 22
(south of the town centre but east of the river, near the
Parc des Expos)
Mondays to Saturdays 9.30am to noon and 2 to 7pm,
Sundays and bank holidays 10am to noon and
2.30 to 7pm.

Vive le Jardin, route de Mont de Marsan,
Le Passage   ☎ 05 53 69 00 00
(west of Agen over the river)
Mondays to Saturdays 9.30am to noon and 2 to 7pm,
Sundays 10am to 12.30pm and 3 to 7pm.

Marmande   Gamm Vert, route de Bordeaux   ☎ 05 53 20 44 35
Mondays to Saturdays 8am to noon and 2 to 7pm.

Jardinerie Jay, route des Isserts   ☎ 05 53 64 30 12
Open every day.

Nérac   Gamm Vert, route de Bordeaux   ☎ 05 53 97 66 00
Mondays 2 to 6.30pm, Tuesdays to Saturdays 8am to noon
and 2 to 6.30pm (closes at 6pm Saturdays).

Villeneuve-sur- Brico Bati Jardi Leclerc, La Justice   ☎ 05 53 01 58 58
Lot   (on the Leclerc retail park east of town)
Mondays to Fridays 9am to 12.30pm and 2 to 7.30pm,
Saturdays 9am to 7.30pm.

Gamm Vert, route de Bordeaux   ☎ 05 53 49 65 70
Mondays to Saturdays 9am to noon and 2 to 7pm.

Hypermarkets

Agen   Carrefour, Boé   ☎ 05 53 77 66 00
(on the south side of town)
Mondays to Saturdays 9am to 8.30pm (Fridays till 9pm). Within
the complex you can hire carpet cleaners and floor polishers as
well as order domestic heating fuel. There's also a florist's,
mobile phone shop, cafe, photographic shop, business card
machine and photo booths.

Villeneuve-sur- Auchan, route de Bordeaux, Bias   ☎ 05 53 49 62 00
Lot   Mondays to Saturdays 8.30am to 10pm. Within the complex
are a chemist's, dry cleaner's, hairdresser's, optician's, mobile
phone shop and a key and heel bar.

Leclerc, route de Fumel   ☎ 05 53 01 58 58
Mondays to Saturdays 9am to 8.30pm, Fridays until 9pm.
There's a chemist's, travel agent's, cafe/bar, photo booth and
business card machine.

Kitchens & Bathrooms

Specialist kitchen and bathroom shops can often be found on the large
retail parks (see page 275).

Agen	Cuisines Mobalpa, 852 avenue Maréchal Leclerc 🖳 *www.mobalpa.fr*	☎ 05 53 96 22 02
Marmande	Cuisines Pérène Socomex, 102 rue de la Libération	☎ 05 53 89 09 38
Villeneuve-sur-Lot	Bati-Seul, route d'Agen, RN21 🖳 *www.bati-seul.com*	☎ 05 53 70 44 81

Markets

Agen	Wednesday and Sunday mornings at Place du Pin, Saturday mornings at Place Jasmin.
	Organic market at Place des Laitiers every Saturday morning.
	Main fair on the first Monday in June.
	Foie gras market on the second Monday in December.
Casseneuil	Tuesday and Sunday mornings.
Casteljaloux	Tuesday and Saturday mornings.
Duras	Mondays and Saturdays all year and Thursdays June to September.
Eysses	Sunday mornings.
Foulayronnes	Saturday mornings.
Fumel	Tuesday, Friday and Sunday mornings.
Lauzun	Saturday mornings.

Marmande	Tuesday and Saturday mornings.
	Night market on the second and fourth Thursdays in July and August.
Mézin	Thursday and Sunday mornings.
Miramont-de-Guyenne	Fridays in July and August only.
Monflanquin	Regular market on Thursdays with aditional markets on Tuesdays and Saturdays from June to September.
Nérac	Saturday mornings.
	Evening market on Tuesdays from June to September.
Tonneins	Wednesday, Friday and Saturday mornings.
Tournon d'Agenais	Tuesdays.
	Night market on Fridays in July and August.
Villeneuve-sur-Lot	Tuesdays and Saturdays with a fair the second and fourth Tuesdays of the month.
	Organic market Wednesday mornings at Place d'Aquitaine on the left bank of the river.

Model Shops

Nérac	La Boîte à Fumée, 43 rue Gambetta ☎ 05 53 65 65 70 Model railways, trains and accessories. Open Wednesdays to Saturdays 9.30am to noon and 2.30 to 6.30pm.

Music

Agen	Macca Music, 12 rue de Raymond ☎ 05 53 66 60 14 Open Tuesdays to Saturdays.
Marmande	Musico'Case, 56 rue de la République ☎ 05 53 20 68 04 Mondays 2 to 7.15pm, Tuesdays to Saturdays 9am to 12.15pm and 2 to 7.15pm.

Organic Food

Agen	Bio Coop, 108 boulevard Liberté ☎ 05 53 96 42 71 Mondays 11am to 3pm, Tuesdays to Saturdays 10am to 7pm.

Marmande	La Fontaine Bio, 60 rue de la République	☎ 05 53 93 54 45

Nérac   La Clairière, 3 cours Romas   ☎ 05 53 65 30 48
Tuesdays to Saturdays 9am to 12.15pm and 3 to 7pm
(closes at 6pm on Saturdays).

Villeneuve-sur-Lot   Naturellement Vôtre, ZAC Parasol   ☎ 05 53 70 48 87

Retail Parks

Agen   'Parc des Expositions', Boé
(on the south side of Agen)
Shops include:

- Carrefour – hypermarket;

- Castorama – building materials and DIY;

- Challenge 1 – motorbikes;

- Conforama – furniture, household appliances and electrical goods;

- Darty – electrical goods;

- Expert – electrical goods;

- Galerie du Salon – living room furniture;

- Go Sport – sports goods;

- Jardiland – large garden centre;

- McDonald's – fast food.

Marmande   (on the south-west outskirts of the town)
Shops include:

- Aubert – baby goods;

- Fly – furniture and household accessories;

- La Halle aux Chaussures – shoes;

- Leclerc – hypermarket;

- Joué Club – toys;

- Mr Meuble – furniture;

- Mr Bricolage – DIY;

- Sport 2000 – sports store;

- Vélo Oxygen – Bicycles and outdoor pursuits.

Villeneuve-sur-Lot	(on the east of the town) Shops include:

- Brico Bati Jardi Leclerc – gardening and DIY;

- Buffalo Grill – steak house;

- Conforama – furniture, household appliances and electrical goods;

- Gifi – gifts and household accessories;

- Intersport – sports goods;

- King Jouet – toys;

- Leclerc – hypermarket;

- Les Halles aux Tissus – fabrics.

Second-Hand Goods

Agen   Le Grenier d'Emma, 9 rue Emile Sentini ☎ 05 53 47 85 00

Passé Simple,
132 boulevard de la République   ☎ 05 53 95 66 38

Marmande   Dépôt Vente du Marmande,
92 avenue Jean Jaurès   ☎ 05 53 64 63 51

Nérac   Brocante Antiquités, rue Gambetta   ☎ 05 53 65 05 50
(in a small side street nearm the town centre)

Villeneuve-sur- Au Plaisir du Passé,
Lot   route de Monflanquin   ☎ 05 53 70 47 46

Sports Goods

Agen   Décathlon, ZAC de Gardes, Boé   ☎ 05 53 98 55 66
🖳 *www.decathlon.fr*
(on the retail park south of the town)
Mondays to Thursdays 9.30am to 7.30pm, Fridays and
Saturdays 9.30am to 8pm.

Marmande	Sport 2000, route Bordeaux	☎ 05 53 89 36 90

(by Leclerc on the south-west outskirts of town)
Mondays to Thursdays 9.30am to 12.30pm and 2 to 7.30pm,
Fridays and Saturdays 9.30am to 7.30pm.

Nérac	Eco Sports, 27 cours Romas	☎ 05 53 97 25 95

(in the town centre)
Mondays 2 to 7pm, Tuesdays to Fridays 9.30am to noon and
2 to 7pm, Saturdays 9.30am to 7pm.

Villeneuve-sur-Lot	Intersport, route de Fumel	☎ 05 53 01 58 67

(on the Leclerc retail park on the east side of town)

Swimming Pool Equipment

General	Pool Serve, Domipech, Prayssas	☎ 05 53 95 98 62

This company is run by a UK qualified pool engineer and
builds, refurbishes and maintains pools from its base in
Lot-et-Garonne.

Marmande	Oasis Piscines, Champagne	☎ 05 53 64 01 99

Construction, installation, maintenance and repairs.

Pont-du-Casse	Génération Piscine, route de Séguran	☎ 05 53 67 52 66

(north-east of Agen)
Sale of kit-pools and consumables plus design and
maintenance service.

Sports

The following is just a selection of the activities available, the large towns
having a wide range of sports facilities. Full details are available from the
tourist office or the mairie.

Aerial Sports

Flying

Agen	Aéro Club de l'Agenais, Aérodrome d'Agen la Garenne	☎ 05 53 96 36 67

Contact Mr Gratiolet.

Cavarc	Aéroclub de Cavarc	☎ 05 53 36 85 99

Flights over some of the châteaux in the area.

Marmande	Aérodrome de Marmande, Carpète	☎ 05 53 64 26 36

Introduction and sightseeing flights.

| | Centre Vol à Voile de Marmande, Aérodrome de Marmande Gliders. | ☎ 05 53 20 86 29 |

Montpezat Base ULM ☎ 05 53 95 08 81
💻 *www.ulmstex.com*
(east of Villeneuve-sur-Lot)
Microlights.

Nérac Club ULM ☎ 05 53 65 91 38
Microlight centre with trial flights, sightseeing flights and pilot training. Bar, restaurant and playground. Open every day of the year from 8am to noon and 2 to 7pm. Trial flight €25. Contact Mr Dureau for further details and booking.

Villeneuve-sur-Lot Aérodrome de Rogé, route de Tournon ☎ 05 53 70 43 07
Tourist flights and a 1,050m airstrip for private aircraft.

Aéro Club Villeneuvois, Aérodrome de Rogé, route de Tournon ☎ 05 53 40 00 59
Contact Mr Morin.

Parachuting

Agen Para Club de l'Agenais, Aérodrome d'Agen la Garenne ☎ 05 53 68 23 00
Contact Mlle Huc.

Marmande Cercle Parachutiste Marmandais, Aérodrome de Marmande, Carpète ☎ 05 53 83 48 41

Archery

Agen Archers de Boé, Château d'Allot ☎ 05 53 68 20 71
(on the south side of Agen)
Contact Mr Tovo.

Gavaudun LCS Nature Evasion ☎ 05 53 40 83 55
(in the north-east of the department)
Archery, rock climbing, canyoning and potholing.

Marmande Archers Club Marmandais ☎ 05 53 89 29 84
Contact Mr Duranteau.

Nérac Archers du Roy, rue Chenevoy ☎ 05 5365 87 97
Contact Mr Faget.

Villeneuve-sur-Lot Archers des Deux Rives ☎ 06 86 64 68 80
Minimum age nine. Contact Mr Coeymans.

Badminton

Agen	ASPTT Badminton, Contact Mr Lavaud	☎ 05 53 98 28 39
	✉ asptt47.agen@wanadoo.fr	
Marmande	Badminton Club Marmandais	☎ 05 53 83 09 97
	Contact Mr Recoules.	
Nérac	Badminton de Nérac	☎ 05 53 65 33 60
	Contact Mr Labanhie.	
Villeneuve-sur-Lot	Club de Badminton	☎ 05 53 40 32 98
	Minimum age eight. Contact Mr Houviez.	

Canoeing & Kayaking

Agen	Aviron Agenais	☎ 05 53 68 28 94
	Canoe hire.	
	Canoë-Kayak Club Agenais,	
	2 quai du Canal	☎ 05 53 66 25 99
	Contact Mr Cabrérizo.	
Marmande	Marmande Kayak Nature	☎ 05 53 93 30 30
	Canoe hire.	
Nérac	'Maintenant', route de Thouars,	
	Feugarolles	☎ 05 53 67 46 67
	(directly south of Montpon on the D708)	
	Two-person canoe €10, one-person €5 for half a day. Open all year.	

Canyoning

Gavaudun	LCS Nature Evasion	☎ 05 53 40 83 55
	(in the north-east of the department)	
	Canyoning, archery, rock climbing and potholing.	

Clay Pigeon Shooting

Agen	Société de Chasse de Boé,	
	Le Petit Lacassagne	☎ 05 53 68 07 78
	(on the south side of Agen)	
	Contact Mr Raynal.	
Marmande	Ball Trap Marmandais, la Vallée	☎ 05 53 94 53 32
	Contact Mr Toucan out of office hours.	
Villeneuve-sur-Lot	Ball Trap Club Villeneuvois	☎ 05 53 84 63 93
	Minimum age 12.	

Climbing

Agen	Escalade d'Agen Contact Mr Pradal.	☎ 05 53 68 21 25
Gavaudun	LCS Nature Evasion (north-east of the department) Rock climbing, archery, canyoning and potholing.	☎ 05 53 40 83 55
Marmande	Horizon Vertical, le Broy Contact Mr Primault.	☎ 05 53 83 85 46

Cycling

The tourist offices in this department have details of 23 cycle routes, many having sections along the Lot river.

General	Comité Départemental de Cyclotourisme, 27 rue Hoche This is the organisation for road cycling in the department.	☎ 05 53 98 05 79
	UFOLEP, 108 rue Fumadelles The departmental group for mountain biking.	☎ 05 53 77 05 34
Agen	ASPTT Cyclotourisme et Cyclosport ✉ asptt47.agen@wanadoo.fr The local cycle touring group. Contact Mr Schück.	☎ 05 53 98 28 39
	VTT Club de l'Agenais, Maison de la Nature, 29 rue Baudin The local mountain biking group. Contact Mr Théron.	☎ 05 53 66 06 54
Marmande	Association Sportive des Cheminots – Cyclisme Contact Mme Guardiola.	☎ 05 53 20 45 68
	VTT Club Marmandais Val de Garonne Local mountain biking club.	☎ 05 53 64 13 85
Nérac	Cyclotourisme de Nérac Contact Mr Bachère.	☎ 05 53 65 46 28
	VTT The local mountain biking club. Contact Mr Lacombe.	☎ 05 53 65 21 42
Villeneuve-sur-Lot	Union Cycliste Villeneuvoise Contact Mr Berbiguie.	☎ 06 08 46 66 40

Fencing

Agen	Société Encouragement Escrime Agen, Gymnase Donnefort, 225 avenue Léon Blum	☎ 05 53 87 66 65
Marmande	Escrime Club Marmandais, Terrasse des Capucins Contact Mme Edwards-Pougnet.	☎ 05 53 94 86 57
Villeneuve-sur-Lot	Académie d'Escrime Contact Mme Firemans. Minimum age six.	☎ 05 53 36 48 59

Fishing

If there's a lake locally, permits will be on sale at a nearby *tabac* or at the mairie; some tourist offices also sell permits. Fifteen-day permits can be bought between 1st June and 30th September.

General	Fédération de Lot-et-Garonne, 44 cours 9ème de Ligne, Agen	☎ 05 53 66 16 68
Agen	Association de Pêche de l'Agenais, La Mairie, Le Passage	☎ 05 53 66 94 62
Aiguillon	Plage sur le Lot, rue de la Résistance Fishing lake.	☎ 05 53 88 15 40
Bajamont	Lac de St Arnaud (north-east of Agen) Fishing from the end of June to August.	☎ 05 53 95 61 48
Damazan	Lac du Moulineau	☎ 05 53 79 42 98
Marmande	Club des Pêcheurs à la Mouche de Sainte Bazeille Fly fishing. Contact Mr Ducan.	☎ 05 53 64 50 24
	Lac de Beaupuy Five-hectare (12-acre) fishing lake. Permits can be bought from tabacs in the area	
Nérac	Société de Pêche 'Les Gaules d'Albret' Contact Mr Vergnes.	☎ 05 53 65 23 59
Penne d'Agenais	Lac de Férié (east of Villeneuve-sur-Lot)	☎ 05 53 41 30 97

| Villeneuve-sur-Lot | Pêcheurs à la Ligne
Contact Mr Mathau. | ☎ 05 53 70 55 08 |

Golf

| Casteljaloux | Golf de Casteljaloux,
route de Mont-de-Marsan | ☎ 05 53 93 51 60 |

18 holes, par 72, 5,916m. Pro shop, bar and restaurant. Covered and open driving range, golf carts for hire. Green fees €20 mid-week, €25 weekends.

| Castelnaud-de-Gratecambe | Golf de Castelnaud | ☎ 05 53 01 60 19 |

9 and 18-hole courses. Centered around a hotel, this club offers group and individual lessons and courses. There's also a partially covered driving range, clubhouse, golf shop and restaurant. Open all year.

| Marmande | Golf de Marmande, Levant de Carpète | ☎ 05 53 20 87 60 |

9 holes, par 69, 5,469m. Pro shop, bar and restaurant, large indoor and outdoor driving ranges, golf carts for hire. Closed Tuesdays in winter. Green fees from €16 to €19.

| Tombeboeuf | Golf Club de Barthe | ☎ 05 53 88 83 31 |

9 holes, par 36, 2,813m. Pro shop and bar, small covered driving range, golf carts for hire. Green fees from €18 to €20.

Horse Riding

| Agen | Ferme Equestre d'Augé, Laplume
(south of Agen) | ☎ 06 87 11 72 94 |

Open all year for lessons and hacks, from one hour to all day; in the summer overnight rides available.

| Fargues-sur-Ourbise | Centre de Randonnée Equestre
d'Albret | ☎ 05 53 83 33 78 |

Lessons and hacks, from one hour to all day. Riding tours available for two to six days with either camping or hotel accommodation. English spoken.

| Marmande | Club Hippique du Marmandais,
'Les Barthes', Montpouillan | ☎ 05 53 93 65 82 |

Open all year, for lessons (beginners and experienced riders), hacks and competitions.

| Nérac | Ferme Equestre du Petit Galopin, Serres,
Lannes | ☎ 05 53 65 89 02 |

(south of Nérac)
Hacks on ponies and horses for novices and experienced riders of all ages. Open all year (by appointment) from 8am to 9pm in the summer and 10am to 6pm the rest of the year.

| Penne d'Agenais | Domaine de Lamothe | ☎ 05 53 40 04 45 |

Penne
d'Agenais
Domaine de Lamothe   ☎ 05 53 40 04 45
(east of Villeneuve-sur-Lot)
Lessons, courses, exams and hacks, by the hour or all day.
Also stabling and breeding. Open all year 9am to 8pm
every day.

Jetskiing

Agen
Jet Club Boé, Illots, Boé   ☎ 06 03 01 29 39
(on the south side of Agen)
Contact Mr St Etienne.

Judo

Agen
Judo Club Agenais, Gymnase Donnefort,
225 avenue Léon Blum   ☎ 05 53 66 38 81
Contact Mme Dagassan.

Marmande
Ecole de Judo Marmandais   ☎ 05 53 93 98 07
Contact Mr Gava.

Nérac
Judo Club d'Albret   ☎ 05 53 65 32 92
Contact Mme Benoît.

Villeneuve-sur-
Lot
Judo Club Villeneuvois   ☎ 05 53 40 31 93
Contact Mr Hautefage. Minimum age five.

Motorcycle Riding

Agen
Union Motocycliste Agenaise   ☎ 05 53 68 52 00
Contact Mr Dumas.

Bavaria Moto Club, rue Llanelli,
ZAC Agen Sud   ☎ 05 53 48 28 17
✉ bavariamotoclub@aol.com
Contact Mr Vicentini.

Marmande
Moto Club Marmandais   ☎ 05 53 89 61 66
Contact Mr Bares.

St Sernin-de-
Duras
Moto Sport Loisirs, Courtaou   ☎ 05 53 94 18 68
(north of Marmande, near Duras and next to lake Castelgaillard)
Both motorbikes and quad bikes can be taken round this
course. Introductory sessions and courses; motocross and
grass track. Open all year by appointment. From €35
per person.

Villeneuve-sur-
Lot
Auto de Guyenne et Villeneuvois   ☎ 06 22 12 82 45
Motor bike club, minimum age 18. Contact Mr Marchand.

Potholing

Agen	Groupe Spéléologique et Archéologique Agenais, Maison de la Nature, 29 rue Baudin	☎ 05 53 66 41 19
	Contact Mr Benkemoun.	
Gavaudun	LCS Nature Evasion	☎ 05 53 40 83 55
	(in the north-east of the department) Potholing, archery, canyoning and rock climbing.	

Roller Skating

Agen	There's a skate park alongside the river Garonne on 'Voie-sur-Berge'.	
Marmande	Lyns Roller Hockey Marmandais	☎ 05 53 64 48 33
	Contact Mr Duriez.	
	Roller Skating Club Marmandais	☎ 06 67 49 54 06
	Contact Mr Boin.	

Rowing

Agen	Aviron Agenais, Cité la Salève, rue Jean Laffore	☎ 05 53 68 28 74
	Contact Mr Romat.	
Marmande	Aviron Marmandais, 26 terrasse des Capucins	☎ 05 53 20 66 99
	Contact Mr Motron.	
Villeneuve-sur-Lot	Aviron Villeneuvois 'Rames'	☎ 05 53 70 96 76
	Contact Mr Delsuc.	

Sailing

Agen	Yacht Club d'Agen, 53 quai du Canal	☎ 05 53 66 46 06
	Contact Mr Routaboul.	

Scuba Diving

Agen	Club Subaquatique Agenais	☎ 05 53 65 00 27
	Contact Mr Merle.	
Marmande	Club Sub-Aquatique Marmandais	☎ 05 53 93 92 15
	Contact Mr Marle.	

Shooting

Marmande	Société de Tir Marmande/Fourques	☎ 05 53 20 18 58
	Contact Mr Da-Ros.	

| Nérac | Tir d'Albret | ☎ 05 53 65 63 16 |

Contact Mr Suarez.

| Villeneuve-sur-Lot | Société de Tir | ☎ 05 53 70 05 00 |

Minimum age nine. Contact Mr Pettini.

Swimming

| Agen | Aqua'Sud, avenue d'Italie | ☎ 05 53 48 02 63 |

| Marmande | Aquaval, rue Portogruaro | ☎ 05 53 20 40 53 |

This swimming complex has a 25m training pool, Jacuzzi and water toboggan.

| Nérac | Piscine Municipale, boulevard Pierre de Coubertin | ☎ 05 53 65 03 89 |

Outdoor pool open only in summer.

| Villeneuve-sur-Lot | Piscine de Malbentre, rue de Malbentre, Pujols | ☎ 05 53 70 97 26 |

(on the south-west side of the town)
An indoor pool that becomes an outdoor pool in the summer, when the roof is opened. Opening hours vary according to school holidays.

Tennis

| Agen | Amicale Laïque – Section Tennis, 275 rue Duvergé | ☎ 05 53 87 78 80 |

Contact Mme Blandamour.

| Marmande | ASPTT de Marmande – Tennis, Complexe Carpète | ☎ 05 53 89 69 00 |

Contact Mr Soubies.

| | Tennis Club Marmandais | ☎ 05 53 20 86 78 |

| Nérac | Tennis Municipaux, rue de Nazareth | ☎ 05 53 65 14 26 |

(alongside Parc de la Garenne, on the east bank of the river)

| | Tennis Club d'Albret | ☎ 05 53 65 03 39 |

Contact Mr Bequin.

| Villeneuve-sur-Lot | Tennis Club, route d'Agen | ☎ 05 53 70 48 78 |

Contact Mr Cruz.

Waterskiing

| Boé | Waterfun, Pont Bourbonnais | ☎ 05 53 96 20 67 |

(on the south side of Agen)

Courses in waterskiing and wake-boarding. Open mid-April to end of October every day from 8am to 8pm.

Frespech	Aux Avirmes	☎ 05 53 95 79 70

This club is on a private lake with a slalom course and clubhouse. Full equipment provided. Open from mid-April to the end of August 9am to 8pm. Courses from €75 per day.

Villeneuve-sur-Lot	Yacht Motor Club Villeneuvois	☎ 05 53 40 29 73

Minimum age nine.

Tourist Offices

General   Comité Régional du Tourisme d'Aquitaine,
23 Parvis des Chartrons,
33074 Bordeaux   ☎ 05 56 01 70 00
🖳 *www.tourisme-aquitaine.info*

Comité Départemental du Tourisme
Lot-et-Garonne, 271 rue Péchabout,
Agen   ☎ 05 53 66 14 14
🖳 *www.lot-et-garonne.fr*
🖳 *www.cc-val-de-garonne.fr*

Agen   107 boulevard Carnot   ☎ 05 53 47 36 09
🖳 *www.ot-agen.org*
🖳 *www.ville-agen.fr*
September to June Mondays to Saturdays 9am to 12.30pm and 2 to 6.30pm; July and August Mondays to Saturdays 9am to 7pm, Sundays 10am to noon.

Marmande   Kiosque Gambetta,
boulevard Gambetta   ☎ 05 53 64 44 44
freephone within Aquitaine ☎ 08 00 47 20 47
🖳 *www.mairie-marmande.fr*
September to June Tuesdays to Saturdays 9am to noon and 2 to 6pm. July and August Mondays to Saturdays 9am to 7pm.

Nérac   7 avenue Mondenard   ☎ 05 53 65 27 75
🖳 *www.ville-nerac.fr*
October to April Tuesdays to Saturdays 9am to noon and 2 to 6pm; May, June and September Tuesdays to Saturdays 9am to noon and 2 to 6pm, Sundays 10am to noon and 3 to 5pm; July and August Tuesdays to Saturdays 9am to 1pm and 2 to 7pm, Sundays and bank holidays 10am to 12.30pm and 3 to 5.30pm.

| Villeneuve-sur-Lot | 47 rue de Paris | ☎ 05 53 36 17 30 |

💻 *www.ville-villeneuve-sur-lot.fr*
September to June Monday to Saturday 9am to noon and 2 to 6pm; July and August Monday to Saturday 8.30am to 12.30pm and 2 to 6pm, Sundays 9am to 1pm.

Tradesmen

Architects & Project Managers

| General | Adams Gautier | ☎ 05 49 64 42 96 |

💻 *www.adamsgautier.com*
This is a British/French team of experienced architects, who also organise surveys and building permits and carry out project management for new builds, renovation, landscaping and pools.

Builders

| Agen | Valla Pierre, 18 rue Voltaire | ☎ 05 53 66 50 06 |

💻 *www.pierre-valla.com*

| | Confort Toit, boulevard Prés Carnot | ☎ 05 53 95 78 18 |

New builds and renovation.

| Auradou | JP Biette, Grezac | ☎ 05 53 70 91 04 |

(south-west of Villeneuve-sur-Lot)
English-speaking firm dealing with restoration and new builds: interiors and exteriors, walls, fencing, re-pointing and rendering.

| Marmande | Constructions André Mary, 133 avenue Jean Jaurès | ☎ 05 53 64 15 05 |

General building and renovation.

| Nérac | Reno Bat, le Fréchou | ☎ 05 53 65 20 04 |

| Villeneuve-sur-Lot | Avibat, 28 boulevard Danton | ☎ 05 53 49 48 86 |

Carpenters

| Agen | Menuiserie Ebenisterie, rue des Ambans | ☎ 05 53 66 06 57 |

| Marmande | Jolibert Claude, Maussacre | ☎ 05 53 64 63 21 |

| Nérac | Christian Beschi, route de Lavardac | ☎ 05 53 65 85 62 |

| Villeneuve-sur-Lot | SIGA, ZI Rooy | ☎ 05 53 36 24 10 |

Chimney Sweeps

| Agen | Sani Chauff, 16 rue Garonne | ☎ 05 53 95 98 07 |

| Marmande | Pierre Coutou, Résidence Eaubonne | ☎ 05 53 64 25 53 |

| Nérac | Raymond Daniel, Cassarel | ☎ 05 53 65 24 99 |

| Villeneuve-sur-Lot | Boussignac Sarl, 86 avenue Jean Claude Cayrel | ☎ 05 53 40 21 80 |

Electricians

| Agen | Pottier Emmanuel, 172bis avenue Michelet | ☎ 05 53 87 85 01 |

General electrics, heating, plumbing and emergency call-out.

| Marmande | Ortolan,17 rue Jean Jacques Rousseau | ☎ 05 53 64 65 66 |

Heating, electrics and air-conditioning.

| Nérac | Capeletto & Fils, ZA Larrousset | ☎ 05 53 97 00 75 |

| Villeneuve-sur-Lot | Pierre Vignes, 30 rue de Grelot | ☎ 05 53 70 45 26 |

General electrics and alarm systems.

Plumbers

| Agen | Renov'Services, 361 avenue Joseph Amore | ☎ 05 53 47 13 06 |

| Marmande | Wendel, route de Bordeaux | ☎ 05 53 64 04 06 |

Tiling, bathrooms and heating.

| Nérac | Michel Bacharel, 10 rue Bourbonette | ☎ 05 53 65 04 65 |

| Villeneuve-sur-Lot | Boussignac, 86 avenue Jean Claude Cayrel | ☎ 05 53 40 21 80 |

Translators & Teachers

French Teachers & Courses

| Agen | Maison de l'Europe, 6bis rue de Strasbourg | ☎ 05 53 66 47 59 |

🖳 *www.maisoneurope.fr.fm*
Various subjects taught, including French.

	Les Nouveaux Cours Pascal, place du Maréchal Foch Open Mondays to Saturdays.	☎ 05 53 66 38 23
Bourglon	Corine Rouleau, Valorme 🖳 *www.valorme.com* (south of Marmande) Residential French courses.	☎ 05 53 93 51 81
Villeneuve-sur-Lot	AVF, 8 place de la Marine French conversation on Wednesday mornings 10 to 11am.	☎ 05 53 70 35 34
	L'Action Atelier de Langue Française, 5 rue Bernard Palissy Mondays, Tuesdays, Thursdays and Fridays 2 to 5pm.	☎ 05 53 71 46 76

Translators

Foulayronnes	Daniel Garrigou Traductions, 21 allée Georges Brassens ✉ info@danielgarrigoutraductions.fr (just north of Agen) Liaison with artisans also carried out, but not simultaneous interpreting.	☎ 05 53 66 47 40
Le Passage	Joanne Dunning, Guiral (east of Agen)	☎ 05 53 87 86 69

Utilities

Electricity & Gas

Électricité de France/Gaz de France (EDF/GDF) is one company for the whole of France but operates its gas and electricity divisions separately. The numbers below are for general information; emergency numbers can be found on page 59.

General	EDF Services Lot-et-Garonne 🖳 *www.edf.fr*	☎ 08 10 33 47 10

EDF/GDF local offices are listed below (there are no direct telephone numbers for these offices; you must dial the above number).

Agen	69 avenue Henri Barbusse	
Cancon	rue Nationale	
Casteljaloux	30 avenue 8 Mai 1945	
Fumel	place Aristide Briand	
Marmande	41 avenue Charles Boisvert	
Nérac	4 rue Martyrs de la Résistance	
Villeneuve-sur-Lot	avenue Henri Barbusse	
Boé	Gaz du Sud Ouest, rue Lacarrérotes 🖳 *www.gso.fr*	☎ 05 53 68 39 69

Heating Oil

Agen	Louda, 29 rue Cornières	☎ 05 53 66 58 41
	J.P. Péchavy, 1 rue Marceau	☎ 05 53 98 03 70
Boé	Rieux, 4 ZAC Rigoulet	☎ 05 53 96 43 45
Marmande	Alvéa, Montpouillon	☎ 05 53 89 89 89

Water

The main water supply companies are listed below. If you aren't covered by one of these, your mairie will have details of your water supplier.

Fédération Départementale d'Adduction d'Eau Potable et d'Assainissement du 47, 997 avenue Docteur Jean Bru, Agen	☎ 05 53 68 44 00
Générale des Eaux, 1456 avenue Colmar, Agen	☎ 08 11 90 29 03
Syndicat de la Brame	☎ 05 53 68 44 01
Syndicat du Nord du Lot et de la Garonne	☎ 05 53 68 44 02

SAUR	place des Cornières, Castillonnès	☎ 05 53 40 52 83
	rue Jean Orieux, Duras	☎ 05 53 40 52 83

	ZAC Village d'Entreprises, Foulayronnes	☎ 05 53 40 52 87
	5 avenue Georges Leygues, Fumel	☎ 05 53 40 52 84
	boulevard Georges Clémenceau, Monflanquin	☎ 05 53 40 52 88
	ZAC Nombel, Sainte Livrade-sur-Lot	☎ 05 53 49 77 00
	ZI Bordeneuve du Rooy, Villeneuve-sur-Lot	☎ 05 53 40 52 83

Wood

Barbaste	Noval Emmanuel, Pot de Lèbe (on the edge of the forest, west of Agen)	☎ 05 53 97 26 40
Casteljaloux	L'Escaille, 44 avenue Libération (south of Marmande)	☎ 05 53 93 41 61

INDEX

M

O

P

R

LIVING AND WORKING SERIES

Living and Working books are essential reading for anyone planning to spend time abroad, including holiday-home owners, retirees, visitors, business people, migrants, students and even extra-terrestrials! They're packed with important and useful information designed to help you **avoid costly mistakes and save both time and money.** Topics covered include how to:

- Find a job with a good salary & conditions
- Obtain a residence permit
- Avoid and overcome problems
- Find your dream home
- Get the best education for your family
- Make the best use of public transport
- Endure local motoring habits
- Obtain the best health treatment
- Stretch your money further
- Make the most of your leisure time
- Enjoy the local sporting life
- Find the best shopping bargains
- Insure yourself against most eventualities
- Use post office and telephone services
- Do numerous other things not listed above

Living and Working books are the most comprehensive and up-to-date source of practical information available about everyday life abroad. They aren't, however, boring text books, but interesting and entertaining guides written in a highly readable style.

Discover what it's *really* like to live and work abroad!

Order your copies today by phone, fax, mail or e-mail from: Survival Books, PO Box 146, Wetherby, West Yorks. LS23 6XZ, United Kingdom (☎/▤ +44 (0)1937-843523, ✉ orders@ survivalbooks.net, 💻 www.survivalbooks.net).

BUYING A HOME SERIES

Buying a Home books are essential reading for anyone planning to purchase property abroad and are designed to guide you through the jungle and make it a pleasant and enjoyable experience. Most importantly, they're packed with vital information to help you **avoid the sort of disasters that can turn your dream home into a nightmare!** Topics covered include:

- Avoiding problems
- Choosing the region
- Finding the right home and location
- Estate agents
- Finance, mortgages and taxes
- Home security
- Utilities, heating and air-conditioning
- Moving house and settling in
- Renting and letting
- Permits and visas
- Travelling and communications
- Health and insurance
- Renting a car and driving
- Retirement and starting a business
- And much, much more!

Buying a Home books are the most comprehensive and up-to-date source of information available about buying property abroad. Whether you want a detached house, townhouse or apartment, a holiday or a permanent home, these books will help make your dreams come true.

Save yourself time, trouble and money!

Order your copies today by phone, fax, mail or e-mail from: Survival Books, PO Box 146, Wetherby, West Yorks. LS23 6XZ, United Kingdom (☎/🖷 +44 (0)1937-843523, ✉ orders@ survivalbooks.net, 🖥 www.survivalbooks.net).

ORDER FORM 1

Qty.	Title	Price (incl. p&p)*			Total
		UK	Europe	World	
	The Alien's Guide to Britain	£6.95	£8.95	£12.45	
	The Alien's Guide to France	£6.95	£8.95	£12.45	
	The Best Places to Buy a Home in France	£13.95	£15.95	£19.45	
	The Best Places to Buy a Home in Spain	£13.95	£15.95	£19.45	
	Buying a Home Abroad	£13.95	£15.95	£19.45	
	Buying a Home in Florida	£13.95	£15.95	£19.45	
	Buying a Home in France	£13.95	£15.95	£19.45	
	Buying a Home in Greece & Cyprus	£13.95	£15.95	£19.45	
	Buying a Home in Ireland	£11.95	£13.95	£17.45	
	Buying a Home in Italy	£13.95	£15.95	£19.45	
	Buying a Home in Portugal	£13.95	£15.95	£19.45	
	Buying a Home in Spain	£13.95	£15.95	£19.45	
	Buying, Letting & Selling Property	£11.95	£13.95	£17.45	
	Foreigners in France: Triumphs & Disasters	£11.95	£13.95	£17.45	
	Foreigners in Spain: Triumphs & Disasters	£11.95	£13.95	£17.45	
	How to Avoid Holiday & Travel Disasters	£13.95	£15.95	£19.45	
	Costa del Sol Lifeline	£11.95	£13.95	£17.45	
	Dordogne/Lot Lifeline	£11.95	£13.95	£17.45	
	Poitou-Charentes Lifeline	£11.95	£13.95	£17.45	
					Total

Order your copies today by phone, fax, mail or e-mail from: Survival Books, PO Box 146, Wetherby, West Yorks. LS23 6XZ, UK (☎/▤ +44 (0)1937-843523, ✉ orders@survivalbooks.net, 🖳 www.survivalbooks.net). If you aren't entirely satisfied, simply return them to us within 14 days for a full and unconditional refund.

Cheque enclosed/please charge my Amex/Delta/MasterCard/Switch/Visa* card

Card No. _ _ _ _   _ _ _ _   _ _ _ _   _ _ _ _

Expiry date _____   Issue number (Switch only) _____

Signature _____   Tel. No. _____

NAME _____

ADDRESS _____

_____

_____

* Delete as applicable (price includes postage – airmail for Europe/world).

ORDER FORM 2

Qty.	Title	Price (incl. p&p)*			Total
		UK	**Europe**	**World**	
	Living & Working Abroad	£14.95	£16.95	£20.45	
	Living & Working in America	£14.95	£16.95	£20.45	
	Living & Working in Australia	£14.95	£16.95	£20.45	
	Living & Working in Britain	£14.95	£16.95	£20.45	
	Living & Working in Canada	£16.95	£18.95	£22.45	
	Living & Working in the European Union	£16.95	£18.95	£22.45	
	Living & Working in the Far East	£16.95	£18.95	£22.45	
	Living & Working in France	£14.95	£16.95	£20.45	
	Living & Working in Germany	£16.95	£18.95	£22.45	
	L&W in the Gulf States & Saudi Arabia	£16.95	£18.95	£22.45	
	L&W in Holland, Belgium & Luxembourg	£14.95	£16.95	£20.45	
	Living & Working in Ireland	£14.95	£16.95	£20.45	
	Living & Working in Italy	£16.95	£18.95	£22.45	
	Living & Working in London	£13.95	£15.95	£19.45	
	Living & Working in New Zealand	£14.95	£16.95	£20.45	
	Living & Working in Spain	£14.95	£16.95	£20.45	
	Living & Working in Switzerland	£16.95	£18.95	£22.45	
	Renovating & Maintaining Your French Home	£13.95	£15.95	£19.45	
	Retiring Abroad	£14.95	£16.95	£20.45	
	Rioja and its Wines	£11.95	£13.95	£17.45	
	The Wines of Spain	£13.95	£15.95	£19.45	
				Total	

Order your copies today by phone, fax, mail or e-mail from: Survival Books, PO Box 146, Wetherby, West Yorks. LS23 6XZ, UK (☎/▤ +44 (0)1937-843523, ✉ orders@ survivalbooks.net, 🖳 www.survivalbooks.net). If you aren't entirely satisfied, simply return them to us within 14 days for a full and unconditional refund.

Cheque enclosed/please charge my Amex/Delta/MasterCard/Switch/Visa* card

Card No. __ __ __ __   __ __ __ __   __ __ __ __   __ __ __ __

Expiry date _____   Issue number (Switch only) _____

Signature _____   Tel. No. _____

NAME _____

ADDRESS _____

_____

_____

* Delete as applicable (price includes postage – airmail for Europe/world).

OTHER SURVIVAL BOOKS

The Alien's Guides: *The Alien's Guides to Britain* and *France* provide an 'alternative' look at life in these popular countries and will help you to appreciate the peculiarities (in both senses) of the British and French.

The Best Places to Buy a Home in France/Spain: The most comprehensive and up-to-date homebuying guides to France or Spain.

Buying, Selling and Letting Property: The most comprehensive and up-to-date source of information available for those intending to buy, sell or let a property in the UK and the only book on the subject updated annually.

Foreigners in France/Spain: Triumphs & Disasters: Real-life experiences of people who have emigrated to France and Spain.

How to Avoid Holiday and Travel Disasters: This book will help you to make the right decisions regarding every aspect of your travel arrangements and to avoid costly mistakes and disasters that can turn a trip into a nightmare.

Lifelines: Essential guides to specific regions of France and Spain, containing everything you need to know about local life. Titles in the series currently include the Costa del Sol, Dordogne/Lot, and Poitou-Charentes.

Renovating & Maintaining Your French Home: The ultimate guide to renovating and maintaining your dream home in France.

Retiring Abroad: The most comprehensive and up-to-date source of practical information available about retiring to a foreign country – contains profiles of the 20 most popular retirement destinations.

Wine Guides: *Rioja and its Wines* and *The Wines of Spain* are the most comprehensive and up-to-date sources of information available on the wines of Spain and of its most famous wine-producing region.

Broaden your horizons with Survival Books!

Order your copies today by phone, fax, mail or e-mail from: Survival Books, PO Box 146, Wetherby, West Yorks. LS23 6XZ, United Kingdom (☎/▤ +44 (0)1937-843523, ✉ orders@ survivalbooks.net, 🖳 www.survivalbooks.net).

NOTES

NOTES

NOTES

NOTES